Making American Tradition

MAKING AMERICAN TRADITION

Visions and Revisions from Ben Franklin to Alice Walker

CUSHING STROUT

Rutgers University Press
New Brunswick and London

Library of Congress Cataloging-in-Publication Data

Strout, Cushing.
   Making American tradition : visions and revisions from Ben
Franklin to Alice Walker / Cushing Strout.
     p.   cm.
   ISBN 0-8135-1516-5 (cloth)   ISBN 0-8135-1517-3 (pbk.)
   1. American literature—History and criticism. 2. National
characteristics, American, in literature. 3. Influence (Literary,
artistic, etc.) 4. Literature and history. I. Title.
PS169.N35S76 1990
810.9—dc20   89-37765
                                                      CIP

British Cataloging-in-Publication information available

To
the memory of John William Miller
(*1895–1978*), professor of philosophy
at Williams College from 1924 to 1960

"All I can do with the theme
is tell a story. . . . The story
contains argument but is not
contentious in itself. It can't
prove anything; it can only
show something."

John William Miller, *The Philosophy of History*

Contents

Acknowledgments   ix

Introduction   American Literary History and Its Remaking   1

Chapter 1   Upward Bound: Hawthorne, Melville, James, Fitzgerald, and the Myth of Franklin   9

Chapter 2   In Hawthorne's Shadow: The Minister and the Woman in Howells, Adams, Frederic, and Updike   22

Chapter 3   "Mediumistic Existence": The Female Trance-Speaker in Hawthorne, Howells, and James   40

Chapter 4   Complementary Novels of Manners by James, Wharton, Howells, and Cahan   52

Chapter 5   Pragmatic Godfather: Emerson, Whitman, and William James   72

Chapter 6   "Gentle William" and Warren's Willie   88

Chapter 7   Refractions of History: Lowell's Revision of Hawthorne and Melville in The Old Glory   100

Chapter 8   Twain, Doctorow, and the Anachronistic Adventures of the Arms Mechanic and the Jazz Pianist   117

Chapter 9   American Dilemma: Lincoln's Jefferson and the Irony of History   133

Chapter 10   "Working on the Circumstances": Twain's Huck, Faulkner's Chick, and the Negro   152

Chapter 11   Invisible Men and Native Sons
              in Wright and Ellison   164

Chapter 12   The Wise Man (Niebuhr), the Prophet (King),
              and Civil Disobedience   177

Chapter 13   "I, Too, Sing America": Alice Walker's
              Visible Woman, Meridian   196

Notes   209

Index   239

Acknowledgments

SOME OF the material in this book has appeared elsewhere in different form. I have written on Edith Wharton's relation to Henry James in "James's Lady and Wharton's Age," *The Hudson Review* (Autumn 1982); on Robert Penn Warren's relation to William James in "*All the King's Men* and the Shadow of William James," *The Southern Review* (Autumn 1970); and on Robert Lowell's relation to Hawthorne and Melville in "Refractions of History: Lowell's Revision of Hawthorne and Melville in *The Old Glory*," *The Southern Review* (Summer 1989). I am grateful to the editors of both journals for letting me rework the articles for this book.

The cover design is based on "Eagles with Shields" by John Haley Bellamy (1836–1914) of Kittery Point, Maine. The work is in the Webb Gallery, Shelburne Museum, Shelburne, Vermont, and I am grateful for the Museum's permission to use a reproduction of it.

I have benefited from the suggestions made to the Rutgers University Press by one of its readers, a fellow literary historian, Marcus Cunliffe, and from a reading of chapter five by my friend and colleague, Joel Porte. I have profited also from the courtesy of librarians at the Stetson Library, Williams College; the Mugar Library, Boston University; and the Houghton Library, Harvard University.

As always, my wife Jean has given me the advantage of her ear, her commentary, and her encouragement. My former secretary, Dianne Ferriss, fortunately for me has cast her keen eye on every page of this manuscript.

Making American Tradition

Introduction

American Literary History
and Its Remaking

ONE OF the extraordinary things about American literature is how late it came to be regarded as a national tradition. Even as late as 1941, the English novelist H. G. Wells thought it was ridiculous for any American to call himself a professor of *American* literature.[1] We now see Canada and Australia energetically struggling to achieve recognition of their own literary traditions, and such efforts should not only arouse our sympathy but remind us of our own long struggle.

At the very time of Wells's disdainful remark and for the next thirty years, an influential group of critics in New England and New York universities developed a common vision of our literature as distinguished from an English literary tradition. Ironically, the most striking feature of their vision was its kinship with a formulation first made by a young aristocratic Frenchman who visited America in 1831 and published his speculations about modern literature in the second volume of his classic *Democracy in America* (1840). Alexis de Tocqueville, while describing America, was always thinking about Europe; indeed America interested him not so much for itself as for its typological role as a society less revolutionary than France and more democratic than England.[2] In spite of his penchant and talent for generalizing, he knew that American literature of the future would have a different character from "the American literature of today," and he warned that "no one can guess that character beforehand."[3] Yet, he was persuaded that a prediction could be made about the basic difference between modern democratic literature and the traditional literature of aristocracies. It was this prediction, which only became widely recognized a hundred years after he made it, that intrigued the American critics who were trying to develop the notion of an American literary tradition.

Tocqueville's idea presupposes that literature will reflect the nature of modern society in which the social space between the individual and the state would increasingly be emptied of the aristocratic forms of life that had previously filled it. In an inevitably democratic world the sources of literary art would center around the nature of man himself, seen against the background of nature or God rather than of society. Reflecting on the examples of Chateaubriand, Lamartine, and Byron, rather than upon any American writers, he prophesied that modern poets by focusing on "passions and ideas" in "the hidden depths of man's spiritual nature" would illuminate by exaggeration "certain dark corners of the human heart."[4] Escaping from society and history, democratic and romantic writers, in contrast to aristocratic and classic ones, would find their subject in "man himself, not tied to time or place, but face to face with nature and God."[5] F. O. Matthiessen's *American Renaissance: Art and Expression in the Age of Emerson and Whitman* (1941) applied Tocqueville's prophecy to the two poets whom he took to be representative of the age, and in the next two decades a host of influential critics (W. H. Auden, Lionel Trilling, R. W. B. Lewis, Richard Chase, Richard Poirier, Marius Bewley, Charles Feidelson, Harry Levin, Daniel Hoffman, and Quentin Anderson) found Tocqueville's literary reflections to be highly pertinent to their own vision of the American "romance" as a form supposedly distinguishable in its metaphysical symbolism about mythicized characters from the more empirically, socially, and historically differentiated English form of the "novel."[6]

This school of interpretation virtually created the classic canon of American literature and ended forever the long period of neglect and condescension that had kept American literature a poor country cousin in English departments. It was an historic achievement, but it has had its price. Such a Tocquevillean vision minimized or neglected the close attention to time and place even in those writers, such as Hawthorne, who seemed most illustrative of Tocqueville's prediction about attention to "the hidden depths of man's spiritual nature" and "certain dark corners of the heart," and it neglected Southern, black, and female writers for whom social context has always been an essential focus. Moreover, the Tocquevillean image of our literature was influential precisely because it assimilated our nineteenth-century writers to the dominant literary taste of our own day, seeing them either as precursors or contemporaries of the alienated fiction of our own time. Edmund Wilson, near the end of the 1920s, had pointed to the path that would be followed when he called for a criticism that would see how Hawthorne, Melville, and Poe "anticipated, in the middle of the last century, the temperament of our own day and invented methods of rendering it."[7] A major answer to Wilson's call came in 1953 with Charles Feidelson's *Symbolism in American Literature,* which substituted for Matthiessen's theme of our classic writers' "devotion to the possibilities of democracy" a new aesthetic focus on "their devotion to the possibilities of symbolism." Feidelson was candid in saying that his interest lay in seeing them "as a proving ground for the issues to which the method of modern literature is an answer."[8]

This version of what Herbert Butterfield has called "the Whig interpretation of history," justifying our predecessors by the extent to which they anticipated ourselves, certainly kept earlier American writers alive in our world, rescuing them from antiquarianism, but Whiggism is also an insidious source of anachronism, not to mention complacent dogmatism about the virtue of our present tastes. There is something paradoxical about this deformation in this case because the critics who took the Tocquevillean image seriously were committed in principle to a historical form of comparative criticism (in contrast to current ahistoric forms of theorizing that cast doubt on all national traditions), even if they made remarkably few empirical comparisons with specific examples of English writers.

In recent years influential literary critics in the universities have been fascinated not with historical comparisons but with continental theorizing about "structuralism" and "post-structuralist deconstruction," which has foregrounded langauge and its tropes as fundamental. Unfortunately, as I have witnessed at my own university, "English departments," as the novelist Cynthia Ozick has pointed out, "have set off after theory, and use culture as an instrument to illustrate doctrinal principles, whether Marxist or 'French Freud'."[9] Whether in response to Derrida or Foucault, many fashionable critics assume, What could any canon mean but "reactionary, racist, sexist, elitist closure"? In the politicized academy "all categories are suspect, no category is allowed to display its wares without the charge of enslavement by foregone conclusion and vested interest."[10]

The editor of *Reconstructing American Literary History* (1986) assumes that European critical theories have "broken down, worn out, or at best opened up" any consensus on either the term *literary* or the term *history*. The task of reconstruction he delegates to those trained in the 1960s or later, those who will know how to proceed by "making a virtue of dissensus."[11] But the historical consciousness must take account of both continuity and agreement as well as of discontinuity and disagreement. It cannot legitimate only one way of looking at these two dimensions of history.

It is instructive that scholars in Black Studies and Women's Studies, who have complained about the narrowness of traditional canons, now find themselves creating their own canons. One of my colleagues, celebrating an anthology of black women's writing, justly observes that it demonstrates how works configure into a tradition "because writers read other writers and *ground* their representations of experience in models of language provided largely by other writers to whom they feel akin." Only in this way can we "know a literary tradition."[12]

That is also true of our classic nineteenth-century writers, who sometimes not only read but met each other. The most famous example is Herman Melville's encounter with Nathaniel Hawthorne for five days at the Red House in Tanglewood. Melville praised Hawthorne's "power of blackness" (akin to his own) and spoke of his own "infinite fraternity of feeling" for him.[13] Both writers went their own ways, but Melville was given the confidence to carry on and deepen the implications of his own work in *Moby Dick*.

The study of literary influence has been revivified by a subtle awareness of the differing ways one writer can relate to another.[14] One example Harold Bloom has made familiar in his provocative Freudian theory of poetic influence is the unconscious competitive anxiety in a "strong" poet's ambivalent relationship to his misunderstood predecessor. For Bloom, the rule applies to "strong" readers as well, so that what seems to be an historical procedure turns out in his hands to be a creative one that does not ask, "Am I getting this right" but rather, "What can it do for me, what can I make it mean?"[15] A recent cartoon in a newspaper caricatured the theory by showing a man typing with Shakespeare's critical face at his elbow, while the writer pleads, "Will, could you ease up?" Responses to earlier writers need not, however, always be so tense and rivalrous. The later writer may find a point of departure in the earlier text for many different positive reasons, which only the particular case will make clear. William Dean Howells in 1907 made the modern point that "there is no creation; there is only recreation. Or we may reverse the paradox and say there are no fathers, there are only forefathers."[16] Yet "the influences operating upon originality are always original" in the case of a "union between the original mind and other original minds."[17]

My concern is not to typify the connections by a general theory, but rather to see how what Melville called "the shock of recognition" can illuminate by comparison the particular nature of the two texts, each throwing light on the other. The philosopher Maurice Mandelbaum has implicitly defined my procedure in noting that the literary historian "searches for a connecting link between works that seem similar and yet puzzlingly different, but there is no guarantee that any such link ever existed: Genuine innovation, as well as influences, must be taken into account." In a literary history, as he says, "the question of influence and the spread of influence stands at the heart of the problem of continuity."[18] We sometimes imagine (and textbooks tend to do so) that the mere existence of written works by a variety of authors constitutes a tradition. But only the retrospective interpretations of the critical historian, linking the works to some envisaged common theme or technique, can define tradition. Yet such stories are often vulnerable to the vice of subordinating the past to present concerns and ideas, regardless of those held by the authors. The accounts may be brilliant narratives, but they suffer from a lack of modesty in failing to take the authors more seriously than they do their own critical categories. A more modest and historical way of defining the existence of a tradition would be to see how writers themselves make it come alive whenever they respond in their work to previous writers. If that never happened, tradition would be only an invention of the critic.

When the detective's acolyte in Umberto Eco's *The Name of the Rose* realizes that books often speak of other books, he says in wonder that "it is as if they spoke among themselves."[19] Indeed, it is, but not because they speak only about themselves. Comparing texts highlights, for one thing, the fact that the prior writer's example is only one of the elements in the later writer's experience, which provides the context in which the earlier text has its force. Comparisons can be otiose, "yet it sometimes happens that a comparison closely pursued leads the mind to an instructive difference," as Jacques Barzun has remarked, because it "helps to mark a change of direction in culture." What is required for fruitful comparison is a connection showing "many points of congruence up to the sought-for point of disparity."[20] That is what I hope my examples will represent for the reader.

The value of such an analysis cannot be yet another grand theory. In the end, "all that history can teach us at last is that there *is* history. . . . That is all the facts are good for." In a democratic society, the philosopher John William Miller adds, "anyone, not only the hero, may define himself historically . . . indeed, he can do no other. Everyone is both heir and executor of the estate."[21] My chapters aim to facilitate that inheritance.

My subjects in this book are well known, in contrast to the recent forays into the unfamiliar literature of minorities, and their intellectual and artistic level is high, in contrast to much of more popular culture. My selection runs the risk, therefore, of arousing the same animus that animates some of the dominant social historians who are disdainful of studying "important people, significant events, and successful historical movements," as historians traditionally have done.[22] I am inspired, however, by Gertrude Himmelfarb's call for a written history with a sense of "renewed excitement in the drama of events, the power of ideas, and the dignity of individuals— 'not only in things that are trivial but in the things that really matter.' "[23] As she points out, there is a tendency among some literary historians of popular culture to be "dismissive of great books and great thinkers, to think that reality is better reflected in second-rate and third-rate thinkers than in first-rate ones." From this point of view importance is found in the technology of publishing, the composition of the reading public, and the economics of the market—in "everything, that is, except the ideas in the book itself."[24] In this respect I find Alfred Kazin's formulation exemplary: "It might be sufficient to say here that I have never been able to understand why the study of literature in relation to society should be divorced from a full devotion to what literature is in itself, or why those who seek to analyze literary texts should cut off the act of writing from its irreducible sources in the life of men."[25]

The very idea of a national literature is now tainted by the political suspicion directed at the idea of the nation itself, as if national identity were the same thing as ideological nationalism. Radicals treat the concept of nation (except in the Third World) as a mere reflection of the hegemonic rule of oppressing classes; and even the conservative philosopher Michael Oakeshott rejects the idea of a history of France, for example, because only if the author has "abandoned the engagement of an historian in favour of that of an ideologue or a mythologist shall we find in it an

identity—*La Nation* or *La France*—to which the differences that compose
the story are attributed." But, as Himmelfarb points out, it was a pioneer
social historian of France, critical of nationalism, who eloquently acknowledged: "I was born in France. I have drunk of the waters of her
culture. I have made her past my own. I breathe freely only in her
climate, and I have done my best, with others, to defend her interests."[26]
In Marc Bloch's declaration I find precisely reflected my sense of my
relation to my own country.

My selection of subjects is not meant to be definitive of a canon or a
method, nor does it necessarily focus on the best prose work of a writer.
American literary ancestry may not tell us much about many valuable
works: Willa Cather's late novel *The Professor's House* is in some respects
reminiscent of Henry James's short story "The Jolly Corner." Both emphasize houses in symbolic relation to a male protagonist's mid-life crisis;
both protagonists finally fall into unconsciousness and are saved by
women; and both stories are critiques of commercialism. Yet, Cather is
not at all Jamesian in her way of opening up the novel to the outdoors
with an adventuresome student's discovery of an Indian city on a mesa.
That central episode is kin to her characteristic fiction about pioneers.
Mary McCarthy's *The Oasis,* a satire on a utopian community of literary
intellectuals, recalls the debate in Hawthorne's *The Blithedale Romance*
about calling his satirized utopian community "The Oasis," the one
"green spot in the moral sand-waste of the world." Yet, her biographer
notes that two European intellectuals, Nicola Chiaromonte and Arthur
Koestler, were the strongest influences on her novella.[27]

My choice of topics arises out of my experience of teaching courses on
American literary and intellectual history. In doing so, I discovered telling relationships between texts, devoted to themes that had attracted me
in the first place: The lure of upward mobility; religion and the lovers'
triangle; reforming the relation between the sexes; the conflict of manners among regions, classes, and countries; American pragmatism; fictionalizing history; and the American dilemmas of slavery and race. I
have made bridges to connect my chapters, but there is no single theme
to connect them. The only constant is my comparative method of relating visions and revisions in the making of tradition.

In medieval England the collective term for writers was "a worship of
writers," perhaps because of their need for patrons. For my book the
more appropriate term would be "a resonance of writers." It points to the

noncausal relationships between them and their works, the vibrations in meaning between them that follow from looking at them in pairing relation to each other, especially when a later writer has taken an earlier text or writer as a self-conscious point of departure. My comparisons of prose writers and texts make them march in pairs, two by two, into the ark of the American covenant, but in doing so, they make visible the historically dynamic and creative nature of the tradition.

Some readers may be surprised to find a philosopher, a theologian, and four statesmen in the company here of so many literary artists, but while I know how to distinguish literary and historical sides of the street, I have spent my academic life moving back and forth from one side to the other and so I can never isolate them from each other. Moreover, anyone with an eye for style will recognize that Franklin, Jefferson, Lincoln, William James, Reinhold Niebuhr, and Martin Luther King, Jr., whatever else they may be, are eloquent writers. Other readers may be surprised at the extent to which my nonfictional writers represent liberal values, particularly at a time when "conservative" is the honorific term in our politics and "radical" is the honorific one in the groves of academe. But, the connection of liberal values to the central events of our Revolution, Civil War, and civil rights movement is a matter of history, whatever the politics of the historian may be. If this be heresy in our current academic climate, where it is the fashion to say that "everything is ideological," let us make the most of it.

A critic has recently objected that the idea of an American literature distinct from British literature was "concocted to express political animosities and is based on the notion that there are two worlds, one Old and one New." He argues instead for "a single, complex, English-speaking culture" and for looking at books not as historical events, rooted in the soil that gave them birth, but as literary objects that "tend to flee their places of origin and associate themselves with their generic, thematic, structural, and stylistic counterparts from other countries." The true framework for studying writing in English, he insists, is "a stateless modernism."[28] It is another possible study, but his dogmatic monism fails to see that whenever an American writer responds to a native predecessor, the event is both literary and historical. No literary work is the exclusive possession of any single history, but my story of such events may serve to redress the abstractness of a merely linguistic orientation and to join the "divided realms" of literature and history.

Chapter 1

Upward Bound: Hawthorne,
Melville, James, Fitzgerald, and
the Myth of Franklin

NOTHING is more characteristic of our contemporary literary sophisti-
cation than the treatment of autobiography as a form of fiction. When
Philip Roth, for example, wrote his novelist's autobiography, *The Facts,*
he included one of his fictional characters, whose role is to cast doubt on
the authenticity of his creator's account. It is of course true that autobiog-
raphies are highly selective and that their formal organization is not a
matter of simply reflecting what actually happens. (The same can be said
of maps, which are not therefore in principle unreliable—unless you read
them literally.) Even at the beginning of American autobiography with
Benjamin Franklin, the author makes it manifest and explicit that he is
presenting himself to illustrate a national theme. He was so understood
by Hawthorne, Melville, James, and Fitzgerald, who alluded to his memoir in fictions connected to his theme.

Begun when he was sixty-five as a family history for his mature,
illegitimate son, Franklin's memoir became, through the urgings of
friends, a politically pertinent document. Benjamin Vaughan, Franklin
tells us, implored him to see his story not only as a model of self-
education in industry, frugality, and temperance, but as the representation of a life connected to the "manners and situation of a rising people,"
a living proof that social origin is irrelevant to "happiness, virtue, or
greatness," and a concrete demonstration that the virtuous principles
claimed for the Revolution really did have an influence on a man who
from infancy "loved justice, liberty, and concord" in a way consistent

with his mature behavior since the middle 1760s as a spokesman for the colonies.[1] Writing Franklin at the end of the war, Vaughan saw in his friend's autobiographical project the prospect of making England once again think well of America. Written in the press of public business, the memoir went some way in meeting these objectives by detailing Franklin's self-made scheme for making private virtues into public habits, particularly useful for those no longer energized by Christian faith, and recounting his many public services to the organization, improvement, and defense of community life, as well as his internationally recognized contributions to natural science. Yet, taken up at four different times, the memoir is fragmentary, unfinished, and misleadingly truncated by stopping on the eve of the crucial years of his struggle with British statesmen over the future of the colonies and his eventual commitment to the emerging Revolution. Designed to establish the virtue of the Revolution, it never gets around to portraying the Revolutionary Franklin.

The result has been to narrow Franklin's extraordinary range of talents to fit the cultural myth of the self-made man's rise to fame and fortune, emphasizing the Puritan economic virtues of industry and frugality at the cost of obscuring Franklin's powerful literary, intellectual, and political talents and achievements. In a sense, Franklin as a personality has been a victim of his own success in portraying himself as a hero of the success story, only one of his many roles.[2] These roles are unified by his early ambition to be a writer and the sustained use of his literary talent to promote his civic programs, to write up his experiments, to satirize English imperial arrogance, to conduct his diplomacy, and to produce polished "bagatelles" for the admiring ladies of the Paris salons. Not for nothing did he have a godfather and uncle Benjamin who wrote poetry, collected sermons in his own shorthand, and wrote marginalia in his many volumes of pamphlets on public affairs.

Franklin's success as representative of the colonies in England was finally cut short when he was scorned in the Privy Council for his role in circulating the Hutchinson letters. Written by colonial officials, lamenting the seditious tendencies of the colonies, the letters stirred a hornet's nest of patriotic indignation. He had hoped the letters would convince the colonists that the British ministry had been misguided rather than ill-intentioned; it was a more serious misjudgment than any of the errata he candidly acknowledged in his memoir. The letters, widely published, whipped up demands for removing Thomas Hutchinson, governor of the Massachusettts Bay Colony, and led to Franklin's loss of his postmastership. He was compelled to return to America, where he had practically abandoned his wife and where his illegitimate son, to Franklin's bitter dismay, had become a Tory.

Hawthorne borrowed five volumes of Franklin's works at about the time he was working on "My Kinsman, Major Molineux," and his hero Robin parallels Franklin in leaving home, taking a boat, meeting a strumpet, resting at a church, and seeking the help of influential royal authorities. In both cases, the young men discover that they have to depend primarily on their own efforts rather than on their patrons to rise in the world. Hawthorne in his *Biographical Stories for Children* (1842) pointed out that Franklin "generally profited more by his misfortunes than many people do by the most favorable events that could befall them."[3]

Robin's experience, however, is much more confused and disorienting than Franklin's; it is like a dream, which in this case, as dreams are popularly held to do, foretells the future. Hawthorne supposed that when Franklin slept in the Quaker church he could not even have dreamed of his remarkable future. Hawthorne has his young hero of the 1730s anachronistically swept up, as if in a dream, in a Revolutionary crowd of the 1770s. Robin joins the crowd by the contagion of its excited derision of his uncle, rather than by any deliberate choice on his part. Franklin by contrast rationally explored his ideas about the British Empire, until his humiliation in the Privy Council over his role in circulating the Hutchinson letters compelled him to return home. Hawthorne's story undercuts any complacent enthusiasm for the Revolution, which had enjoyed its fiftieth birthday shortly before he wrote it, by reminding his countrymen of the price paid in terms of the persecution of some admirable men who happened to be loyal to British authority.

A veteran of the Revolutionary War, captured by the British at Bunker Hill, taken to England, and escaped to fight under John Paul Jones in the famous battle of the *Bon Homme Richard* with the *Serapis,* Israel Potter lived much of his exile among the London poor and was able to return home only fifty years after the Revolution. Melville's fictionalizing of this hard-luck story is distinguished by its portraits of Benjamin Franklin, Ethan Allen, and John Paul Jones as different American types. The most memorable of these sketches is the portrait of Potter's encounter

with Franklin in Paris. Indeed, the novel seems to be a kind of reply to
Franklin's memoir in the form of a biography, for while the former is a
celebrated account of a Yankee who rises from poverty and obscurity to
wealth and international eminence, illustrating at the birth of the nation
what would become an enduring national myth, the latter is the story of a
poor and obscure Yankee whose remarkable adventures leave him finally
positioned even lower at the bottom of the ladder and more obscure than
when he began them. In Melville's *Israel Potter: His Fifty Years of Exile*
(1855), two patriots of the Revolution meet each other in Paris and their
meeting links sharply divergent histories. Melville drily notes in his preface that Potter's name does not appear in the volumes of Jared Sparks,
whose *Library of American Biography* included only the distinguished; he
published in ten volumes the *Works of Benjamin Franklin; with Notes and a
Life of the Author* (1836–1840).

Melville's fictionalized biography, dedicated to the Bunker Hill Monument and published on the anniversary day of the famous battle, begins
with a hero who, like Franklin, runs away from home and eventually
joins the Revolution. Franklin records that he never imagined as a young
man that he would some day come to stand before five kings and even sit
down to dinner with one; and Melville observes in mirror-like fashion
that when Potter became an assistant chain bearer to a party of royal
surveyors bordering the Connecticut River, he never imagined "that the
day was to come when he should clank the king's chains in a dungeon,
even as now he trailed them a free ranger of the woods."[4] Wounded at
Bunker Hill and captured by the British from a brigantine, the young
soldier escapes to become a laborer in the king's gardens at Kew, where
he is surprised to have a friendly audience with his Majesty. English
friends of America send Potter on a secret mission to carry papers to
Franklin in Paris.

Melville's Franklin gives Potter *Poor Richard's Almanac* and a *Guide to
Paris,* gifts of a "household Plato" who is said to have "politic grace" of
mind and "pastoral simplicity" of manners, a mix of the Bible's serpent
and dove. He is also described less sympathetically as one of the
"labyrinth-minded, but plain-spoken Broadbrims" who are "keen ob-
servors of the main chance."[5] He is too much for Potter, who finds
himself talked out of having wine or a flirtation with the chambermaid
by a sententious sage. Feeling somewhat tricked, Israel ruefully reflects:
"It's wisdom that's cheap, and it's fortune that's dear. That isn't in Poor

Richard; but it ought to be." He slams down the *Almanac* with its moralizing saw, "God helps them that help themselves."[6] Franklin promised his
good offices in helping Potter to return home, but a steady accumulation
of misfortunes, public and private, leave Israel bereft of this hope and
unable to comply with "the mild man of wisdom's words" to avoid
elation at the prospect of pleasure and to respect without depression the
omens of ill.[7]

Melville's satire of Franklin's moralizing is tempered by noting Franklin's "levity of tranquility" that does not allow him to take himself too
seriously and by citing his extraordinary ability to play many roles while
being "master of each and mastered by none—the type and genius of his
land. Franklin was everything but a poet." *Israel Potter* prefigures a modern reductive conception of him as a canny and devious bourgeois, but
Melville candidly acknowledges (as his literary descendants tend to forget) that "very little indeed of the sage's multifariousness will be portrayed in a simple narrative like the present." Instead, he will appear in
his "far lesser lights, thrifty, domestic, dietarian, and it may be, didacti-
cally waggish."[8] Melville later on in the narrative shows Franklin in
another light by having him, because of his "rare insight into rare natures," suggest letting Captain John Paul Jones rove without instructions
as a "prowling *brave*" who is by nature a solitary warrior.[9] No bourgeois,
Jones is a rakish gallant and a savage fighter, yet Melville has the *Bon
Homme Richard* named for Franklin's *Almanac* character at Potter's suggestion, because Franklin's French negotiations have organized the fleet.
Jones, who befriends Israel as a loner like himself, despises prudence;
nevertheless, he incongruously wants to wear a copy of *Poor Richard*
round his neck for a charm.

In Melville's account the victory of the American ship, "gorged with
slaughter," is ambiguous because, overcome by fire and water, it sinks
out of sight "like Gomorrah," and the battle's fury provokes the suspicion that civilization is really "an advanced stage of barbarism." In this
light Jones is a prophetic warning that "intrepid, unprincipled, reckless,
predatory, with boundless ambition, civilized in externals but a savage at
heart, America is, or yet may be, the Paul Jones of nations."[10]

Melville adds yet another American type to his repertory in Ethan
Allen, a Vermont frontiersman, envisaged as "essentially Western," a
prefiguration of "the true American one," which Melville assumes, as
Frederick Jackson Turner would at the end of the century, must be

Western. Melville's Allen, captured by the British, is frank, bluff, hearty, convivial, strong, and intrepid, a pagan rather than a Puritan New Englander.[11] In this respect *Israel Potter* points forward to James's *The American.*

James's hero, Christopher Newman, draws on both the Franklin and Allen images projected in Melville's generalizing of the American character. Newman has always had his eye on the main chance, and he can be admired for it in America in contrast to the disreputable role that Noemie Nioche must play in French society as an upwardly mobile adventuress. Mrs. Tristram, a Philadelphian living in the Parisian American community, sees Newman as "the great Western Barbarian, stepping forth in his innocence and might, gazing awhile at this poor effete Old World, and then swooping down on it." His relaxed and simple response to the unfamiliar experience of European art strikes an Englishman as too puritanical, but to a puritanical Unitarian minister from Boston, Newman seems to be a pagan. James himself describes the hero of this "intensely Western story" in more Franklinesque terms as "a born experimentalist" who once found himself penniless in a strange city and might have marched along the San Francisco street as Franklin did Philadelphia's, "munching a penny loaf," if he had only had one for "the performance." Later, in Paris, Newman meets a woman whose father had fought with French troops in the American Revolution and whose husband had actually seen "the great Dr. Franklin."[12]

The connection in one sense points up a contrast: Newman is quite without Franklin's unusual literary, political and scientific gifts. In another sense, it is an appropriate reference: Franklin was in Paris to make an alliance with the French and so is Newman, though his project is entirely personal. Moreover, Franklin in his early forties gave up business for public affairs and scientific inquiry; and Newman has turned his back on commerce to enjoy the sights of the European tour, discovering as a final result that "his commercial imagination was dead." The story is set in 1868, but James wrote it in 1876 when he was living in Paris and must have been aware that it was for Americans a centennial year.

Critics have been alert to discover the ways in which the novel is in dialogue with European writers, whether Alexander Dumas's play *L'Étrangère,* with its unflattering portrait of an intrusive American, or Turgenev's *A Nest of Noblemen,* with its heroine who also enters a convent where her lover comes for a mute farewell. The Russian had a repertory of heroes whose function, as James described it, was to be "conspicuous as failures, interesting but impotent persons who are losers at the game of life." James had befriended Turgenev in Paris, where both were outsiders, and the American was drawn to the Russian's idea of a central figure who (in James's words) is "usually a person in a false position, generally not of his own making, which according to the peculiar perversity of fate, is only aggravated by his effort to right himself."[13]

These connections are helpful, but they may obscure the pertinence of James's own experience of France. In 1878, he wrote for the *Nation* an article, "American Abroad," in reply to a criticism of them. He pointed out that Americans as members of a commercial democracy inevitably were outsiders to European society. Their ignorance of European society was at least balanced by a certain amount of imagination about Europe, unlike the European's ignorance of America. In this respect, "the American in Europe may be spoken of as a provincial who is terribly bent upon taking, in the fullness of ages, his revenge."[14] The conclusion retroactively underlines the extent to which the novelist looked sympathetically at Newman's restrained impulse to gain revenge against the Bellegardes for their snubbing of him as a merely commercial person.

Franklin, rich in American public honors, could nevertheless write Madame Lavoisier in 1788 that none of these blessings could make him forget his nine years of happiness in Paris: "And now, even in my sleep, I find that the scenes of all my pleasant dreams are laid in that city, or in its neighbourhood."[15] James, however, five years after he had gladly left Paris, remembered coming to see that there he would be "an eternal outsider."[16] This difference shapes his story. Newman, standing outside the convent wall behind which Claire de Cintré has retreated forever, has his first experience of a limit that he cannot overcome by ingenuity, resolve, or wealth. He had failed economically before and recovered again; however, from this failure of his quest for a wife, who would represent the aristocratic Old World to perfection, there is no recouping his loss. He can only come to terms with it by taking satisfaction, as he comes to do, in realizing that "the woman within was lost beyond recall. . . . Everything was over, and he too at last could rest."[17]

James's version of the success story revises it by establishing its limits. Newman is too historically naive and ignorant about French aristocratic society to understand the improbability of his romantic quest, and he is too intent on seeing his marriage to Claire as the acquisition of what he calls "the best article in the market," the symbol of "the greatest victory over circumstances," to understand her psychology.[18] When her family rejects Newman as "a commercial person," she is faced with reconciling her Catholic obedience to the religion of family with her distaste for her family's wish to marry her off again to another titled person of their own choosing. She solves it by abstracting herself from any possible marital choice. Newman, baffled by this "dusky, old-world expedient" of her becoming a nun, can only imagine that she was physically forced to enter the convent, which appears to him as a prison. (James has foreshadowed this ending in his hero's first glimpse of Claire's house, which looks to him like a convent.) In this sense, Mrs. Tristram was right; Newman is a barbarian in his ignorance of the world that he hopes to conquer.

But James's revision of the success story is also faithful to another associated myth, the idea of Nature's Nobleman. Franklin himself had cannily exploited its charm for European intellectuals when he appeared in the salons with his fur cap and his invented bifocals, the very image of a Solon from the wilderness. It is another version of the democratic idea about the unimportance of social origins; its protagonist is always, like a knight, a man with a code. In fiction the theme is most influentially developed in James Fenimore Cooper's mythmaking about his Natty Bumppo, reared by Indians and Moravians. It is carried on in the twentieth century by innumerable Westerns and private-eye films when their heroes have a stubborn integrity. James invokes the myth by having Newman eventually repudiate his chance to take revenge on the Bellegardes. Was it "Christian charity or unregenerate good nature" that enabled him to "let the Bellegardes go"?[19] James pretends not to answer the question, but the plot answers it for us. Newman plans to tell a duchess about Madame de Bellegarde's conspiracy to murder her husband, but disdain for her conceited gossiping society changes his mind. Why should he care what the duchess thinks of the Bellegardes? Later, he is ashamed to have wanted to hurt them because they hurt him, but "such things were really not his game." He strolls out of the church, where he has been contemplating the miscarriage of his quest, "like a good-natured man who is still a little ashamed."[20]

He tells Mrs. Tristram that he has had satisfaction enough in having frightened them with what he might do with his knowledge of their guilt; but she believes that they had successfully counted on his "remarkable good nature" never really coming to the point of taking revenge. But it is not so much amiability as American disdain for European intrigue that motivates him. In this respect, James's novel serves the traditional myth of American diplomacy about the innocent nation that must always be wary of being gulled by sophisticated and corrupt European diplomats. There is a continuity in Newman's career. He had earlier disdained revenge when wronged in a commercial matter by a rival. His European adventure recapitulates that same "mortal disgust" in a new milieu.

In that first experience of his rejection of revenge Newman had driven out into the country and looked at the "first green leaves on Long Island," feeling a "new man" inside his old skin and longing for "a new world."[21] Curiously enough, it is "the fresh green breast of the new world" that is also the subject of Nick Carraway's meditation on Long Island at the end of F. Scott Fitzgerald's *The Great Gatsby*. Other echoes of *The American* are much louder. Jay Gatsby, the self-made rich man of obscure origins, is obsessed, as Newman was, with marrying a woman who is symbolic of the mystery that privileged wealth "imprisons and preserves." Fitzgerald's is also a story of a Westerner's quest in the East, and the cultural symbolism of the two regions is transferred to East and West Egg, Long Island. The Buchanans, linked to Yale and old money, live at the East end; Gatsby, linked to a Western pioneer, Dan Cody, who has brought the violence of the brothel and the saloon to the East, lives at West Egg in a garish mansion, bought with dubious new money, derived from bootlegging. He throws large parties while looking yearningly at the green light on the end of Daisy's dock.

The story also evokes Franklin's memoir when Gatsby's father proudly displays his son's Hopalong Cassidy book with Gatsby's inscribed schedule for self-improvement and its references to studying inventions and electricity. This evocation, of course, dramatizes the vast difference between the eighteenth-century model and the corrupted twentieth-century exemplar of the self-made man. But, as in James's novel, the representatives of Eastern stability, propriety, status, and privilege are much more radically flawed: Tom Buchanan is attracted to pretentious racist ideologies and has sordid extramarital affairs, while Daisy is really as common as her name and is quite inadequate to Gatsby's romantic dream of her. Having killed her husband's mistress in a car accident, she lets Gatsby take the blame so that the dead woman's husband kills him in revenge. Fitzgerald's fashionable 1920s scene appropriately features its own wasteland, "a valley of ashes" over which presides a giant advertisement for an oculist, a face that is only a pair of eyes with no other human features.

Amid this squalor, Gatsby's "creative passion" for his dream of Daisy and his faithfulness to his invented idea of himself as an acceptable suitor, ultimately seem admirable to Nick, even though he thinks Jordan Baker is "too wise" to carry "well-forgotten dreams" from age to age.[22] Nick knows that Gatsby is sentimentally dedicated to repeating the past by recapturing the moment when Daisy first flowered for him, as if she never loved anybody else. We never know whether, like Nick, Gatsby finally sees through Daisy or instead maintains his dream until the end. What is clear is that Nick himself generalizes the story to represent a commentary on his historical distance from the time when the New World flowered before the eyes of the Dutch sailors who discovered Long Island. Gatsby's dream of Daisy's green light is analogous to their sight of the "fresh green breast of the new world," something commensurate—unlike Daisy—to man's capacity for wonder. In Nick's meditation, the continent then and for the last time answered to the "last and greatest of all human dreams," the vision of a brave New World in America. Nick thinks that Americans now, like Gatsby, fail to realize that the dream is already behind them, contemporary reality no longer being capable of pandering to it.

Nick, who has himself been seeking an Eastern success in the bond business, concludes that all of the main characters in the story, being Westerners, are somehow unadapted to Eastern life, and he plans to return to the Middle West. Fitzgerald, in an interview given after he had published his novel, reinforced Nick's somber pessimism by appealing to Spengler's popular *Decline of the West* and complaining that the good American, while admirable as an individual, collectively speaking is "a mass product without common sense or guts or dignity." Taunting the reporter, Fitzgerald scorned American identification of money with greatness and declared that "the best of America drifts to Paris" because of France's "intelligence and good manners." This dream of the East, which matches the dreams of both Newman and Gatsby, is offset, however, by his final appeal in the interview to "the birth of a hero," who will be of age when a national testing-time comes, to redeem the country. Fitzgerald, in Spengler's portentous vein, spoke of Mussolini as "an omen for America" at some imminent time when we would have "to fight for our race." Yet, Fitzgerald portrayed the redeeming hero as someone who would come out of "the immigrant class, in the guise of an east-side newsboy" with a mother who knows her son will be a hero.[23] The prophecy is classically, almost parodically, fitted to the American myth of the self-made man, in spite of the novelist's Spenglerian gloom, and it goes far towards explaining Fitzgerald's profound sympathy with Gatsby as a person who, in spite of his criminal connections, is better than everyone else around him.

These variations on the theme of the self-made man evoke and revise Franklin's original account in his memoir. Hawthorne's short story connects his character with the fate of "a rising people," as Benjamin Vaughan believed Franklin's story would illustrate, but the major event of the rise that Hawthorne portrays is a divisive and violent mockery of British authority. In "My Kinsman, Major Molineux," young Robin may be shrewd enough, like Franklin, to rise without the patronage of his uncle, as his guide suggests in the last line of the story, but the Revolution he has joined in repudiating the colonial past has entailed, as the narrator tells us, a savage humiliation of an honorable man. What is troubling about the ending is Robin's amnesia about his search for his uncle during a nightmarish experience of joining the mob in its mocking of him. It is as if Robin were setting out on the future without having any past as a basis for his new identity. Joyce A. Rowe, in a study of classic American novels, suggests further that "it is as if Ben Franklin himself were standing beside Robin."[24] But Franklin tells us in his autobiography that it was his father who first turned his children's attention to "what was good, just, and prudent in the Conduct of Life," and the son sometime in the 1750s placed a marble marker over the grave of his parents and wrote the inscription for it, honoring their piety, prudence, and virtue.[25] He had fled his home in Boston to make his fortune in Philadelphia, but it was not part of his mythmaking to repudiate his sense of indebtedness to the past.

Melville's satire is self-consciously reductive of Franklin's actual multifariousness and genius in the interest of commemorating a Revolutionary patriot who never experiences a rise to fame and fortune because of hardships that transcend the limitations of Poor Richard's wisdom. James's romance portrays a classic post-Civil War self-made hero, who as a representative American blend of innocence and experience is typically Western and a man of business, though quite without any of the ruthlessness found in the actual millionaires of the period. James's version dramatizes the limits of the success story, introducing the idea of the need for the uncultured and provincial hero to make his peace with a failure that has no remedy. It is an acute comment on what is conspicuously lacking in the standard myth. With Fitzgerald, echoing both James and Franklin, but substituting for their humor a poignancy and pathos of his own, the self-made man has become a shady character, redeemed only by a romantic passion that is hopelessly out of phase with his actuality. Fitzgerald's story makes his contemporary self-made man derive remotely from Franklin, but Gatsby is even further than Newman from the eighteenth century when the Revolution, in which Franklin played such an important role, aimed to carry out in political terms the dream of a new society.

It is worth emphasizing that these writers are attracted to the theme of cultural polarity between East and West as it works in the American imagination, the differing appeals of tradition and opportunity. Their heroes find their opportunities by hitching their wagons to a Western star and moving to a more mobile society, but they remain vulnerable to the lure of the East wind, blowing from a more traditional quarter.[26] Hawthorne's hero is drawn to seek patronage from a high-ranking member of the court party. Melville's hero, though much victimized by his foreign experience, is impressed by the civility of King George, whom he considers to have been maligned by the patriots. Even in Franklin's life there is a forecast of this ambivalent attraction of East and West, for he himself spent eighteen years on Craven Street, London, enjoying the fact that this "petty island, which compared to America, is but a stepping stone in a brook," nevertheless, had "in almost every neighborhood, more sensible, virtuous, and elegant minds than we can collect in ranging a hundred leagues of our vast forests."[27] He had even hoped to settle in England, until he was charged in the Privy Council with malice and bad faith. By 1775, he had given up all hope of imperial union and was convinced instead of "the extreme corruption prevalent among all orders of men in this old, rotten state" in contrast to "the glorious public virtue so predominant in our rising country."[28]

These were the terms all American patriots could agree on in the Revolutionary years. By the time of Fitzgerald's story it is clear that the polarity still survived in his distinction between East Egg and West Egg, but the old patriotic sense of the American/European contrast was now for Fitzgerald as archaic as the age of discovery.

It is possible to think of Gatsby as linking up both the naturalistic tradition of Franklin and the idealistic tradition of Emerson, two versions of self-reliance, one by a self-made businessman, civic leader, scientist, and diplomat, the other by a self-made poet.[29] From this point of view the tale dramatizes the bankruptcy of both the economic and the poetic versions of self-reliance. As a self-made man, Gatsby is a criminal, not the Napoleon of business whom his father imagined his son was destined to become; and as a lover, Gatsby is a fantasist. But this Franklin/Emerson polarity is much too neat, as if Emerson had no Yankee shrewdness and Franklin had no imaginative aspirations. True, Emerson did see a lack of "fiery grain" in Franklin, but the poet was himself cannily concerned to get his legal benefits from his dead wife's estate so that his intellectual career could be based on the security of the legacy.[30] Franklin, for his part, pursued science as a dedicated experimentalist, not merely as a utilitarian inventor.

Fitzgerald may seem to have corrected the success myth by sending Nick Carraway back home to the Midwest at the end of the story. But it is there that he has rejected a "certain girl" by mail, and he rejects another, Jordan Baker, before he returns. It is from this position of a far from splendid isolation that he indulges in the concluding speculation that it was the Dutch discoverers of Long Island who, "for the last time in history," met with something commensurate to man's "capacity for wonder."[31] Franklin's own rise entailed duties and pleasures abroad that in effect made him virtually abandon his wife when she needed him most. His smiling detachment provoked Carl Becker to maintain that only in nature did Franklin meet "a disinterestedness matching his own."[32] But this evaluation makes far too little of his commitment to the Revolution. It was so strong, in fact, that he harshly never forgave his son for becoming a Tory. Nothing actual, however, can evoke Nick's commitment, and his generalizing of Gatsby's fate is consistent with this incapacity, which Nick defends as a mark of his single virtue of honesty. Nick's romantic pessimism is the other side of Gatsby's romantic optimism. Going home again, in this context, is "a rejection of that mutual sympathy which is the only real liberation from the wheel of endless longing and endless failure that Nick insists is our inevitable American fate."[33] Such sympathy was more of an ideal for Hawthorne than it was for any other evoker of Franklin's memoir.

Chapter 2

In Hawthorne's Shadow: The Minister and the Woman in Howells, Adams, Frederic, and Updike

NO MATTER how our literary past has been viewed, Hawthorne has the distinction of having always been seen, ever since *The Scarlet Letter* (1850), as a classic American writer.[1] Frequently painted and photographed, he sat for a sculpture that, his son complained, made him look like a "combination of Daniel Webster and George Washington."[2] The references are appropriate: for our history, he has been a literary hero comparable to what Webster and Washington were as political heroes for Hawthorne's generation. The length of his shadow is illustrated by the fact that when Malcolm Cowley wanted to give Ernest Hemingway and William Faulkner classic status, he associated them both with Hawthorne for having what Melville had first called "the power of blackness."[3]

It is remarkable that the man who became the nineteenth century's exemplar of the American writer is best known for a novel about a minister's adultery in which the woman is the most memorable and sympathetic character. Unlike most adulterous heroines of nineteenth-century novels, she is allowed to survive and her illegitimate child is given a happy future after the events of the novel are over. Not surprisingly, modern feminists have responded to her because Hawthorne himself presented her as a flawed believer in a day when there would be a female apostle of a new truth that would "establish the whole relation between man and woman on a surer ground of mutual happiness." He also saw her from the beginning of the story as walking in the footsteps of the Puritan Anne Hutchinson, whom the minister John Cotton had

22

much admired before she became treated as a scandal. She had posed a threat to the established church and magistrates for her antinomian heresy, which disturbed a crucial Calvinist balance by celebrating election by God's grace at the expense of sharply reducing the value of performing good works. Moreover, she implied that she had immediate revelations from God. Even more pertinently for Hawthorne's purpose, she also threatened the establishment as a female preacher who did not "know her place."[4] Hawthorne was an ardent admirer of Sir Walter Scott's historical novels, and *The Scarlet Letter* pays close attention to many aspects of its setting in the 1640s, but its symbolic use of Hester Prynne points the story both backwards and forewards in time. In this way it tends to loosen the character from her period and so gives the issues of the novel a power of suggestion to later writers who deal with marital triangles. They would deal with contemporary issues in a contemporary setting, but the shadow of Hawthorne's triangle would fall upon them.

Howells wrote his publisher about *A Modern Instance* (1882) that he intended to treat tragically a theme "only less intense and tragic than slavery," the "enormous fact" in American life of divorce.[5] The American Bureau of Labor made a report on divorce for 1867 to 1886, in which year it had reached over 25,000. Citing this report, the *Encyclopaedia Britannica* (11th edition) made Howells's point indirectly when its article on divorce concluded: "The prevalence of divorce in the United States among the native population, in urban communities, among the New England element, in the middle classes of society, and among those of the Protestant faith, indicates how closely this social phenomenon is interlaced with much that is characteristic and valuable in American civilization." Howells's novel dealt with precisely these elements. He deliberately set his story in the middle 1870s because the disputed election of 1876, with its charges of corruption, made an appropriate background for his portrait in the foreground of a deeply flawed marriage. As its female victim, Marcia Hubbard, discovers, since the minister failed to ask for the legal form for a declaration of intent, the union was tainted with fraud from the beginning.

The couple in the failed marriage are thoroughly ordinary, and Howells at one point spoke of "we new men" in describing a club of young journalists like Bartley Hubbard, the delinquent husband; this use of the pronoun helps explain the credibility of the novel's portrait. Howells

understood how different Henry James was from himself: "His best efforts seem to me those of romance; his best types have an ideal development, like Isabel and Claire Belgarde and Bessy Alden and poor Daisy
and even Newman."[6] Howells admitted the influence of French fiction,
particularly Daudet, on the new school that James represented, but funda-
mentally, he asserted, "the new school derives from Hawthorne and
George Eliot rather than any others."[7] Critics have usefully discussed *The
Portrait of a Lady* in relation to both Hawthorne and Eliot, and *A Modern
Instance* has been compared both to James's novel and *The Scarlet Letter.*[8]
Howells might have included himself in the new school, whose arrival he
saluted in an essay on James, in so far as Hawthorne was also for him a
profoundly important predecessor. Indeed, characteristically, Howells later countered Henry James's Anglophile laments about the absence of
differentiated manners in America, as a resource for fiction, by praising
"the simple, domestic, democratic qualities in Hawthorne."[9] Howells
saw in Hawthorne a crucial aspect of himself as a writer.

Hawthorne as a writer had turned to the Puritan world precisely
because he knew that its assumptions were no longer dominant. The
drama of Hawthorne's triangle depended upon its context of a powerful
orthodoxy that set severe limits to individualism of any kind. Howells
emphasized the extent to which the 1870s by contrast represented "a
rather chaotic liberality" in which religion was no longer "a fact of
spiritual experience," and the spirit and functions of the churches had
become deeply secularized as the churches "embraced and included the
world." Bartley Hubbard as an opportunistic newspaperman complacently accepts the modern gospel of "giving people what they want" as
a justification for journalistic sensationalism, and the same principle has
come to dominate the churches. Typically, when Marcia Gaylord has to
choose a church for the christening of her baby, the only criterion she
can think of is to find one "where the best people went." The unfashionable Mrs. Halleck, who still understands religion in the Calvinist terms
of a "saving experience," can make no headway at all in conversing
with this "ruinous open-mindedness." (Mark Twain, who had been
brought up where Presbyterian Calvinism was a reality, told Howells
that he thought this scene was very funny; the humor must be lost on
many contemporary readers.)

Ironically, Squire Gaylord's deistic "infidelity" is in some respects
closer to the spirit of the Puritans because he is similarly committed to

doctrine and to moral severity, and as a dominating patriarch, he makes his wife and daughter live "soft and snug in the shelter of his iron will and indomitable courage." When his daughter pleads with him to be forgiving towards her irresponsible husband, the squire disdainfully observes that forgiveness cannot change the consequences that have been set in motion by their marriage. As a lawyer, he defends his daughter, in a countersuit for divorce from her deserting husband, with a zestful relish and is determined to show Bartley Hubbard "that there is a God in Israel yet!" Feeling as wronged by his daughter's marriage as Hawthorne's Chillingworth was by Hester's adultery, the squire is also bent on revenge and can only be restrained by his daughter's mercy and his own physical collapse from a stroke.

Howells's heroine has none of Hester's speculative boldness or her public humiliation; she constantly forgives her husband for his derelictions and has none of a modern feminist's pride or independence. Marcia Gaylord's marriage to the charming but characterless Hubbard is as unthinking and mistaken as Hester's was to the old scholar of the occult. Whereas Hawthorne audaciously endowed Hester with a forbidden but genuine love, consummated outside the covenant of marriage (and outside the pages of the novel), Howells much more circumspectly provided Marcia with a lover (Ben Halleck) who, out of respect for the marriage bond, never breaks his suffering silence to declare his feelings for her; instead, he even urges her to return to her husband when she has left him after a quarrel. In the end, he leaves the law to become what Arthur Dimmesdale always was—an orthodox minister who guiltily loves a married woman. But Dimmesdale with candor and remorse finally exposed his sin in public, according to the Puritan demand for confession, and he had the satisfaction in his "triumphant ignominy" of dying while ending his hypocrisy and acting out the imperatives of his faith. Halleck, on the other hand, who had failed his family's hopes that in being sent to college in Maine, rather than to Unitarian Harvard, he would carry on the family's orthodox religion, finally is driven to cure his doubts by accepting everything in his "inherited belief" in the spirit of having "fled to it as to a city of refuge." Worn out with the strain of living with his unconfessed love and the uncertainties of reasoning about morality, he had "known the terrors of the law, and he preached them to his people; he had known the Divine mercy, and he also preached that" in the backwoods of Maine. Dimmesdale's confession was sanctioned by the faith he had always publicly, if hypocritically, maintained; Halleck's new-found orthodoxy registers his exhaustion.

Hester's heretical attempt to persuade Dimmesdale (with only tempo-rary success) that their love had "a consecration of its own" is echoed weakly by Howells not in the passive and ignorant Marcia, but in Ben Halleck's unsuccessful attempt to convince himself and his friendly legal adviser, Eustace Atherton, that only love can justify maintaining the marriage bond. His conservative friend, who considers divorce a social crime against the institution of marriage, never accepts this justification for Ben. Nor does Hawthorne let Hester escape to Europe with her lover, as she planned to do, and sends her back finally to put the "A" on her dress again long after the community no longer required it of her. Only in this voluntary act does she possibly express by an outer act any inner "penitence," which Hawthorne, like the Puritan community, carefully distinguishes from external "penance." Hester's final act embellishes her dignity as a character taking responsibility for her deeds. For Ben Halleck "his love was to have been a law to itself, able to loose and to bind, and potent to beat down all regrets, all doubts, all fears that questioned it," but like Hester he finds that his hope is a "delusion." He is compelled to play the parts of both Hester and Arthur. Halleck's contriteness and turning to orthodoxy, however, seem morbidly self-punishing, on the one hand, and weakly acquiescent, on the other.

Howells characteristically has prepared us for this view of Halleck by letting us overhear the moral commentary of two women on Atherton's stern moralizing about Ben. Many critics have been persuaded that How-ells seems to retreat into Atherton's view because he notes, in the author's realistic vein, that "it isn't a question of gross black and white, mere right and wrong, there are degrees, there are shades." Then the lawyer, who has persuasively maintained that love without marriage is worse in its consequences than marriage without love, draws an unshaded conclusion that for Halleck, whatever the case with some other man, there could only be a "lapse from the ideal" in marrying Marcia, even after her husband has died. The modern reader must surely find much more conge-nial the objections Howells put in the mouth of two women: Ben's sister Olive, a spunky Unitarian who recognizes the travesty of Marcia's mar-riage, endorses the idea of a divorce, and sympathizes with her brother's emotional agony, and Atherton's more conventional wife Clara, whose common sense insists that what a man wants to have, rather than what he ought to have, is more to the point in marrying. She sees no reason why she and her husband should share Ben's morbid guilt for wishing at one point that he could profit from Marcia's divorce.

In this respect Atherton echoes Dimmesdale's asking Hester if she didn't think that his public confession and death were better than what they had dreamed of in the forest. In Hawthorne's climax Hester had replied; "I don't know! I don't know!" Howells ends his book with Clara asking if her husband is going to write Ben to tell him that he is wrong to think that he can atone for loving Marcia when she was married. Atherton's reply echoes Hester: "Ah, I don't know! I don't know!" The difference is even more striking than the similarity: Hester's doubt keeps faith with her socially and religiously unsanctioned love. Atherton only questions whether he should express his severe moral convictions to his friend.

Both of these agnostic exclamations have generated continuing controversy about the intentions of both writers. Does Hawthorne identify with Hester's romantic dream? Does Howells identify with Atherton's judgment against Ben Halleck? But Hawthorne and Howells are alike in trying to establish a kind of impartiality about the issues they dramatize. Neither author *is* either character; being created, characters necessarily differ from their creators. The course of the stories themselves makes it clear that neither Hester's romantic radicalism nor Atherton's legalistic conservatism is unchallengeable. The important comparative question is whether the balance of forces in the Howells novel can equal the balance of forces in Hawthorne's.

Hawthorne's novel gains its power from its refusal to endorse either Hester or the community that punishes her. Quentin Anderson has made the point best: "Hester's whole perspective on her world is analogous in its falsity and abstractness to the perspective in which she has been placed by those who judged her."[10] Her merely outward form of charity matches Dimmesdale's merely public piety. They are caught in a tragic conflict because both their sexuality and their civilization have grounds for objecting to each other, an issue discussed in Freud's *Civilization and Its Discontents*. Howell's novel has less strength in this respect because Marcia in her provincial naivete and self-deception is too complicit with her victimizer, Bartley Hubbard; and her lover's hidden love is much too hidden to pose any serious problem except to Ben's own agonized conscience. There is no threat to society from his unconsummated passion, and even if Atherton were right that divorce itself threatens social stability (as its increasing frequency might well do a hundred years later), Ben's participation in the process leading to the divorce suit is remarkably minimal. At a time when Marcia believes her husband is dead, Ben comes by accident on the papers advertising Bartley Hubbard's attempt to divorce Marcia on fraudulent grounds of abandonment. Instead of protecting her illusions about her husband, Ben shows her the papers; even then, only her father can shatter her misconceptions about her husband by appealing to her jealousy of a possible rival.

This act of Ben's is all that Howells presents us as a ground for Atherton's judgment against him. Keeping Marcia in her nearly invincible ignorance of her husband's true character is such a bad cause that Ben's refusal to do so, even if colored by some self-interest, cannot fairly be faulted, as the narrator puts it portentously, for succumbing to "the enemy of souls." It is one thing to show Ben as an agonized conscience without religious guidance; it is another for the narrator to stand in judgment on him for his action. Atherton in his arguments with Ben about his hopeless love insists that "It's our deeds that judge us." But, Ben's deeds are never dubious enough to constitute a judgment against him—except on grounds of his feeling too much morbid guilt. Dimmesdale is also a weak and guilty person, but he has something to be genuinely guilty about.

From this comparative point of view, Atherton's severe abstract moralism suggests the context of Howell's title: "at the last possible moment, the phrase about the fat, pretentious justice of *As You Like It*, 'full of wise saws and modern instances,' drifted into Howells' mind, and he telegraphed his title to Gilder."[11] Seen in this light, the lawyer Atherton's moralizing may appropriately be described as "pretentious." He seems to be a throwback to a world that does not any longer exist; how can one make such unqualified moral judgments in a world in which there is a "chaotic liberality" in religion?

This question animated many Victorians whose ethical anxiety increased in proportion to their agnosticism. Puritanism was ruled out both for Hawthorne and Howells, and neither author was traditionally religious. The law itself in providing for divorce implied that marriage was not a covenant with God but simply a contract that could be ended by the agreement of both parties. John Stuart Mill, the philosopher of modern liberalism, had expressed this view in a private letter in 1855, but in his public writings even he committed himself to justifying divorce as a relief only in extreme cases.[12] Howells dramatized an extreme case with ordinary beginnings, but he also portrayed a woman whose ignorance about herself and her husband kept her, for most of the book, devoted to him in spite of his faults, thus inhibiting the suit of the responsible third member of the triangle. How could he claim that the marriage was invalid when the long-suffering wife still blindly clung to her morally feckless husband? Even in a non-Puritan world the son of a traditionally Christian family could feel the force of Atherton's point. But that problem, for the reader, disappeared with the divorce and the husband's death. The lover's continuing obsession with it has only a psychological, not a moral interest, while Hawthorne's genius was to fuse them together in a convincing way.

Even though contemporary reviewers tended not to read his tragedy as a historical novel,[13] Hawthorne had the advantage of distancing his story in the Puritan age; its authoritarian orthodoxy gave force to the lovers' sin at the same time as it created sympathy for the heroine and a sanctioned resolution for the hero. Howells paid the price of his belief that the American world of respectable magazines in which he published would not tolerate a contemporary version of *The Scarlet Letter.*[14] Still, his portrait of a marriage without love and a love without marriage could stand for a current version so long as adultery itself was not part of the story. He used the terms "pathetic" and "tragically" in contemplating his intentions for his novel, and what we finally hear is the note of pathos rather than of tragedy. Howells had no interest in reconstructing Hawthorne's Puritan setting; "realism" was the world of the present. Yet Howells suggests through Atherton and Halleck the shrewd cultural observation that distorted remnants of the Puritan conscience still survived in New England, even in the much-relaxed liberal era of the 1870s, which also produced young men on the make and ignorant provincial girls without any visible means of support by principles or traditions.

One novel, virtually restricted to private publication, Henry Adams's *Esther* (1884), follows Hawthorne in telling the story from the heroine's perspective. Adams invokes his predecessor directly by having his heroine come from a branch of the old Puritan Dudleys, her father taking a fancy to her name "when he met it in Hawthorne's story." This reference to "Esther Dudley" is a rather cryptic clue compared to the association of Esther with the Hester of Hawthorne's more famous story, but both names have their bearing. The old Puritan Thomas Dudley, first deputy-governor of the Massachusetts Bay Colony, was father to Anne Bradstreet, the Puritan poet of religious faith and family life. He was a loving and indulgent father, as she was an admiring daughter, who celebrated him in the poem whose lines are carved on the Dudley gate at Harvard College. Esther's emotional relation to her father is similar, and she is also artistically talented—as a painter. Her artistic tutor perceptively describes her as a "lightly-sparred yacht in mid-ocean," sailing gaily along "though there is no land in sight and plenty of rough weather coming." Appropriately enough, Anne Bradstreet herself had noted in one of her moral meditations: "A ship that beares much saile, and little or no ballast, is easily overset; and that man whose head hath great abilities, and his heart little or no grace, is in danger of foundering."[15] Esther's position is risky because while she is in love with a minister, who urges her to accept his faith, she herself shares the scientific agnosticism of her cousin, a professor of paleontology. Her intellect and her feelings are split, and she stubbornly refuses to sacrifice one to the other, thus making marriage to either the minister or the scientist an impossibility. She dislikes churchgoing as much as her father. Her romantic triangle, like Hester's, is defined by her relationship to a scientist and a minister, although it is only potentially a sexual one.

Hawthorne's Esther Dudley would seem at first glance to be quite irrelevant as a prototype for Adams's Esther. Hawthorne's character is an old royal pensioner, living in Boston's Province House and keeping alive her anachronistic loyalty to the king after the Revolution has outmoded her. Lord Howe has given her a key to present to the royal governor, who she ardently hopes will return, and she almost gives it by mistake to the republican Governor Hancock. Her only resemblance to the modern Esther would seem to be temperamental: the spinster loyalist's "immutable resolve" to maintain her political faith is as stubborn as the modern Esther's determination not to sacrifice her intellectual doubts about religion to the pressure of her suitor's belief.

At a psychological level, however, Adams could have seen an analogy between his heroine and the political conservatism of Hawthorne's Esther. The psychological point is that the latter is as fixated on the king, a political father figure, as Adams's Esther is on her actual father. When she realizes that he is dying, she finds it "worse than anything she had ever imagined; she wanted to escape, to run away, to get out of life itself, rather than suffer such pain, such terror, such misery of helplessness."

Her engagement to the minister is only temporary; she breaks it off in fidelity to her own disbelief in the church. Her agnosticism, seeking forms of truth more impersonal than Christianity's, is mixed with a troubling self-hatred. "I despise and loathe myself," she cries out to the minister, "and yet you thrust self at me from every corner of the church as if I loved and admired it."

Esther at this point comes painfully close to illustrating the actual psychology of Marion Hooper Adams, whose depression after the death of her father ended in suicide by poisoning herself with the chemicals Adams had given her for her hobby of photography. Adams bought up the extant copies of his novel (published under a pseudonym) in tragic awareness of how percipient he had been about his wife's psychology. His friend Clarence King had prophetically pointed out that Adams had "left his heroine no alternative but suicide to escape the trap into which her intellectual scruples and her emotions had placed her."[16]

Beyond her particular fate, Esther illustrates "the woman question" in so far as she is expected to follow a man who has defined an ideal—in this case the minister. Refusing him, she flees to Europe with her female companion. In Hawthorne's novel, it is Hester's daughter who claims a future for herself by going to Europe. Adams, no more than Hawthorne, however, could imagine what an intellectual woman could successfully do with her life, and he feared that the new woman might be sexless, lacking the qualities of either a Venus or a Virgin. In this respect Hawthorne's Hester is a clear precedent for Adams's Esther.

Hawthorne expressed his doubts about intellectual women when he wrote about Anne Hutchinson in his *Biographical Sketches*. He introduced his historical remarks by throwing cold water on the idea of welcoming female writers: "Woman, when she feels the impulse of genius like a command of Heaven within her, should be aware that she is relinquishing a part of the loveliness of her sex, and obey the inward voice with sorrowing reluctance, like the Arabian maid who bewailed the gift of prophecy." He acknowledged that Mrs. Hutchinson was "a woman of extra-ordinary talent and strong imagination" as a reformer in religion. But her ideas, he insisted, were a threat to Puritan unity and public safety. Unlike his contemporaries, who generally saw in her case the proof of Puritan illiberality, Hawthorne believed that "the principles of an illiberal age indicated the very course which must have been pursued by worldly policy and enlightened wisdom." Her claim to be "commissioned to separate the true shepherds from the false" among the Puritan ministers promoted a diversity that would have "scattered them from the land to which they had as yet so few attachments, or, perhaps, have excited a diminutive civil war among those who had come so far to worship together."[17] By the time of *The Scarlet Letter,* this threat to union must have seemed more plausible to Hawthorne in the contemporary light of the growing sectional tensions over slavery. His portrait of Hester Prynne reflects his critical view of both Mrs. Hutchinson and of female writers by underlining the emotional and moral price that Hester paid for her bold individualism in love and thought by wandering in a "dark labyrinth" and losing her femininity.

In the introduction to his novel, Hawthorne dramatizes himself as experimentally putting the remnant of Hester's historic letter *A* on his own breast. It is a sign of his link to her through the power of imagination that he shares with Mrs. Hutchinson and Hester. Equivalently, because Henry Adams, as a mere spectator of the political world in which his ancestors had played such notably large parts, did not conform to the Victorian standard of masculinity as a form of power, he could imagine heroines who suffered from that cultural prejudice. As an agnostic naturalist, like Esther's scientist-friend, Adams went beyond Hawthorne in sympathy with a woman's intellectual skepticism. At Niagara Falls, Esther finds nature's eternity, infinity, and omnipotence in the falling water and endorses the idea of immortality as "having one true thought": What is true in us, as she puts it, will pour into a grand reservoir of truths, just as the falls pours into the basin beneath. Yet, even less than Hester can this troubled heroine carry out a prophetic feminist role. All she can do is maintain the integrity of her unbelief in the church.

Adams had been a professor at Harvard with William James, who in the 1880s defended "the will to believe" against the contemporary scientific agnosticism that ignored the need of religious "overbeliefs" as "truths of orientation" providing a basis for action, which could not wait until all the evidence was in. Adams implicitly replied to James in *Esther* by presenting someone who refused the risk of faith and took the risk of doubt instead. She could not make herself believe in what she did not believe, even though she had vital reasons for wishing to do so.

Harold Frederic also presupposed *The Scarlet Letter* when he wrote his novel with the Hawthornian-sounding title, *The Damnation of Theron Ware* (1896), which deservedly made his reputation both here and in

England, where he had become a foreign correspondent for the *New York Times* in the year that Adams published *Esther*. But unlike Adams, or their predecessors, Frederic turned the triangle to the purposes of serious comedy. Whereas Adams had dramatized an honest doubter, Frederic dramatized a dishonest doubter as another modern type. His upstate New York protagonist is an uneducated, married Methodist preacher, whose infatuation with a flirtatious devotee of hedonistic Hellenism, Celia Madden, is actually no more serious than his intellectual speculations. Stimulated by his association with Celia and her intellectual friend, the Catholic priest Father Forbes, Ware modernizes his old-fashioned religion into a skeptical form of liberalism that subverts his Christian belief without his ever realizing it. Fancying that he is progressing, he is actually declining. It is as if Frederic had conflated Hester and Arthur in Theron Ware, but by giving him the most dubious aspects of both. The Roger Chillingworth of the novel is the insidious Dr. Ledsmar, an authority on Assyriology, a scholar whose satanic aspect is suggested by his having written a book on the anthropological history of serpent worship. He is a cynical materialist who is experimenting on his Chinese servant with doses of opium, but unlike Chillingworth, he has no marital relationship to the woman whom the minister imagines he loves.

One reviewer saw "more than a mere touch of the vanished hand that wrote 'The Scarlet Letter' " in Frederic's novel, and he acknowledged Hawthorne as one of his heroes.[18] Van Wyck Brooks in a modern edition of *The Damnation* observed that Henry Adams might have seen in Celia Madden the force in the power of sex that he found largely absent in America.[19] But she also represents the New Woman who insists that she belongs to no one and belongs to herself "as much as any man." She is a nominal Catholic who puts into her religion, as she avows, whatever she likes, as Ware under her influence increasingly does with his Protestantism. Their relationship is most reminiscent of Hawthorne's novel in the scene when "once more a minister sits in the forest with the woman he loves as she lets down her hair to catch the sunlight filtering through the trees," and Theron is moved by Celia's kiss also to dream of escape by sailing away with her.[20] But the crucial revision Frederic has made in Hawthorne's materials is evident in the comically ironical fact that the minister's dream is inspired by a kiss that is "a swift, almost perfunctory caress." Moreover, it is a dream corrupted by being inextricably linked in his mind with his awareness that "she was very rich."

Following Celia and Father Forbes to New York City, where his provincial prejudices lead him to suspect them of enjoying a tryst, Ware is crushed to discover that they have ceased to be entertained by him, now that he has lost his innocence and exposed his mistrust. They dismiss him as a bore. The pragmatic Soulsbys, who engineer Methodist revivals with an eye to theatrical effects, take pity on him and deflate the significance of his fall by reminding him that he has always been a deeply flawed man without a true calling for the ministry. Frederic has artfully given us clues from the beginning to expose the minister's clay feet—his financial irresponsibility, his unfairness to his wife, his commercial motive for writing, and his opportunistic preaching of either conservative or liberal version of the gospel, depending on his audience. When we last see him, he is recovering and contemplating a political career in the West, one that is sure, like the ministry, to call again on his talent for oratory and self-deception.

The fall that Frederic measures is not a moral one within the minister but an historical one in America, the distance between Ware's superficial enlightenment and the time of the older generation of circuit-riding Methodists (whom we glimpse only in the first chapter) when "a plain and homely people had been served by a fervent and devoted clergy." Ware's preaching has rhetorical power, like Dimmesdale's sermons, and both are hypocrites; but Hawthorne's minister was no provincial: he came from a venerable English university, bringing his learning into "our wild forest-land." His adultery was no flirtation; and measured by his orthodox Calvinism, it was a genuine fall. The Hawthornian point in Frederic's novel is that he invokes an earlier and more substantial generation, for in *The Scarlet Letter* Hawthorne similarly observes:

> It was an age when what we call talent had far less consideration
> than now, but the massive materials which produce stability and
> dignity of character a great deal more. The people possessed, by
> hereditary right, the quality of reverence; which, in their
> descendants, if it survive at all, exists in smaller proportion, and
> with a vastly diminished force in the selection and estimate of
> public men.

Hawthorne conceded that the change might be for both good and ill, but if the primitive statesmen of the Puritan era were not often brilliant, they had fortitude and self-reliance in times of peril enabling them to stand "like a line of cliffs against a tempestuous tide."[21] Frederic invokes a

Methodist generation of preachers that once had similar traits, which had atrophied in his own time, so that the easy false "enlightenment" of Theron Ware was a Protestant temptation.

Frederic had an accurate sense of the way in which modernist forms of Protestantism were, in fact, allying themselves with science, evolution, and historical criticism of the Bible, jettisoning traditional Christian doctrine in the process and presupposing a sentimental confidence that change is inevitably progress. Lyman Abbott, for example, a major molder of liberal social and religious thought through his editorship of *The Outlook,* accepted Darwinian evolution as if it could be used to justify his optimism that "God is steadily displacing the animal" in man; and Henry Ward Beecher, subject of a successfully contested adultery charge, acknowledged that traditional Calvinism, which was his heritage, was for him "like an armor which had lost its buckles and would not stick on."[22] They were more talented, influential, and substantial than Theron Ware ever was, but they had contributed to the intellectual climate in which he could so thoroughly deceive himself.

Hawthorne's triangle is a vivid presence in John Updike's novel *Roger's Version* (1986), but its comic spirit makes it a close kin to Frederic's story. As Updike's title suggests, he proposes to look at the triangle not from Hester's or Arthur's point of view, but rather from the perspective of the cuckolded husband. Roger Lambert is a former minister who has become a divinity school professor, specializing in scholarship about heresies. (This specialty will have much point in the climax.) Updike's use of the names Prynne and Chillingworth in *A Month of Sundays* merely reminds the reader that adultery is a theme he shares with Hawthorne; but in *Roger's Version* the references are further developed with the allusive names of Dale Kohler and Esther Lambert, and the reader is bidden to consider seriously the novel's relationship to its classic predecessor.

Hawthorne's novel dealt with adultery as an aspect of his historical subject of Puritanism; it did not otherwise appear in his work. Updike, however, persistently thematizes adultery in a suburban context as a contemporary subject, which, he said, "if I have not exhausted it, has exhausted me. But I have persisted . . . with the conviction that there was something good to say for it, some sad magic that, but for me, might go unobserved."[23] Updike has called *The Scarlet Letter* "our classic novel of religious conscience and religious suffering."[24] *Roger's Version* also deals with adultery in the context of religion. It is not conscience and suffering, however, but an intellectual debate about God that interests the author, who himself is a Christian believer willing to profess the Apostles' Creed;[25] and his characters are motivated mainly by libido rather than by conscience.

Updike's updating of Hawthorne is relentlessly contemporary; it doubles the adultery and then some. Esther's marriage to Roger, we learn, was preceded by their affair, which broke up his earlier marriage, forcing him to leave the ministry; and later she becomes erotically entangled with Dale Kohler, a graduate student in divinity who is also a computer expert and a fundamentalist Christian. Roger Lambert's mother, he tells us, was pregnant with him when she had an affair with a man who became her second husband; and Roger himself will succumb to the sexual teasing of his sluttish niece, Verna, daughter of his half-sister and mother of a half-black illegitimate child. By giving the child the name of Paula, reminiscent of Hester's Pearl, and making her mother a profane and promiscuous child abuser, smoking dope and living on welfare, Updike sharply reminds us of the temporal distance between the Boston of his story, with its tangled skein of family disorder, and the Boston of Hawthorne's Puritans or his contemporaries.

Updike's title not only indicates his narrator; it also emphasizes his angle of vision. Roger tells us that he not only enjoys theology, but finds "kindred comfort and inspiration in pornography," and his own imagining of the couplings between his wife and his student has a voyeuristic specificity. It is not irrelevant that he refers to the influential theologian Paul Tillich as "another fool of love," because Tillich himself was a womanizer with a compulsive taste for pornography, as Updike has pointed out in a review of his work.[26] This lubricious aspect of Roger's vision radically differs, of course, from Hawthorne's severely restrained treatment of Hester's sensuality. Updike's tactic might seem to suggest that he is only telling us about Roger's salacious imagination, but eventually his visionary narrating turns out to be virtually verified by Verna's own report that Dale has been enjoying sex, as described, with someone in his neighborhood. Her revelation turns Roger's vision into actual second sight. This unexplained mystery has the effect of making the reader uneasily wonder if the author himself is not hiding behind Roger's paranormal voyeurism.[27]

Updike has spoken of his earlier novel *Couples* as being about sex "as the emergent religion, as the only thing left," and in a discussion of sex in fiction he casually refers to "the delicious triadic scene in *The Devil in Miss Jones*," a pornographic movie.[28] Recounting his avid reading at age fourteen of Edmund Wilson's "The Princess with the Golden Hair" in *Memoirs of Hecate County,* banned in New York state, the story that gave him his "most vivid glimpse of sex through the window of fiction," Updike notes that Wilson's European sexual realism sets down "no sexual detail in simple celebration, to please and excite himself," but always to illuminate the social and psychological condition of his characters.[29] Updike's own writing about sex, while it sometimes focuses on realistic detail in a clinical way reminiscent of Wilson's cold eye, more often does have a celebratory and lyric quality.

In one sense, nevertheless, the author is not hiding at all: adultery is for him an especially compelling case of the phenomenon he finds central as a result of man's "paradoxical position in the Universe as a self-conscious animal." Only in being loved do we find "external corroboration of the supremely high valuation each ego secretly assigns itself." Accordingly, "this exalted area, then, is above all others the one where men and women will insist upon their freedom to choose—to choose that other being in whose existence their own existence is confirmed and amplified." Updike moves from this libertarian premise to the conclusion that "the enforced and approved bonds of marriage, restricting freedom, weaken love." The minor premise that carries him to it is simple: "The heart *prefers* to move against the grain of circumstance; perversity is the soul's very life."[30] In this idea there is much more than a glimmer of the traditional Christian concept of original sin. We begin to understand why adultery is such an obsessive subject for him: in that act the perverse heart prefers to move against the confines of the social contract. This assertion, which Hawthorne's novel powerfully chastens, reappears, clothed in Christian garments, in Updike's reflections on love in the Western world.

Much of *Roger's Version* is given over to a long, brilliantly argued debate between Roger and his student about the Christian God. Updike's updating of Hawthorne takes knowledgeable account of the new fundamentalists, who are often literate in some aspect of science or engineering and seek to put their creationism on scientific grounds. Dale in this case is a computer whiz, trying to derive God from concepts of high-energy physics and the Big Bang cosmology, inventing new versions of the teleological argument from design, and vainly manipulating his computer graphics in the hope of replicating ultimate reality. His computer jargon is exaggerated to the point of tedium, but he is a vividly comic creation of a contemporary type.

Updike's Roger, who works in a building named for the Puritan Thomas Hooker, who held relatively liberal views on some theological matters, is a scholar of heresies, as was his Hawthornian original, but the 1980s Roger is an admirer of Karl Barth, his "rascally pet," who has taught him that God is the Wholly Other who does not stand "at the end of some human way." Roger is scandalized by Dale's reduction of God to the status of a fact, as if he were an object among other objects; and he also admires Barth and Tertullian for their insistence that "the flesh is man." Updike's comic sense contrives his narrative to segue from this Christian reflection to Roger's vivid imagining of his wife performing fellatio with Dale.

Esther, like Hester, is much younger than her husband and is also talented (like Adams's Esther she is a painter). But Updike has drastically updated her so that her sexual voracity is finally too much for the student fundamentalist, and Hester's Pearl is transformed into Verna's Paula, the victim of child abuse. Dimmesdale ended in "triumphant ignominy," while Updike's Dale abandons his quasi-scientific-religious project for a thesis under the crushing impact of his affair with Esther and the intellectual onslaught of a skeptical scientist, who breezily explains, in a flurry of technical jargon, why the universe is merely "blind chance plus math." Updike cleverly ties together this scientific argument and his expansion of Hawthorne's triangle to four by having the scientist explain why four dimensions are necessary:

> "A lesser number of spatial dimensions, it just so happens,
> couldn't provide enough juxtapositions to get molecules of any
> complexity, let alone, say, brain cells. More than four, which is
> what you have with space-time, the complexity increases but not
> significantly: four is plenty, sufficient. O.K.?"
> Dale nods, thinking of Esther and myself, himself and Verna.
> Juxtapositions.[31]

Another ironic stroke of updating is that in Updike's story it is not the Dimmesdale figure, but the heretical and satanic Chillingworth figure, who seems to maintain the Christian faith. Updike makes this radical revision by having Roger succumb to the sexual invitations of the nineteeen-year-old niece, whom he is protecting from the consequences of her child abuse and promiscuity, and who finds him attractive because of his aura of evil. By the depth of his fall he can appreciate with a new vividness the infinite majesty of God. His Barthian faith in the Other has previously been tried, as he tells Dale, by the Other allowing so much evil that "he turns out to be a monster." But after Roger has become complicit, as he puts it, with incest, adultery, and child abuse by having sex with Verna, he has a spiritual vision that God's silence allows us to "enjoy and explore our human freedom"; and he finds a proof of His existence in the "immense distance measuring our abasement" before God's majesty. Updike gives another crucial, comically ironic twist, however, to his account of Roger's vision by showing that only later does this specialist in heresy come to see that what he took to be his faith is actually a traditional Christian heresy—"committing deliberate abominations so as to widen and deepen the field in which God's forgiveness can magnificently play," a forbidden form of tempting God.

What has really happened, as Roger finally realizes, is that

> I had been contaminated, if not by herpes or AIDS, by DSS; from my corbelled limestone academic precincts I had been dragged down into that sooty brick parish of common incurable muddle and woe from which I had escaped twice before, in leaving Cleveland and in leaving the ministry.[32]

When Verna decides to return to Cleveland, with his financial assistance, he is able finally to conclude: "Things had indeed worked out very well." *Roger's Version,* for all its revisionist resonance with *The Scarlet Letter,* is in spirit more akin to Harold Frederic's intellectual comedy, *The Damnation of Theron Ware,* in which the fallen minister, entangled in the late Victorian arguments over religion, also returns to the "incurable muddle" of ordinary life. If Ware had been tempted by an easy modern religious liberalism into scuttling his Christian faith, Roger was tempted by his skewed appropriation of Barth's orthodoxy to fall into his version of a traditional heresy. Seen in this light, *Roger's Version* makes a third corner in a triangle that includes *The Scarlet Letter* and *The Damnation of Theron Ware.*

Chapter 3

"Mediumistic Existence": The Female Trance-Speaker in Hawthorne, Howells, and James

FOR A quarter-century after 1947, influential American critics tended to agree with Lionel Trilling's comparison of Hawthorne and William Dean Howells with Henry James. It served the broad purpose of distinguishing an American tradition of "desocialized" romance from the more concrete, socially dense English novel of manners. Trilling spoke of "the lack of social texture" in Hawthorne's work, of Howells's inability to take the social subject "with full seriousness," and of Henry James being alone among our classic writers in knowing how to "scale the moral and aesthetic heights in the novel" by using "the ladder of social observation."[1] Nearly twenty-five years later, a friend and colleague of Trilling's at Columbia University, Quentin Anderson, marked the waning of Trilling's theme by turning it 180 degrees around, arguing that *The Scarlet Letter* is "much more closely akin to the novels of Jane Austen, George Eliot, or Trollope than it is to the late James," because the New Englander, unlike James, viewed society "as the unique ground of our triumphs and defeats." By then, Trilling himself, in his growing discontent with modernism, had come to take a much more positive view of Hawthorne and Howells.[2]

Neither Trilling's nor Anderson's formulations, however, each depending upon a neat polarity, deal with the matter of how both Howells and James happily found in Hawthorne's work a welcome point of departure for some of their own fiction. The first person to see a linkage of Hawthorne, Howells, and James was the philosopher William James. He wrote his brother Henry in 1870:

> It also tickled my national feeling not a little to note the resemblance of Hawthorne's style to yours and Howells's, even as I had earlier noted the converse. That you and Howells with all the models in English literature to follow, should needs involuntarily have imitated (as it were) this American, seems to point to the existence of some real American mental quality.[3]

T. S. Eliot in 1919 wrote about a close analogy between "the sort of experience which develops a man and the sort of experience which develops a writer. . . . This relation is a feeling of profound kinship, or rather of a peculiar personal intimacy, with another, probably a dead author. . . . It is a cause of development, like personal relations in life. Like personal intimacies in life, it may and probably will pass, but it will be ineffaceable."[4] He could have applied this idea to the relation of Howells and James to Hawthorne as a pervasive influence on their own work. Instead, Eliot discussed Hawthorne and James in terms of their representing a kind of leisured New England genius (despite James being a New Yorker), interested in "the deeper psychology" and using a dramatic method that enabled them to see characters "through the relation of two or more persons to each other." Eliot did recognize a Hawthorne influence on James at least at the beginning (*Roderick Hudson*) and the end (*The Sense of the Past*) of his career. The former novel resonates with Hawthorne's *The Marble Faun* and the latter (unfinished) with Hawthorne's uncompleted manuscript "The Ancestral Footstep." American artists in Italy and an Anglophiliac American in England, respectively, are their common subjects. But Eliot's main point was to treat James as a successor to Hawthorne in the sense of fulfilling potentialities that "poor Hawthorne" could only suggest. Eliot conceded that Hawthorne, with his erudition in colonial history, had a much more "acute historical sense" than James, who had only "a sense of the sense." Eliot ended his essay, nevertheless, by imagining Hawthorne "coming to a mediumistic existence again" in order to express his satisfaction that James had been given the opportunities that the New Englander had never had.[5] Oddly enough, one link between Hawthorne, Howells, and James would be their fictional interest in performing mediums.

In taking this line, Eliot unconsciously reflected the covert message of James's own highly qualified tribute to his predecessor in *Hawthorne* (1879). More often than not, as John Carlos Rowe has remarked, critics have defined a Hawthorne-James tradition in James's "own terms of comparison and contrast—terms invented by James before he himself had written the major works on which most of these critics would base his effective transcendence of Hawthorne's provinciality, mechanical allegory, or unresolved internal conflicts."[6] James's *Hawthorne,* portraying him as "morbidly provincial" in an "innocent" and "thin" America, compared to a sophisticated and "thick" Europe, set the stage for the reader to appreciate James's own position as a cosmopolitan person, living in a more complex post-Civil War era and practicing his art with a more modern sense of "realism." Eliot thought James's *Hawthorne* was tenderly affectionate, but it patronizes his predecessor and never acknowledges an indebtedness to him nor predicts how recurringly important Hawthorne's example would be in James's long career. *Hawthorne* would not be James's last reckoning with him. Peter Buitenhuis has shown precisely how James's view of Hawthorne's importance underwent several changes, all influenced by James's shifting attitudes toward America and his own work. Yet modern critics have followed in Eliot's steps by assuming that, as F. O. Matthiessen put it in *American Renaissance* (1941): "James, in a sense, started where Hawthorne left off."[7]

The earliest and most convincingly cited example of this version of the relationship is a pairing of James's *The Bostonians* with Hawthorne's *The Blithedale Romance.* Since then, critics have also connected this earlier work to several other novels and short stories of James, and they have seen even more connections between *The Scarlet Letter* and other Jamesian stories. The familiar pairing has the advantage of looking like a close affinity, even at a first glance, as Matthiessen first noticed in 1941 without developing the comparison very far. Moreover, its very persuasiveness points up the limits of the link as a warning against its tendency to obscure the extent to which James was responding also to his own experience of American culture and his participation in the international literary movement of realism. (Harold Bloom's theory, for example, ignores this danger by his dogma that strong poetry always arises "out of a loving conflict with previous poetry, rather than out of conflict with the world." He concedes that there is a "referential aspect" to poetry, but it is always "masked and mediated" by "another poem."[8])

In a literal sense, however, James did begin where Hawthorne left off, for the New Yorker reached his majority six weeks after the New Englander died, an event of powerful import because James learned of it in "fusion" with news of Lincoln's death. Reflecting late in life on this moment, James felt that Hawthorne had "proved to what use American matter could be put by an American hand" so that "an American could be an artist, one of the finest . . . just by being American *enough,* by the felicity of how the artist in him missed nothing, suspected nothing, that the ambient air didn't affect him as containing."[9] That ambient air was the common subject of *The Blithedale Romance* and *The Bostonians,* and both writers, as Richard H. Brodhead has observed in *The School of Hawthorne,* dealt with the private dramas lurking beneath public ideologies so that "the energies of sexuality, voice, and political conviction transform themselves into one another."[10] Similarly, in spite of James's commitment to a kind of social realism, making something specific out of the degraded Boston reform movement, in contrast to Hawthorne's presentation of four characters none of whom really believes in the specific purposes of the Blithedale community, the result in both novels is to make psychology more individual and more aberrant than it is social or normative. Even in this respect, James does not seem more modern than Hawthorne, for, as Alfred Kazin has remarked, Hawthorne's characters seem to be more like "self-enclosed modern types derived from the lonely crowd" than they do the legendary figures of romance.[11] Hawthorne called it a romance, but, Kazin reminds us, it ends in catastrophe.

James himself never mentions his relation to Hawthorne's book (though he had read it and criticized it), citing instead his debt to Daudet's *Evangéliste.* Nor does he suggest any relation to Howells's *The Undiscovered Country* (1880), and James says nothing about his own earlier short story "Professor Fargo" (1874), which also involves a critical view of mesmerism. Indeed, in this respect all three writers, whatever their relation to each other, responded as artists to the continuing American interest among reformers in mesmerism, clairvoyance, and spiritualism.

No literary influence is needed to account for this shared subject matter. Hawthorne knew about this occult subject from his sister-in-law Elizabeth Peabody, her friend Caroline Sturgis, and his father-in-law's use of hypnotism in dentistry. Howells knew about it from being an editor and friend of the spiritualist reformer Robert Dale Owen; Howell's title resonated with Owen's *The Debatable Land between This World and the Next* (1871). Henry James noted in his autobiography that his father had debated spiritualism with their good friend Caroline Sturgis, and he himself attended in 1863 an exhibition by the medium Cora Hatch.[12] Yet the idea of influence does come into play because of the way this shared historical material is treated. Howells, who had as a young writer reverently visited Hawthorne on a pilgrimage to New England from the Middle West, confessed that his favorite Hawthorne novel was *The Blithedale Romance,* and *The Undiscovered Country* explicitly describes its central situation of an innocent female medium, dominated by her father, in an atmosphere of fraud, as being "worthy of Hawthorne."[13] It portrays a Shaker community to match Hawthorne's picture of Brook Farm; just as Hawthorne had actually participated in the utopian experience so had Howells vacationed in a Shaker colony.

Hawthorne's skeptical narrator, Miles Coverdale, has a counterpart in Edward Ford, the skeptical journalist of Howells's story, and both men come to fall in love with a medium, Hawthorne's myterious Veiled Lady and Howells's Egeria Boynton. Ford has almost as much trouble coming to recognize his love for the medium as Coverdale, who only reveals it on the last page. In both cases there is a bondage between the performer and the showman who presents her. In both novels, too, there is an important matter of the subjection of women in American society because an ethic of sacrifice, suffering, and domestic labor substitutes for their exercise of choice.

In Howells's novel, the medium's father sees no happy life except in subordination to those she loves and in "sacrificing herself to their pleasure, their pride and ambition," precisely what his daughter unhappily finds to be her fate as a medium in "slavery" (as she calls it) to her father's obsessive quest to prove the reality of spiritualism. Hawthorne's Coverdale sees in Zenobia not only a sexually attractive woman but a natural "stump-oratress" who, as a reformer, had "an instinctive sense of where the life lies" and therefore naturally attacks "the relation between the sexes." Her story about the magician and the Veiled Lady is meant to illustrate her becoming a "bond-slave" to him. Zenobia complains to Coverdale that grown women in being assigned to marriage as the center of their life lack a man's capacity for choice, a point that in the Howells novel Ford makes to the medium's father. Howells may have read "Professor Fargo" as well because in his manuscript he changed his journalist's name from "Gifford" (used by James) to "Ford." But James's portrait of the music-hall professor, who seduces the deaf and mute daughter of a down-at-the-heels performing mathematician, thus turning "spiritual magnetism" into sexual attraction and sending the father into an asylum, is much harsher than anything in Howells's story.[14] With his feeling for the ordinary and the average Howells makes his story much less fanciful than Hawthorne's treatment of the mysterious Veiled Lady. Instead of Zenobia's melodramatic, moving suicide and the dangling-man Coverdale's last-minute confession of his love for Priscilla—neither of which events is very credibly motivated, though they have the virtue of surprising us—Howells tidies up everything in a quotidian way by having the lovers happily marry and spend a month every summer in the Shaker colony, while Egeria's father gives up spiritualism for Christianity.

Howells in his spiritualist novel did accomplish an important purpose defined by a critical reader when he wrote him: "You have silenced those of us who begged you to write a genuine American story." While working on the novel, Howells himself had written James Russell Lowell: "I have come to understand fully what Hawthorne meant when he said to me that he would like to see some part of America on which the shadow of Europe had not fallen." That shadow had not fallen on *The Blithedale Romance* either, as it usually did in Hawthorne's other novels. Similarly, James gave a prospectus of *The Bostonians* to his publisher that stressed his plan "to make the whole thing as local, as American as possible, and as full of Boston: an attempt to show that I *can* write an American story . . . a tale very characteristic of our social conditions."[15]

James set his story in the 1870s (as his predecessors' tales had also been set in the recent past), but he deliberately invoked an earlier antebellum era through his use of Miss Birdseye as an exemplar of the golden age of New England reform in sharp contrast to the vulgarities and corruptions of the current age. He was attacked by his brother for drawing her in an uncomplimentary way from the actual example of Elizabeth Peabody, and, while he protested unconvincingly both that he hadn't and that the picture was highly complimentary, she was in fact a very appropriate figure for him to invoke as a survivor from the earlier era. She had been interested in spiritualism, transcendentalism, abolitionism, and women's rights; she was a friend of Margaret Fuller; her sister married Hawthorne, who sent *Twice-Told Tales* to Miss Peabody and later rebuked her for not minding her own business. Bronson Alcott summed her up appropriately as "one of the most generous souls that I have known, and a part of the life of New England."[16]

Her biographer had no trouble recognizing her in James's portrait, just as James himself saw that Margaret Fuller was at least the "starting point" for Hawthorne's Zenobia. Moreover, James had direct access to the golden era through his friendship with Caroline Sturgis, who had flirted with Emerson, circled in Margaret Fuller's orbit of intense friendships, become interested in spiritualism, and married into the prominent New York abolitionist family of the Tappans. She had even boarded for a time with the Hawthornes at the Old Manse in Concord.[17] Given his invocation of this earlier New England era, which Hawthorne had dramatized in his novel, James might have expected his knowledgeable readers to make the connection not only between the eras but between the two texts.

He did not need the example of Howells's *The Undiscovered Country* for his father-daughter mediumistic couple; after all, James's "Professor Fargo" had preceded Howells in dramatizing the vampirish bondage in such performers, as Hawthorne had first done. James had written Howells to compliment him on his having chosen "a larger and heavier" subject than any he had yet tried, but at the same time he did not think it fruitful—"and I suspect that much of the public will agree with me."[18] Ironically, his prediction would apply forcibly to his own treatment of the mediumistic subject in *The Bostonians,* but James may have thought he had given it a more fruitful theme by focusing on the women's rights movement rather than on spiritualism, as Howells had done.

Actually, as Howard Kerr has shown in detail, the trance-speaking of mediums was historically linked to the suffrage movement. The trance-speaker Cora Hatch, whom James had heard in 1863, was (like James's Verena) managed by her father, and she, too, often spoke on behalf of women's emancipation. Like Verena, she was a beautiful blond with a melodious platform voice. James's portrait of the seedy milieu in which spiritualists operated had its justification in the career of this medium, who divorced a mesmeric physician with charges in court of sexual irregularity and bondage, and in the even more notorious case of Victoria Woodhull, a radical suffragist and proponent of free love, who at the spiritualist convention in 1872—the very time of James's novel—charged the popular minister Henry Ward Beecher with adultery and hypocrisy.[19]

Given these historical matters, it might seem that Hawthorne's novel is irrelevant to James's; yet the latter invoked the former's era in Miss Birdseye; and it also dramatized in the Verena-Olive relationship the intensities of female friendship that Hawthorne had hinted at in portraying Priscilla as coming to the utopian community to be the emotional slave of her half-sister Zenobia. Both history and texts are entwined. Moreover, James's comments in *Hawthorne* on *The Blithedale Romance* point toward his own differing and later treatment of similar material. He wished there was more "appeal to our own vision of the world—our observation," as well as more satire of the "strange types of radicalism," and he found "least felicitous" that portion of the story dealing with Priscilla and her "mysterious relation" to Zenobia, her mesmeric gifts, and her "divided subjection to Hollingsworth and Westervelt, and her numerous other graceful but fantastic properties—her Sybilline attributes, as the author calls them."[20]

In all these noted respects, James revised Hawthorne in *The Bostonians* by a detailed kind of descriptive realism about settings, a more biting satirical treatment of the Boston reformers, and a more psychologically explicit treatment of the emotional life in the charismatic medium, who was torn between two dominating suitors for her love, the fanatical feminist, Olive Chancellor, and the conservative, masculine Southern ideologue, Basil Ransom. In Hawthorne, the sexually magnetic Zenobia is jealous of the submissive Priscilla's love for the fanatical, egotistical reformer Hollingsworth, a consummate male chauvinist, and Zenobia is the victim of an earlier bad marriage with a dominating unfeeling husband. In James, the sexuality of Olive is repressed and displaced into her domination of Verena, who has Zenobia's charismatic charm and Priscilla's passivity. James's Ransom is as complacently male chauvinist as Hollingsworth, but he is a reactionary rather than a reformer. James's triangle simplifies the more complicated Hawthornian pattern of four characters.

Hawthorne's perception of the emotional dynamics in the Priscilla-Zenobia relationship probably derived from his acquaintance with women like Margaret Fuller, Elizabeth Peabody, and Caroline Sturgis. "Even taking into account the habitual grandiloquence of the transcendental discourse and the freedom of emotional expression in a pre-Freudian age," George Dimock has pointed out, Margaret Fuller expressed her affections for Caroline Sturgis with "importunate intensity." Sturgis struggled for independence from her mentor, and Fuller once spoke of their friendship having become "redeemed from 'the search after Eros.' "[21]

James, also, could draw on personal experience for his own more graphic and extensive presentation of the morbid intensity in Olive's tutelage of Verena. In his family the most spectacular genius was masculine, the most spectacular neurosis, feminine: the psychic retreat of his sister Alice into a crippling invalidism and an emotional possessiveness of her faithful companion and Boston Brahmin, Katharine Loring, that demanded her undivided attention. Alice had broken down massively in 1878 when she learned of her brother William's engagement to another (healthy) Alice. In her diary for 1892, the hysterically paralyzed Alice dated this earlier event as marking the time of her having faced a "ceaseless possible horror" and having felt "the dark waters" closing over her, leaving her with "neither hope nor peace." (Her brother Henry had even projected an unwritten story about a peculiarly intense affection between a brother and a sister.) His suspicion of the love that Alice's biographer finds in Alice's tenacious dependence on her companion was well grounded in his intuition of its morbidity and is justified by the findings of contemporary analysts that failure to achieve a firm sexual identity is part of a hysterical structure and results (like Alice's invalidism) in caricatures of either the masculine or the feminine role.[22] No doubt there were "Boston marriages," as these female friendships were called, that were not morbid, but James's sister arrived in England while he was writing *The Bostonians* and he spent several weeks with her in the summer of 1885. Olive's possessiveness is too neurotically desperate to be blandly assimilated to friendship, just as Zenobia's suicide is an excessive response to Hollingsworth's winning of Priscilla.

Indeed, both writers tend to understand feminism itself in a reductively psychological way insofar as their accounts tend to illustrate Coverdale's idea that "women are not natural reformers, but become such by the pressure of exceptional misfortune." Yet, when Zenobia drowns herself, Coverdale reflects that Professor Westervelt might have been right in imagining a grand future for her as an actress. That a man's love should have been so important to her strikes Coverdale now as the deplorable result of "masculine egotism" in making the success or failure of women depend wholly "on the affections, and on one species of affection, while man has such a multitude of other chances, that this seems but an incident."[23] Moreover, Hawthorne endorses Hollingsworth's tender nursing of the sick Coverdale by having the invalid praise the reformer for his unusual lack of shame in having "something of the woman" in his personality. In this respect, Hawthorne was continuing his own interest in the feminist argument, begun in *The Scarlet Letter* with his identification of the boldly speculative Hester Prynne with the historical figure of Anne Hutchinson, the antinomian preacher whom the Puritan magistrate John Winthrop had condemned for heresy. Zenobia was Hester's successor and like her, the victim of a husband characterized as having traffic with the devil. Hawthorne was unusually capable of giving tender qualities to a male character and intellectual powers to a female one, thus going against the grain of the standard Victorian gender polarizing of intellect and feeling.

By contrast, there seems to be nothing feminist about James's story, and a contemporary feminist critic complains that his treatment of Olive (in contrast to Hawthorne's of Zenobia) reflects "a vicious, unhealthy kind of humor that reveals as much about its author as about his character." Moreover, in spite of its realist's method, James's tale does have something of a fairy-tale quality in having the knight liberate the spellbound princess from the wicked witch.[24] But James recognizes something futile in Ransom's unsuccessful role as a political theorist and something dominating in his ideologized masculinity. His victory over Olive at the Music Hall puts Verena in tears as a prelude to their "far from brilliant" union. James did give a victory to Ransom's claim for a private life over Verena's claim for a public role that would be a vehicle for her oratorical talent; and James also spoke in his notes about intending to show "the decline of the sentiment of sex," precisely what Ransom also laments in his hostility to feminism. Hawthorne's Coverdale was impressed with Zenobia because "we seldom meet with women now-a-days, and in this country, who impress us as being women at all; their sex fades away and goes for nothing, in ordinary intercourse," a point with which Ransom would heartily agree. Yet, one can see in Verena's public role a fulfillment of what Professor Westervelt saw as a tragically lost potentiality in Zenobia. In this sense, James did indeed start where Hawthorne left off.

Hawthorne's criticisms are directed more to the communitarian fallacies of the utopian colony than to Zenobia's feminism in contrast to the way James's satire scores against the feminist reformers. Nevertheless, his posing of the debate between Ransom and Olive, whether he appreciated its force or not, makes an ironic observation about how both parties presuppose the same polarized view of human nature as being divided into active masculine and passive feminine virtues. Ransom accepts Miss Birdseye not only because she is an *"old* old maid" but also because he sees her as "essentially feminine" on account of her "weakness" and "generosity," in contrast to the "false delicacy" and "coddled sensibilities" of genteel culture in the 1870s. (He is unaware, however, that many actual feminist reformers would have made the same criticisms of that genteel culture.) Ironically, his own definition of the "essentially feminine" is mirrored in Verena's public speeches (under Olive's instruction) about how women will "redeem" the public order through their "heart," "generosity," "tenderness," and "sympathy."[25] Both conservative and radical in James's story are captive to the same stereotype about the difference between the sexes. For this reason, *The Bostonians* marks the difference between a Victorian and modern view of this issue.

Even in 1876, Henry Adams, in a lecture in Boston on "The Primitive Rights of Women," blamed the church for having "stimulated or permitted" women's degradation by idealizing the image of woman as "the meek and patient, the silent and tender sufferer, the pale reflection of the Mater Dolorosa." In this respect, at least, Adams and Hawthorne were closer to Freud than James was. Despite Freud's failure in the Dora case (as Erik Erikson has pointed out) to recognize her as a female intellectual, he understood theoretically that the "masculine" and "feminine" traits, which had become culturally identified with the active and the passive, belonged, as a matter of normal psychology, to *both* sexes.[26]

To some extent, *The Bostonians* represents a rewriting of Hawthorne's story by remedying those things James criticized in *The Blithedale Romance.* The result was an uncharacteristic rendering of satiric social detail at a particular postwar historical moment. James ruefully recognized its longueurs, but our critics have been too inclined to take at face value James's own claim to have superseded Hawthorne. T. S. Eliot (who inaugurated this tradition) as an expatriate of Anglified characteristics understandably saw James as more exemplary for him than the New England republican. Paradoxically, however, a biographer of Eliot has noted in his poetry "a distinctively New England self-consciousness," much like that in Hawthorne's alienated observers, Chillingworth, Coverdale, Holgrave, and Kenyon. Eliot suffered from the mix of conscientiousness and skepticism that he called "the Boston doubt." The poet felt that he had escaped it by allying himself with the sensuous and intellectual sensibility of Henry James. When Eliot returned to America in 1933, for the first time since 1914, his speech to the students of Milton Academy enacted James's story "The Jolly Corner" by speaking of wanting to face his youthful self to say "See what a mess you have made of things," while recognizing that neither one liked the other. If he was involuntarily akin to Hawthorne, he voluntarily made himself akin to James.[27]

Chapter 4

Complementary Novels of Manners by James, Wharton, Howells, and Cahan

"WHY, in fact, should I not make a Personal History of American Literature," asked William Dean Howells in 1892, "for thirty years since I have been a part of it?"[1] He had known virtually everyone of note in American literature from Hawthorne and Emerson to Whitman, Twain and James, to mention only the major figures. When he summed up his New England literary life in particular in *Literary Friends and Acquaintance* (1900), he wished he had called it "Literary Friends and Neighbors." The congenial phrase suggests his unusual gift for such friendships. They are not in current fashion. We are too familiar with the anecdotes about the rivalrous relations among the notables of the 1920s, Hemingway, Dos Passos, Fitzgerald, Wolfe, and Lewis. Hawthorne struck a very different note when he confided to his notebook his belief that Melville "has a very high and noble nature, and better worth immortality than most of us."[2]

This was the generous spirit as well of Howells's record of his literary friendships. He was typically at work when he died in 1920 on a complimentary essay about a literary friend, "The American James." In 1911, Edith Wharton, as a devoted friend of James, naturally turned to Howells in trying to gain support for a movement on behalf of giving the next Nobel Prize in Literature to Henry James. (The movement failed.) As an editor of influential literary magazines, Howells himself vigorously defended the new literary realists, here and abroad, in the court of public opinion; and he audaciously took up the case of such an exotic client as

Abraham Cahan, the editor of the major Yiddish journal, the *Jewish Daily Forward,* and a man whose immigrant world on New York's lower East Side was far from the genteel circle Howells knew in New England. Such friendships are consequential for literary history when they enter into the making of literature itself, and for Howells, Cahan, James, and Wharton they bore remarkable fruit.

It is possible, for example, to pair some of their novels in a way that makes one look very much like a reply to the other, as if a dialogue were going on, although unmentioned by either writer. Thus, James's *The Ambassadors* (1903) found the germ of its story in an anecdote about Howells, and its plot puts reverse English on Howells's own middle-aged version of "the international theme" in *Indian Summer* (1886); Cahan's *The Rise of David Levinsky* (1917) is a Jewish and much more urban version of another ironic success story, Howells's *The Rise of Silas Lapham* (1885); Edith Wharton's *The Age of Innocence* (1920), although separated by forty years from its predecessor, reads in many respects like a sequel, done in a spirit much more anthropological, as its title suggests, to James's *The Portrait of a Lady* (1881). These pairings deserve a close comparative look in relation to the question of the nature of literary influence in the making of tradition.

It is now legendary (as well as a matter of record) that James in *The Ambassadors* took off from remarks he had been told that Howells had made in Whistler's garden in Paris to Jonathan Sturges: "Live all you can: it's a mistake not to. . . . This place makes it all come over me. I see it now. I haven't done so—and now I'm old. It's too late. It has gone past me—I've lost it. You have time. You are young. Live!"[3] Howells was then, in June 1894, fifty-seven years old and on his way back to America because his father had suffered a stroke. James heard the story from his young friend Sturges, and the novelist's hero, Lambert Strether, a New England literary editor in his middle fifties, makes a very similar confession to little Bilham at the emotional high point of the novel. Both confessions take place in an artist's garden in Paris.

These facts are clear enough. But the episode is not as simple as it sounds. In the first place, James conceded that he had amplified and improved Howells's original remark of only ten words (later James would refer to it as being only five words). In a letter from the States to his son, studying in Paris to be an architect, Howells said of the episode in

Whistler's garden that it was as well that he had been called home: "The poison of Europe was getting into my soul. You must look out for that. They live much more fully than we do. Life here is still for the future—it is a land of Emersons—and I like a little present moment in mine. When I think of the Whistler garden!" Characteristically, Howells, like so many literary Americans abroad, was ambivalent about the garden; he missed its aura of present enjoyment, but it was a kind of "poison." Howells was writing to his son from Saratoga, which he contrasted with Whistler's garden: "But Saratoga amuses somewhat. Here is an image of leisure, if not leisure." The place was full of sharp American types, "pointed for business, not two ideas in their skulls, but mostly good and kind."[4]

James assured Howells that the garden episode was only a germ that had developed fictionally from the beginning into something quite different from anything like Howells, something "impersonal and independent," even if Howells in one sense had been "responsible for the whole thing." Independent perhaps, but not impersonal: James also wrote another friend that he might find in the novel's "poor old hero" a "vague resemblance" to the author.[5] That is the way Leon Edel sees the novel in his biography: James "could see and hear Howells" in the anecdote, but "he listened as if the message were for him. He felt old. His best years were gone. He was aware of his unlived life rising within—and yet it seemed 'too late.' "[6] James may have projected into his young friend's account his own mid-life anxieties, but he certainly had Howells in mind when in 1901 he wrote in his notebook about an idea for a story: a man, "who, like W.D.H.(say), has never known *at all* any woman BUT his wife—and at 'time of life' somehow sees it, is face to face with it."[7] The notion, he added, flowed into "a small side" of the idea of *The Ambassadors*. In describing the original anecdote about Howells, James had also imagined the "so-possible presence of a charming woman or two, or peculiarly 'European' tradition, such as it had never yet been given him to encounter."[8] This idea would flower into the character of Madame de Vionnet.

What is usually unmentioned, however, is the pathetic condition of the original listener to whom Howells made the speech that James has made famous: Jonathan Sturges. This American journalist and short-story writer, living abroad, had been crippled as a child by poliomyelitis; because of his wizened legs, he required a cane and after 1900 spent much of his time in nursing homes until he died before he was fifty. Edel thinks he had really tried to follow Howells's counsel to "live all you can," but, in light of Sturges's condition, Howells's life seems far less limited than his listener's; Edel himself refers to "the ever-narrowing horizon of Sturges's life."⁹ Moreover, Edel describes Sturges's mood in telling James about the episode in Whistler's garden as deeply downcast because (James believed) he had fallen in love with some woman in France, "and for the first time had had to face the fact that in his crippled helpless state he could not hope for love as other men."¹⁰ It is not clear where the evidence lies for this assertion; James does not mention it in his accounts of the germination of his project, and in the novel James's expansion of Howell's statement to Sturges is made to John Little Bilham, a character who is neither downcast nor crippled.

Howells's message to Sturges seems appropriate enough about the novelist's own feelings at that moment. The approaching death of his father must have reminded Howells of his own mortality and of his family duties, both of which would have weighed heavily amid the leisurely pleasures of the party in Whistler's garden. After his father had died, Howells felt more aged than ever before and confessed to a friend that he sometimes felt as if he were lost in some "dreamy fumbling" about his own identity, "as if it were somebody else," and he sometimes wished it were.¹¹ (James had described him in the anecdote as the "*désorienté* elderly American.") This disoriented mood makes it seem plausible that a few years earlier in the garden he could have blurted out something about the need for younger persons to take advantage of whatever opportunities they had before it was too late for them. But his advice to the young man seems cruelly ironic unless it was made in ignorance of his condition or as a stoical suggestion for him to make whatever he could of his drastically limited life. In any event, it was the drama of Howells not his listener that interested James as a novelist.

The novel goes well beyond its germ in the anecdote by developing the idea that it is too late for the American "ambassador" to "live," except by his having "a little supersensual hour in the vicarious freedom of another."¹² Lambert Strether has his hour by allying himself with the lovers, Chad and Madame de Vionnet, rather than with the representatives of Chad's family who have come over to get him back. The vicarious freedom to see and appreciate is all the freedom or fulfillment that James allows his protagonist. That is the personal signature he stamped on the novel, one traceable to his youth when he characteristically mourned the death of his cousin Minny Temple by writing that he was "perfectly satisfied" to have her "translated from this changing realm of fact to the steady realm of thought."[13] Even so, it is remarkable that James nowhere recognizes the affinity of his story to Howells's earlier novel, *Indian Summer*. The editors of James's notebooks even refer to Strether's "belated Indian summer of awakening" without any reference to it, though it is about the working out of a mid-life crisis on European ground.[14]

James had many reasons beyond the episode in the Paris garden to think of Howells in relation to *The Ambassadors*. Howells's appraisal of James's later work was appearing in the *North American Review* at the same time as *The Ambassadors,* whose publication Howells had encouraged. Thinking about returning to America in 1904 for new literary material, James naturally turned for advice to his old friend Howells and thanked him for the pleasure his remarks "about the *Ambassadors* and cognate topics" had given him. James added that "the international theme" as a literary resource was clearly what he was "*chronically* booked for." It is as if he were marking out his own territory, distinguishing it from the domain of Howells, whom he always thought of as "monarch absolute of the Atlantic to the increase of his profit and comfort."[15] This edgy remark, which went on to figure Howells as a man with a diamond who did not know quite what to do with it, was made in 1871 at a time when they were carving out their careers, and it points to the competitive strain in their relationship.

Howells himself was a pioneer in developing "the international theme," having spent the Civil War years in Italy as American consul; he made his mark as a writer with travel accounts, as James did, and then turned his foreign experience into fictional stories of Americans abroad, three of them written before *Indian Summer*. Like James, he was also much taken with Turgenev's fiction and the international movement of literary realism. James had read and commented on *Indian Summer,* but even in his most generous and appreciative estimate of Howells, written for his seventy-fifth birthday dinner, he did not mention one of the most shapely and witty examples of Howells's talent for writing comedies of manners.

To look at *Indian Summer* in the light of *The Ambassadors* is to see not only a predecessor, but to be struck by the extent to which it is revised by its successor. As William B. Gibson has noticed, the similarity between the two heroes in character, situation, and attitude towards the past is "rather remarkable." Both are editors, both are returning to a Europe they had loved in their youth, both have lost a woman they loved in their

youth, and both had dreamed of raising up a 'temple of taste' " in literature.[16] Thereafter, it is the crucial differences between the novels that are
notable. Colville's experience is to get himself unwisely engaged to an
infatuated young American girl, as if in returning to Florence he could
recapture his youth through her. In the end, he recognizes that an American widow, Lina Bowen, the girl's chaperone, whom he had known in
his youth, is the realistically appropriate wife for him, though neither
woman is any help in enabling him to reach this conclusion. The younger
woman is blinded by her romanticizing, the older by a sense of propriety
about concealing her own interest in Colville. When Colville comes to
his senses, with the help of a shrewd and scholarly expatriate clergyman,
he tells his future wife that he prizes the love she kept from him even
more than the love she could have given him because it would have
meant the loss of her self-respect. This platonic thought, as Howells
wryly notes in his realistic vein, serves him better than subtle art as his
best defense against Mrs. Bowen's accusations. Even so, only her child's
tears at the idea of his leaving brings the moralistic mother to the essential
point of urging him to stay.

Colville's married fate sharply contrasts with Strether's; the latter's
"only logic," he tells Maria Gostrey, who would like to marry him, is:
"Not, out of the whole affair, to have got anything for myself." Colville
at forty-one is a good deal younger, but he is also divided in mind,
unhappy with himself in Europe either as "idler on its modern surface, or
delver in its deep-hearted past," because he is, at bottom, drawn to "the
vast tumultuous American life" on which he has only temporarily turned
his back. Howells even slyly included his relation to James within the
novel by having his own characters discuss the two writers. Colville
suggests that in a romantic mood they might seem to be "a passage from
a modern novel," say "one of Mr. James's." A character responds: "I
hardly feel up to Mr. James. I should have said Howells. Only nothing
happens in that case!"[17] Colville agrees that "that's the most comfortable
way." This persiflage accurately predicts the conclusion in its entirely
credible prosiness with the couple being now in Rome and the affair with
Imogene being "the grain of sand" between them, even though they
agreed that no one was "very much to blame."

In his own version of the middle-aged American abroad, experiencing
an Indian summer awakening, James turned the older woman into a
living reminder, through the furnishings in her apartment, of "some

Napoleonic glamour" that included the major French literary figures of Chateaubriand, Madame de Staël, and Lamartine. His hero is stirred by Madame de Vionnet as an incarnation of this legendary France, a lover whose affair with Chad has transformed him for the better; and she remains for Strether "the finest and subtlest creature, the happiest apparition, it had been given him, in all his years to meet."[18] Chad turns out, however, to be mainly interested in getting into the American advertising business; for all his being polished up by his lover, he is quite unequal to his lover's passion for him. Whereas Colville's Italian Indian summer is, like the season, a brief poignant reminder of past pleasures before the fall comes, Strether had never had a youth to recover, and his awakening is not to the absurdity of his romantic imagination, but to an awareness of the romantic spell cast by Madame de Vionnet and her country. When he discovers the truth of the intimacy between Chad and Madame de Vionnet, it is during his walk into the countryside as if into the picture, painted by a French Romantic painter, that he had first seen in a Boston shop. His only fidelity to the familiar gods of Woollett in New England is to try to persuade little Bilham to marry Mamie Pocock in compensation for Strether's "sacrificing to strange gods" in Europe.

James's passionate pilgrims abroad usually find that the enchanted kingdom is an illusion of their own imaginary idea of Europe, but Strether's vision stays with him to the end as a true sign of "the illusion of freedom." James accents the illusory aspect not so much because of aging's limits (perhaps also as an echo of his awareness of the crippled condition of Howells's listener, Jonathan Sturges), but because Strether's freedom lies in his seeing. What he finally sees is that Mrs. Newsome, the widow who finances his magazine from the money derived from "the greatest product of Woollett," is not a person he will marry. It is a comic portent that Maria Gostrey stops him from ever telling her what this "rather ridiculous" common object of domestic use actually is.

Both novels are centered on a single protagonist's point of view. But Howells's novel progresses mainly through its witty dialogue, while James's develops complexity through three subjective levels: "the characters' awareness of events; the narrator's seeing of them; and our own trailing perception of the relation between these two."[19] Strether's ruminating interior monologues would become increasingly a hallmark of modernist fiction. *Indian Summer* is as tautly economical as *The Ambassa-*

dors is exfoliatingly prolix. Since the anecdote about Howells was the germ of *The Ambassadors,* it is entirely appropriate that James's treatment of it dramatizes his difference from Howells as an artist and a man. For James saw in the impassioned outburst of Howells in Whistler's garden a lament that his drink of the "poison" of Europe, which James had been quaffing for a quarter of a century, was destined to be such a brief one. What James did with Strether was to give him a drink that would sustain his appreciation of Madame de Vionnet. As Strether himself happily puts it: "Of course I moved among miracles. It was all phantasmagoric."[20] For Colville to have said such things would have been a rueful recognition that he had been blinded by his romancing.

From Howells's point of view, as he often said, James's stories are romances. For James the point of creating Strether was that he would have "imagination galore, and that this yet wouldn't have wrecked him." James saw Howells as too definite a character in actuality to be Strether, who had to be "a more fantastic and more moveable shadow" of the living man.[21] The two heroes thus serve quite different purposes, even though they have clear affinities. If we transpose them in our minds, we cannot imagine their plots being switched without violating the laws of their fictional worlds. The idea provokes a smile, rather like the scene in one of the Marx Brothers' movies where Groucho stands before a mirror and sees his reflection at one point diverge from parallelism into an opposite action.

There is no such divide between Howells and Cahan in the matter of technique; both men worked in the vein of social realism, which they admired in the great nineteenth-century Russian writers, who were a native cultural legacy for Cahan and a personal discovery for Howells. Both were men without much formal education and drawn to socialism, though it was a much more active and credible faith for Cahan, who became a major political figure in the workers' movement of the lower East Side, while Howells only briefly attended the Church of the Carpenter, an Episcopal mission set up by the Reverend W.D.P. Bliss, an influential Christian Socialist. On the other hand, Howells and Cahan were not continuously in and out of each other's lives and minds, as Howells and James were. Yet Howells was in a way an immigrant to New England from Ohio as Cahan, more crucially, was an immigrant (and political exile) to New York from Russia. They did not meet until 1892 when Howells sought out Cahan as a spokesman for the concrete world of labor and socialism.

The fictional career of David Levinsky begins in 1885, the same year that Howells published his story about Silas Lapham. Both novelists make self-made businessmen their protagonists and put them in a critical light (James's *The American* is also the story of a businessman, but Christopher Newman is seeking an aristocratic French wife as a symbol of his victory over circumstance. It is an example of "the international theme," and Newman's successor is not Silas Lapham but Sinclair Lewis's Sam Dodsworth, another bewildered American abroad, learning to appreciate and enjoy cultural pleasures he has never known in his successful economic life.)[22] Howells focuses on a Vermont businessman's misguided aspiration to join the stratified society of old Boston, while Cahan spotlights the immigrant Jewish businessman's aspiration to become acculturated to the new secularized, democratized, urbanized industrial world of New York. Both businessmen are shown to indulge in sharp practices that the mores of their earlier backgrounds would not sanction. Moreover, David Levinsky is as out of place in the Hebrew-speaking milieu of advanced literature, socialism, and Zionism, represented by a poet's daughter to whom he is attracted, as he is among pious traditionalists—or as Silas Lapham is among the old aristocrats of Boston.

There is resonance between the endings as well, but it is not an echo. One man is broken by failure, the other by success. Howells says of Lapham: "He was more broken than he knew by his failure; it did not kill him as it often does, but it weakened the spring, once so strong and elastic."[23] Lapham's real rise is his refusal to become complicit with dishonest businessmen, who could rectify the loss of his Beacon Street house by deceiving other investors; and his manhood is restored when he gives up his dream of social success and returns to his farmhouse in Vermont, the locus of his values. Levinsky achieves his economic triumphs in the New York ready-made clothing industry at the price of feeling alienated from his Russian-Jewish identity as a Talmudic student; and as an atheistic believer in Herbert Spencer's Darwinism, he keeps in touch with the memory of his earlier Talmudic self only by giving money to a synagogue and making the intellectual effort to tell his story in such full detail.

Actually, it is one of the subtleties of the novel that his Talmudic self is more of a myth than a reality, for even while he was in Russia he had lost interest in the Talmud and was looking forward to being rich and influential as a revenge against his enemies. The myth of his past survives as his emotional link to his mother, who had been killed by anti-Semites. Unlike Lapham, he never suffers a business failure, but his success never satisfied him: "My past and present do not comport well." The youthful David, pondering the Talmud, seems finally to have more in common with his "inner identity than David Levinsky, the well-known cloak-manufacturer." He even sadly imagines himself "born for a life of intellectual interest."[24]

Howells was in some respects more like Levinsky and Lapham than Cahan was. Levinsky's bad conscience about his success is much like Howells's about his. He was unusually well rewarded for his writing and actually lived in a Beacon Street house, similar to the one Lapham bought and accidentally burned; and Howells was also an outsider to New England aristocracy. He was never complacent about his economic success and was painfully aware (as he wrote his father) that beyond Beacon Street "thousands upon thousands of poor creatures are stifling in wretched barracks in the city here, whole families in one room," and he wondered why "men are so patient with society as they are."[25] Indeed, Howells had first sought out Cahan to gain some first-hand acquaintance with the workers' world, while Cahan for his part, understandably enough, felt in himself "an American sense of having arrived" in meeting the most famous American writer, whose books he had read and reread. As artists they were congenial realists; as social beings they saw each other as representing the other end of the spectrum. Cahan recognized in Silas Lapham, a farmer who became a rich businessman, a type he identified in Yiddish terms as "an American *allrightnik*."[26] But, in Cahan's eyes, Howells was a member of American "aristocratic society."

Cahan, unlike Levinsky, was at home in the new world of New York immigrant politics, Yiddish culture, and the international republic of literary realism; he kept his ties to Russian literature and the international socialist movement. In 1898, Howells saluted Cahan's stories of Yiddish life as being "entirely of our time and place, and so foreign to our race and civilization," a kind of regional fiction comparable to what other "local color" writers were doing for other parts of the country. But, when *The Rise of David Levinsky* was published, Howells (only three years from his death) gave it faint praise and missed the point by calling it "a pretty good autobiographical novel" that is "too sensual in its facts, though he is a good man."[27] Howells missed the crucial differences between the author and his character: the story is Levinsky's autobiography, not Cahan's. Howells's own genteel treatment of the love affair between the son of the Brahmin Coreys and the daughter of the bourgeois Laphams would have benefited from a dose of Cahan's "sensual facts." She is inhibited for chapters by her melodramatic sense of guilt because the son seemed to have been interested in her sister first. Howells's shrewd Mr. Sewell, in the novel's famous dinner-party scene, speaks for the author in criticizing popular fiction for failing to see that "the whole business of love, and love-making and marrying," ought to be "recognized as something natural and mortal," but his realism was too limited to make this idea convincing in the concrete.[28]

Levinsky's persistent difficulty in finding an appropriate sexual partner, not only reflects class and ethnic barriers to his fulfillment but also his own tendency to a "morbid amativeness" (as he calls it), which is stirred by the guilty sexy look in some girls' faces; it is a residue of his youthful Talmudic days when sexual feelings were associated with sin. This strain in Cahan's hero leads forward to the later Jewish-American novel, which greatly expands on this psychological issue. *The Rise of David Levinsky* is a gritty close-grained version of life in the ghetto, but it also transcends its local particularity by anticipating the general American literary theme about the failure of economic success to satisfy inner needs. Whereas Howells's emphasis is on the moral issues that Lapham confronts in his paint business, Cahan's is more heavily placed on the psychological and cultural issues of Levinsky's identity.

Cahan's tribute to Howells in an obituary on his life and work in 1920, twenty-five years after the peak of his career, is closer to the mark than Howells's comment on *The Rise of David Levinsky* three years earlier, but it has its own element of incongruity. The column is full of genuine gratitude for the example of Howells as "one of the greatest figures in the history of American literature" and a person who was a "dimentener mentsh"—a diamond of a man.[29] Cahan calls Howells's *A Modern Instance* his "classic masterpiece" and appreciates his talent in portraying tensions between the newly rich and the wealthy old American families, as in *The Rise of Silas Lapham*. Yet, Cahan's valedictory to the writer who had crucially encouraged the new Jewish-American writing devotes most of the column's space to the evidence for Howells's "socialistic spirit" in such fictional utopias as *The Traveler from Altruria* and *Through the Eye of the Needle,* thinly disguised tracts which do nothing to show Howells's talent for creating comedies of manners. Cahan's deliberate allusion in his title to Howells's novel, however, provokes us to use each book to focus the other, and this process highlights their differing affinities better than their creators could do when they spoke outside their novels.

In her autobiography, Edith Wharton expressed her admiration for *A Modern Instance* and *The Rise of Silas Lapham,* but regretted that Howells himself, because of her timidity and his social aloofness, remained "inaccessible."[30] It was far otherwise with Henry James, who for about a dozen years after the publication of *The Ambassadors* until his death in 1916 was her close friend and frequent traveling companion. Three years after Cahan's novel was published, Edith Wharton looked back from the end of the First World War to the 1870s by writing a kind of historical novel, *The Age of Innocence.* This version of literary realism, in returning to that period, linked her book to the setting of her friend Henry James's *The Portrait of a Lady,* published nearly forty years earlier. The links are much stronger than that, however, though they have nothing to do with the tradition of seeing her as a sort of Jamesian product in the spirit of Percy Lubbock's *Portrait of Edith Wharton* (1947), which engulfed her in the legend of the master by asserting that "she was herself a novel of his, no doubt in his earlier manner."[31] Critical opinion followed suit by categorizing her as a follower of James. Millicent Bell, writing in 1965 about the James-Wharton friendship, broke this spell by observing that, in spite of their devoted friendship, Wharton was much more interested as a novelist than James was in decor, houses, costumes, opinions, in short, "qualities of period and class" alive at "a particular moment in history."[32] Wharton had no use for his later works precisely because, although she admired some of his aesthetic principles, the stories seemed to her lacking in "that thick nourishing human air in which we all move," including "the irregular and irrelevant movements of life."[33] Yet, the old mistake about her lingered on in the artist's design for the cover of Bell's book with its sharp black and white photograph of James in profile at the left and a pointillistic drawing of Wharton in purple at the right, as if she were forever in his shadow.

Bell, like Lubbock, also makes a connection between Wharton and *The Portrait of a Lady* by seeing her as having the qualities of James's American heroines, even though her own protagonists are never "as illumined with a sense of human possibility as Isabel Archer."[34] Bell also concedes that there are Jamesian aspects to *The Age of Innocence,* but she misses the most interesting and illuminating one, first pointed out by a biography of Wharton, which capitalizes on the interest of the women's movement in reclaiming female writers: Cynthia Wolff's *A Feast of Words: The Triumph of Edith Wharton* (1977). Wolff recognizes an "antiphonal" connection between the novels by pointing out that the link of Wharton's Newland Archer to James's Isabel Archer is underlined by Wharton's having one of Newland's friends remark that he looks like a painting, "The Portrait of a Gentleman." James's story of Isabel Archer was Wharton's favorite among his works and the only one of his that ever appeared on her list of favorite books. Moreover, as Wolff adds, both novels involve issues of individual freedom and the sanctity of the marriage bond. Wharton was much in the midst of her memories of James while she was working on *The Age of Innocence* because she was negotiating with his family over the editing of his letters. Therefore, Wolff acutely suggests, "perhaps the central meaning grows out of the complex way in which the novel beckons to Wharton's dearest friend, Henry James."[35]

This case for considering the two novels together can be considerably bolstered by noticing the way in which Wharton's novel deals precisely with what James himself says he did not do in his own. In his later preface to the novel, he noted that he had advised himself to "press least hard, in short, on the consciousness of your heroine's satellites, especially the male." In his notebook plan for the novel he feared that "the weakness of the whole story is that it is too exclusively psychological," and he predicted that "the obvious criticism" would be that he had failed to see the heroine "to the end of her situation." James felt that his book did have the unity of what "groups together," but he added that "the rest may be taken up or not, later."[36] These observations gave Wharton an opening for her own talent to take up "the rest" by putting the psychological in a social context, telling the male side of the story more fully, and seeing the heroine and the hero through to the end of their situation. These are the specific virtues of *The Age of Innocence.*

It begins with the return to America of Ellen Olenska, who is thinking of divorcing a corrupt count. Like Isabel, she is an orphan. It is as if Wharton had asked herself what might have happened to James's heroine after she returned to her hateful husband in Rome at the end of *The*

Portrait of a Lady. The irony of Isabel's fate hinged on her thinking herself unconventional and generous in making a marriage that actually caused her to be (as her cousin laments) "ground in the very mill of the conventional" by a Europeanized dilettante with fraudulent pretensions to unworldliness. When Ellen returns to her home country, she faces the possibility of jeopardizing or supporting a pending conventional but decent marriage between Newland Archer and May Welland. The crux of the plot is Ellen's refusal to embark on an affair with him; and the matching irony in this novel is that when Archer, in his capacity as lawyer, reluctantly gives her conventional advice not to make a family fuss by divorcing her husband, she surprises and disappoints him by taking the advice seriously out of respect for his social code and for the stability of his future life with his wife. Archer, in his own untragic way, is "ground in the mill of the conventional" by marrying the unimaginative May Welland, who had conspired with her family to keep Ellen at bay by making a premature claim of being pregnant.

Isabel's deluded generosity in marrying the coldest of cold fish is counterpointed by Ellen's clear-sighted generosity in respecting the stability of May's life with Newland. Ellen does not share Newland's naive belief that they can be just "simply two human beings who love each other" and tells him that those who have tried to find that freedom from the categories of "wife" and "mistress" have "all got out by mistake at wayside stations: at places like Boulogne, or Pisa, or Monte Carlo—and it wasn't at all different from the old world they'd left behind, but only rather smaller and dingier and more promiscuous." Her mistaken marriage has made her look at the Gorgon and dried her tears, but it has also fastened her eyes open "so that they're never again in the blessed darkness."[37]

Ellen's awareness of this "miserable little country" of the mistress draws on her creator's own experience of love outside of marriage in her three-year affair with Morton Fullerton, the journalist. The biographer, R. W. B. Lewis, who discovered it in her papers, has also noted that James's troubled description in his letters of Edith's "dark vigils" in Paris, contemplating "her deadly marital imprisonment," reflects his own brilliant passage describing Isabel Archer's meditation on her equally disastrous choice of a husband.[38] Edith Wharton's escape was through Fullerton and her divorce in 1913, three years after the sad end of her joyous affair with this charming but promiscuous man.

"The age of innocence" is a phrase applicable to Isabel Archer, but in

her case it is the legacy of a transcendentalist enthusiasm for the possibilities of free expression. James provided her with a minimum of social
circumstances: dead parents, two briefly mentioned married sisters, and
pleasant memories of her grandmother's house in Albany. Her Emersonian wish is "to leave the past behind her and, as she said to herself, to
begin afresh."[39] It is an impulse she shares with Huck Finn, even though
she has been brought up on the music of Gounod, the poetry of Brow-
ning, and the prose of George Eliot. James's heroine is more generic than
she is particular in her cult of free expression. "Her reputation of reading
a great deal hung about her like the cloudy envelope of a goddess in an
epic."[40]

She is surrounded not by society but by displaced persons: Mrs.
Touchett, her aunt, is virtually separated from her husband, who lives
abroad with his son, Ralph; Isabel's successful suitor, Gilbert Osmond,
is an American expatriate in Rome; his former lover, Madame Merle, is
also an expatriated and Europeanized American. Isabel is vulnerable to
making serious mistakes not only because of her romantic imagination,
but also because she lacks social cues and clues in a world of displaced
persons. Newland Archer's marriage, on the other hand, is a New York
tribal rite of the 1870s, part of a social pattern that allows a man a
foolish fling with a married woman before his marriage, abhors the
scandal of divorce, keeps a gentleman out of politics (given over to
immigrants and their bosses), deprecates intellectual interests, and socially ostracizes those whose business failures can be traced to unethical
practices.

Archer is aware that "in reality they all lived in a kind of hieroglyphic
world, where the real thing was never said or done or even thought, but
only represented by a set of arbitrary signs," a system of shared assumptions. (He sounds like a structuralist linguist or semiotician in the American literary academe of the 1960s.) In this society, May's frankness and
innocence, he reflects, "were only an artificial product . . . so cunningly
manufactured by a conspiracy of mothers and aunts and grandmothers
and long-dead ancestresses, because it was supposed to be what he
wanted, what he had a right to, in order that he might exercise his lordly
pleasure in smashing it like an image made of snow."[41] For Archer, Ellen
Olenska comes home trailing some of the same clouds of glory that had
enveloped James's Isabel; but May is no goddess in an epic; she is the
familiar product of a social code.

Isabel and Ellen are alike in making renunciation the crucial action of their lives. Just as Isabel gives up the social and erotic possibilities offered to her by Lord Warburton and Caspar Goodwood, respectively, so does Ellen carry on this rite of sacrifice by giving up her personal emotional claims on Newland Archer. In the end, he too makes his own mild act of renunciation. After the death of his wife, he returns at the age of fifty-seven (Edith Wharton's own age when she began the novel) to Ellen's Parisian apartment, where she has lived her life, separated from her husband, who is now dead. "There is nothing now to keep them apart," but only Archer's son, child of a freer time, actually visits Madame Olenska. She is more real to her former lover as a memory than she would be as a living person, and so he returns alone to his hotel. Wharton has shown us to the end of their situation, as James deliberately did not do in his story, but renunciation is the keynote of both novels.

These melodious resonances include the consistency of the two Archers. Both Isabel and Newland pay a heavy price in their marriages, both resign themselves to the payment, and both miss the chance for a more sexually fulfilling relationship because there are other values to consider. Ellen insists that he has taught her (in spite of himself) not to buy happiness with "disloyalty and cruelty and indifference." Newland knows that his wife has been lacking in imagination, incapable of growth, but he has come to appreciate the "dignity of duty" in contrast to a "battle of ugly appetites." The price he has paid is in missing "the flower of life," which is incarnated in Ellen Olenska as if she were an "imaginary beloved in a book or a picture," the "composite vision of all that he had missed."[42]

The differing temperaments of Newland and Isabel Archer foretell their destinies. Once, seeing Ellen at the end of the Newport pier, he had waited for her to see him first before making himself known, and so he had missed a chance for an intimate meeting she was waiting to grant him. His decision not to go up to Ellen's Parisian apartment is not a moral one at all. It reflects his awareness that too much of his life has flowed under the bridge for him to resume a relationship that was never consummated. He would prefer to keep her in his memory (as Strether does with Madame de Vionnet) as a symbol of what he had missed. Ellen, on the other hand, has the audacity of her grandmother, old Catherine Mingott, who married two of her daughters to Europeans and built a cream-colored stone house near Central Park "when brown sandstone seemed as much the only wear as a frock-coat in the afternoon." Ellen's decision to return Newland's house key to him, rather than back her own claims to happiness, chimes with Isabel's decision to return to her husband.

Isabel comes to feel that what she has done deliberately must be accepted because responsibility means accepting the consequences of one's deeds. The obligations of marriage, she believes, are "quite independent of the quality of enjoyment extracted from it."[43] This brave sense of the free act entailing her suffering is the measure of Isabel's moral grandeur. James gives us a foretaste of the ending, however, when he introduces her as a person having "a certain nobleness of imagination" that was vulnerable to "the danger of keeping up the flag after the place has surrendered; a sort of behavior so crooked as to be almost a dishonour to the flag."[44] Three good men (Warburton, Ralph Touchett, and Goodwood) love Isabel, but she will have none of them. Isabel honors her promise to return to Pansy, the child of her husband's old affair with Madame Merle, yet her moral decision is also alloyed with a rejection of Goodwood's intensity of "hard manhood" that sends her flying from his kiss at Gardencourt, as if she were afraid of her own vulnerability to his power (unique among her suitors) to move her to tears and emotional turmoil. Moreover, her refusal to consider divorce is partly based on her unwillingness to "publish" her mistake before the world, a shame that is mixed with pride. Compared to Ellen's moral decision, Isabel's is more mixed with psychological elements, as James presents it.

Wharton felt that both she and James came from an "Old America" that could appreciate forms that had become anachronistic. The children of the Archers live in a postwar world that is freer from the old rigidities, as it is from the old decencies. His son can marry a girl born of an extramarital affair, conducted by an unethical businessman, and after 1900 only the older people would remember the scandal. It is the son who tells his father that May had revealed, just before she died, her appreciation of his having given up the thing that he most wanted. Archer is "moved indescribably" and realizes that to his son, however, the episode with Ellen is only "a pathetic instance of vain frustration, of wasted forces."[45]

Edith Wharton understood deprivation from the misery of her twenty-eight-year marriage to an unintellectual man who was driven to alcohol, drugs, and promiscuity by his own despair at their incompatibility. James understood it from his essential loneliness and the recurrent failure of his doomed wish for a smashing success in the theater, an aspiration which regularly compromised his literary standards, diverted him from novelistic talents, and plunged him into depressions. She knew that his "theatrical experiments," which she thought mistaken, showed that "he longed intensely, incurably, for the shouting and the garlands so persistently refused to his great novels," for he had the Latin feeling for "*la gloire*," that last infirmity of noble minds and "never quite renounced by his."[46]

From the perspective of our time, the meaning of Edith Wharton's claim that she and Henry James belonged to an "Old America" can be understood in terms of their common difference from contemporary modernity. A contemporary novelist of manners, Cynthia Propper Seton, has comically made the point about the difference in a passage from her novel *A Glorious Third* (1979). When a junior editor in a publishing house explodes against the "*primitivism* of what we call Victorian morality" for taking seriously "a technicality as ludicrously trivial as *virginity*," the heroine Celia, who is out of phase with the 1968 zeitgeist, confesses that "in our world where all the forces seem to be *centrifugal* . . . where everybody in the name of self-realization . . . of freedom . . . is enjoined to get out, break loose, separate . . . divorce . . . where the *newness* of things is what is most highly prized, most celebrated, well I guess I seem to be a curious anomaly." She is indeed, for she cares most "about a continuum . . . the sense that we derive from a past, and there is a future, that there is a catalogue of generations." Both James and Wharton would have understood her down to the ground: "I care about history," Celia roundly says, "but about virginity I don't care a fig."[47]

This feeling for a continuum has nothing to do with the moralistic terms of the Pulitzer Prize that was awarded to *The Age of Innocence*, ironically enough, for presenting "the wholesome atmosphere of American life and the highest standard of American manners and manhood." She wrote Sinclair Lewis, whom the Pulitzer jury had turned down because *Main Street* had offended some people, about her disgust with "the welter of cant and sentimentality" surrounding "Fiction in America."[48] Her own sense of old New York in the novel was realistic enough about its limitations to prevent any nostalgia for its ways.

The final note of Wharton's novel is not social realism, but the poignancy of Newland Archer's memories of his wife and his potential mistress. In James's novel, Isabel's return to her desolate marriage strikes a darker, more tragic note. His conception of her drew on his affection for the high-spirited young American women he knew, but there was a tragic element in the ones he liked best: his cousin Minny Temple died young and Clover Hooper, who became the wife of Henry Adams, died by her own hand. In a letter written in 1870 on the day of Minny's death, praising both women, James also expressed his enjoyment of the manner and approval of the substance in his father's article in the *Atlantic* about marriage.[49] His father's theology identified love with the spontaneous, not the voluntary; contrasted a merely "ritual covenant" with a "real or living one"; and saw in the marriage bond itself a precursor of the time when "the social sentiment" would prevail and achieve the "unity of mankind." Divorce suits, recorded in the newspapers, were mere outlets for revenge by aggrieved parties. The true society was not to be found in any institutions but rather in "a plenary divine righteousness in our very nature." The man in marriage was to overcome the "gross male Adam" in himself by substituting his wife's self for his own because she represents to the imagination "a diviner self than his own."[50]

It is hard to say just what the novelist made out of this idiosyncratic theology, but its identification of marriage and women with the divinity of a loving spontaneity, heralding a millennial future, bears on the novelist's much more secular interest in endowing Isabel Archer with the capacity he admired in Minny Temple and Clover Hooper for possessing "intellectual grace" and "moral spontaneity." His father's views on women denigrated, in orthodox Victorian style, any feminist demands for participation in the realms of thought or power: "For this is the vital difference of the pair, that man for ever asks more, while woman is always intent on making the most of what she has."[51] He also objected to John Stuart Mill's liberal *The Subjection of Women* because it made sexual difference insignificant and denied any "spiritual sanction" to marriage above "the personal welfare of the parties" or their "reciprocal delight in each other."[52] These views in their antifeminism resonate with the satire of feminist reformers in *The Bostonians*, but in their Victorian idealism about women's role, as a ministering angel, in a sacred marriage bond, they seem to have an echo in the novelist's ruling out for Isabel Archer any possibility of divorce or a second marriage as a solution of her problem.

In looking back and forth at the pairings I have made of these six novels we can see how, as in a diptych, "the individuality of each is preserved without losing sight of the hinges that firmly connect them."[53] The pairs, to use a phrase of Melville's about two of his short sketches, have a sort of "inverse similitude." Emerging out of personal as well as literary friendships, these examples illustrate complementarities that constitute one illuminating aspect of literary tradition. They also expose the fallacy of contrasting allegedly asocial American writers in general with English novelists of manners, for these four novelists are all interested in linking their individual dramas to differences in manners in different regions, classes, ethnic groups, or countries. If they have an Emersonian interest in the aspiring dreams of the individual self, they also know as artists how deeply implicated the dreamers are in their social histories.

Chapter 5

Pragmatic Godfather: Emerson, Whitman, and William James

EMERSON'S shadow has been extraordinarily long. Perrry Miller linked him back to the Puritan Jonathan Edwards, seeing both men as examples of the "mystical springs in the New England character." Harold Bloom instead has celebrated Emerson as the literary father of Henry David Thoreau, Walt Whitman, Robert Frost, and Wallace Stevens. Emerson's extravagant eloquence leads critics to speak in hyperbole: "Emerson in many respects *is* American literature"; "The lengthened shadow of our American culture is Emerson's." Even critics who differ profoundly over their evaluation of Emerson's point of view and the value of its influence tend to agree in identifying him as an exemplar of the "hero-poet" who is "an imperialist of the inner lives of other people," speaking for "the imperial self" that denies the relevance of associated life and history.[1]

No rhetorical inflation of Emerson into an American avatar is necessary, however, to acknowledge his importance for Walt Whitman, who called him "Master" in sending him a copy of *Leaves of Grass.* A legendary event in American literary history is Emerson's famous complimentary letter of 21 July 1855, to the poet, from which Whitman, as a newspaperman with a shrewd eye for promotion and publicity, extracted "I greet you at the beginning of a great career" and (to Emerson's irritation) stamped it in gold on the spine of the 1856 edition of *Leaves of Grass.* Whitman, over thirty years later, described their meeting in Brooklyn on 11 December 1855, with memorable understatement: " 'How are you, Mr. Whitman.' 'How are you, Waldo'—the hour's talk or so—the taste of loveableness he left behind when he was gone." Perhaps even more colored by time is the report, published ten years after Whitman's death, that he had said in 1860: "I was simmering, simmering, simmering; Emerson brought me to a boil."[2]

Whatever Whitman may actually have said, the substance of the report is entirely credible. As a reporter and editor, Whitman was present, thirteen years before he wrote "Song of Myself," at Emerson's lecture in New York called "The Poet." He saluted the address as "one of the richest and most beautiful compositions, both for its matter and style, we have ever heard anywhere, at any time."[3] It was in his essay "The Poet" that Emerson, in a familiar passage, said he had looked in vain for a poet "with tyrannous eye, which knew the value of our incomparable materials, and saw, in the barbarism and materialism of the times, another carnival of the same gods whose picture he so much admires in Homer." Such a poet would see the "foundations of wonder" beneath "the banks and tariffs, the newspaper and caucus, Methodism and Unitarianism," and sing of "our log-rolling, our stumps and their politics, our fisheries, our Negroes, and Indians, our boasts, and our repudiations, the wrath of rogues, and the pusillanimity of honest men, the Northern trade, the Southern planting, the Western clearing," and so America would be "a poem in our eyes."[4] It is not surprising that Emerson should see in *Leaves of Grass* precisely the poet he had called for, and his letter to the author expressed his "great joy" in finding "incomparable things said incomparably well, as they must be," and with a "courage of *treatment*" that was inspired by "large perception." Whitman felt in this welcome endorsement the burden of living up to it and confided to his notebook in the following year his anxious but hopeful question: "Will he justify the great prophecy of Emerson?"[5]

Whitman, of course, not only fulfilled Emerson's prophecy; he went beyond it with a sexual candor, a journalist's experience of the city and of war, and a poetic fecundity quite beyond his Master's own capacities. Emerson told a friend that Whitman was "a Mirabeau of a man, with such insight and equal expression, but hurt by hard life and too animal experience." The qualifications measure the difference in the sort of experiences that get into the poems. For all his reservations, however, Emerson referred to *Leaves of Grass* as "the American Poem."[6] Whitman himself, writing for a journal celebrating Emerson's birthday, clearly understood that "the best part of Emersonianism is, it breeds the giant that destroys itself. Who wants to be any man's mere follower? lurks behind every page.

No teacher ever taught, that has so provided for his pupil's setting up independently—no truer evolutionist."[7]

Even so, Jerome Loving, in a recent close study of their relationship, concludes that they both inaugurated the tradition of "self-begetting" (in Harold Bloom's phrase) as an American version of the Romantic Sublime and so, it is claimed, they "cast off the limitations of the human condition and invented the American experience, the exaltation of a spiritual manifest destiny."

When they failed, according to Loving's account, it was because they listened not to the Orphic muse, but turned instead to "the vernacular of the philosopher and its inevitable failure to transcend the limits of empirical knowledge."[8] This judgment blurs Whitman's innovations as a poet, but it also neglects Emerson's appeal for philosophers of pragmatism. Bloom has pertinently warned that "we should never forget that if Emerson fathered Whitman and Thoreau and Frost and (despite that son's evasions) Stevens, his pragmatic strain ensued in William James, Peirce, and even John Dewey."[9]

When Emerson spoke in New York during the first two weeks of March 1842, one member of the audience was Henry James, Sr. His son William had been born only two months earlier. After one of the lectures, the father invited Emerson to his house, where he was taken upstairs to admire the first-born son. Thus began the James family's friendship with Emerson, who often visited them. The father kept up a correspondence with him for many years, often proudly showing his son's letters to his friend; and the father's paper on Emerson was published when William James edited *The Literary Remains of the Late Henry James* (1885).

> Our forefathers walked in the world & went to their graves
> tormented with the fear of sin & the terror of the Day of Judgment.
> We are happily rid of those terrors, and our torment is the utter
> uncertainty & perplexity of what we ought to do; the distrust of the
> value of what we do; and the distrust that the Necessity which we
> all at last believe in, is Fair.[10]

Emerson wrote this entry in his journal for 1841, a year before the birth of William James, who as a young man suffered the same uncertainty, perplexity, and distrust. It was, in fact, a family fate, experienced in different ways and degrees by his father, sister, and three brothers. The year of William's birth and of his father's meeting with Emerson was significant for another reason as well. By then the father, disinherited as a rebellious improvident son by his implacable, Calvinistic, and wealthy father, had broken the will and become an heir at law.[11] His prosperity thus enabled him to go abroad and continue his irresolution about choosing a vocation. It was his confusion and anxiety about this issue which led him to write Emerson in 1842 for advice: should he withdraw to the country in silence as a meditating man or should he "follow some commoner method, learn silence and bring myself first into men's respect" in order that he might better "speak to them"? He unconsciously predicted the outcome by calling this second alternative "rank with earthiness."[12] Two years later he suffered his "vastation" in which he was transfixed by the vision of a fatally threatening invisible "damned shape," and his accounts of his scourging conscience were described in metaphors that suggest his experience of having been cut off from his inheritance by his father's will.[13] Only a conversion to Swedenborgianism could bring peace to the prodigal son.

By pressing so hard on his own son to choose the road that he himself had not taken—a career in science—he prepared the way for the son's own breakdown at about the same age. William James pursued his father's lost ambition with repressed resentment and at the psychological cost of a lengthy breakdown in health and spirits for over a decade. It culminated in his own "vastation," the "panic fear" that he might become as helplessly deranged as the idiotic epileptic patient he had once seen in an asylum.

Both Emerson and James in groping painfully to find their vocations had suffered eye trouble that was also "I" trouble. Emerson struggled to break free of the ministry, calling his ordination "execution day."[14] His voyage to Europe in 1831 served as a moratorium on the way to abandoning his vocational identity as a clergyman and venturing instead on the new and risky path of becoming a lecturer and writer on behalf of his own religion. James challenged his father's scientific plans for him by going to art school, but then soon withdrew and entered Lawrence Scientific School to study chemistry in 1861, when his nervous symptoms, affecting his eyes and back as well as his spirits, erupted. Subjecting himself to working for a medical degree, which he never used, he experienced his version of his father's panic fear. "Whereas Henry's crisis brought him closer to God," Howard M. Feinstein points out,

"William's crisis brought him closer to his father."[15] He could not find himself in medicine nor the acting self in medical materialism's picture of the world.

He had earlier recognized his talent for a speculative life and proposed it as a long-range objective when he was hospitalized by varioloid on a scientific collecting expedition to Brazil. Looking back on the trip many years later, he told Mrs. Agassiz (whose husband had led the expedition) that his "incapacity as a naturalist" was because his "destiny was to be a 'philosopher.' "[16] Though he at last found his path in 1875 by becoming a Harvard professor, it was in anatomy and physiology, not in the subjects of his deepest interests—psychology, philosophy, and religion. He was fifty-seven when he finally cleared the way for his Edinburgh Lectures on religion in 1901–1902 by turning over all his hated, experimental, "brass instrument," laboratory work, to Hugo Münsterberg.[17]

Ralph Barton Perry, a biographer of William James, calls Emerson one of James's "fairy godfathers," whom he knew through the medium of the elder Henry James's "highly interpretive and peculiarly personal" characterization of him.[18] The elder Henry had what Calvinists called "a conviction of sin," a strong sense of being "thoroughly *self*-condemned before God," and what impressed him most about Emerson was the entire absence of this consciousness and the presence instead of "a holy innocence" that "recognized no God outside of himself and his interlocutor, and recognized him there only as the *liaison* between the two, taking care that all their intercourse should be holy with a holiness undreamed of before by man or angel."[19] William James understood his father's criticism and in his own way even endorsed it in *The Varieties of Religious Experience* (1902). But the philosopher and the poet overlapped in outlook at important points.

James shared with Emerson not only a difficult struggle for a vocation and a talent for popular lecturing, but also a strong feeling for nature as a source of serenity and exaltation. James wrote one of his sons in 1900 that scenery wore better than any other element in life: "I have often been surprised to find what a predominant part in my own spiritual experience it has played, and how it stands out as almost the only thing the memory of which I should like to carry over with me beyond the veil, unamended and unaltered."[20] The best illustration of his point is the episode he called his *Walpurgis Nacht* on Mount Marcy in the Adirondacks in July 1898, when he experienced a free associating of whirling images of scenery, his wife, brother Harry, children, and the problem of the Edinburgh Lectures—all fermenting together. It seemed to him a meeting in his breast of "the Gods of all the nature-mythologies" and the "the moral Gods of the inner life. The two kinds of Gods have nothing in common—the Edinburgh lectures made quite a hitch ahead." Now, he told his wife, he understood "what a poet is," the kind of person who could feel the complexity of influences in such an experience "and make some partial tracks in them for verbal statement."[21]

James's account is reminiscent of Emerson's famous reference in "Nature" to walking on a bare common where he experienced "a perfect exhiliration" and was "glad to the brink of fear." James's letting go was not scary, but it was limited and oriented by the pragmatic concern for his work on the Edinburgh Lectures. Emerson's idea of the poet was similar to James's also, a person who can break the chains of ordinary life and enable us to comprehend our relations in a new way because he speaks from "a new energy (as of an intellect doubled on itself), by abandonment to the nature of things."[22]

In the *Varieties,* James's idea of "a subliminal self" (derived from the theorizing of spiritualists and psychologists) played a central role. Religious feeling tapped subconscious energies to put the believer in "friendly continuity" with a "wider life" of meaning, whether through passionate surrenders and "letting go," or heroic sacrifice. Like Emerson, James believed that the higher power, felt as a control in the believer's experience, is "primarily the higher faculties of our own hidden mind."[23] The variety in the *Varieties,* however, goes well beyond the range of transcendentalists to include Catholic saints, Jews, Buddhists, Christian Scientists, Mormons, Mohammedans, Melanesian cannibals, drug-takers, and even atheists. This sometimes lurid material is presented in the spirit of an empirical scientist, calmly hypothesizing about its meaning.

There are, appropriately, several voices narrating the varied stories of distress and relief in the *Varieties.* There is an Emersonian voice of the moral sentiment, the reformer who values "the strenuous life," as Theodore Roosevelt called it, though with James it is not sport of battle that inspires the phrase; instead it is the ideal of voluntary poverty, pacifism, and the "Utopian dreams of social justice in which many contemporary socialists and anarchists indulge," as "slow leavens of a better order."[24] There is also the appreciator (as Emerson was) of regeneration by "letting go," the person who knows that "official moralists," calling for strenuosity of the will, sometimes only make people "two-fold more the children of hell they were before."[25] In this mood he is congenial to Emerson's conception of spontaneity as the root of authentic being, the principle behind his proposal, so offensive to moralists, to write "whim" above the lintel as a standard of conduct requiring neither explanation nor apology. One of Emerson's most quoted phrases is the one about consistency being "the hobgoblin of little minds," and for James all our insights must be provisional because even "the wisest of critics is an altering being, subject to the better insight of the morrow, and right at any moment, only 'up to date' and 'on the whole.' " In defense of opening ourselves to receiving "larger ranges of truth" that are "unfettered by our previous pretensions," he quoted Emerson: "Heartily know, when half-gods go, the gods arrive."[26]

There are also non-Emersonian, characteristically Jamesian voices in the *Varieties*. There is, for example, the astute doctor-psychologist, a clinically minded, post-Emersonian type, who speaks of Binet, Janet, Breuer, and Freud, who have discovered "whole systems of underground life, in the shape of memories of a painful sort which lead a parasitic existence, buried outside of the primary fields of consciousness, and making irruptions thereinto with hallucinations, pains, convulsions, paralyses of feeling and motion, and the whole procession of symptoms of hysteric disease of body and of mind."[27]

There is also another un-Emersonian voice in the *Varieties:* James's book turns, as Emerson's essays do not, on a vital contrast between "the once-born" and "the twice-born" consciousness in which the "sick soul" is converted to a positive espousal of "surrender and sacrifice." The two types, James believes, lead to different religions, the first to optimistic monisms, like Christian Science, which deny the reality of evil, the second to those, like Buddhism and Christianity, in which "the pessimistic elements are best developed." Yet, insofar as the distinction between the two types is merely a psychological one, James conceded that the twice-born might even be converted *away* from religion and moral scrupulosity into "incredulity" or "license," or simply find some new passion such as "love, ambition, cupidity, revenge, or patriotic devotion."[28] But he did not see that even by his own evidence the "mind-cure" monistic optimists of Christian Science were themselves usually "sick" souls who had, like Emerson, come to their visions through internal conflict and self-transformation. His typology of psychological-religious affinity ultimately breaks down.[29] But his sympathy for the twice-born category reflects the powerful influence of his father's experience of self-division and conversion, as well as his crippled father's robust awareness of evil.

Even though William James was trained in medical materialism, evolutionary biology, and the empiricism of John Stuart Mill, he derived from his troubled involvement with his theological father a sympathy for the evangelical Protestant theme of the sinful natural man's new birth in conversion to belief in a supernatural God. James discovered at the age of forty, after his father died, that the theologian had always been an "integral part" of the son's daily consciousness, an inner tribunal that was always in session.[30] He also knew that his father's life as a theologian without a congregation or colleagues, an isolated man plagued by the legacy of bad blood between himself and his own father, had been in this respect a dismaying one.

Introducing *The Literary Remains of Henry James* in 1885, he recognized that his father as "a robust and dogmatizing theologian" had been sadly "left stranded high and dry" in an intellectual world that, before the Civil War, was more congenial to Emerson, and, after it, to a scientifically trained thinker.[31] But he recognized in his father a classic type of the twice-born sick soul: "The experience in question has always been an acute despair, passing over into an equally acute optimism, through a passion of renunciation of the self and surrender to the higher power." The son, however, believed that his father's "most serious enemy" would be found in "the *philosophic* pluralist," who asserts "a pluralism which, in face of the old mystery of the One and the Many, has vainly sought peace in identification, and ended by taking sides against the One."[32]

It is hard not to see this passage as having a personal subtext about the son's relation to his father. In any case, the introduction poses the central issue between monistic religion and pluralistic moralism that the philosopher would face in both *The Varieties of Religious Experience* and *Pragmatism* with a different emphasis in each one, depending on whether he was thinking about his father's example or Emerson's message. Seeking some "healthy-mindedness" in himself, James defined it as residing in "the full and successful exercise of our moral energy," choosing action and giving "a deaf ear to the thought of *being*." It was his father who always made "moralism the target of his hottest attack, and pitted religion and it against each other as enemies of whom one must die utterly, if the other is to live in genuine form." William James drew the issue sharply: "Any absolute moralism is a pluralism; any absolute religion is a monism." The crux is whether evils are seen as alien, real, and subjugable or, instead, seen as "fractions, with a common denominator, of some less fluctuating Unity, enclosing some less partial and more certain form of Good." That is the way of "morbid mindedness" because it needs relief from its sense of "weakness, of helpless failure, and of fear." James conceded that "we are all *potentially* such men. The sanest and best of us are of one clay with lunatics and prison-inmates."[33]

But after his father's death he had experienced relief from his eye trouble and felt himself "a different man," one who was, as the French philosopher Renouvier told him, "called to found an *American philosophy.*"[34] Presiding over his father's *Literary Remains,* he felt that deep thinkers knew that either moralism or religion had to go. The battle was on, and it would be a hot one indeed if "the friends of philosophic moralism should bring to the service of their ideal" a spirit "even remotely resembling the life-long devotion" of his father's "faithful heart."[35] In the winter following his father's death, William wrote "The Dilemma of Determinism," which represented his characteristic blow for freedom against the monisms of both scientific and religious views of the world, the first of his major essays on behalf of an open universe.

The influence of Renouvier, from whom James derived a useful argument on behalf of free will, was writ large in the essays James wrote in the 1880s and 1890s; but in the summer of 1899 he developed a heart lesion from mountain climbing, forcing him to postpone the Gifford Lectures on religion. His renewed sense of weakness and depression made him more sympathetic now to the insights of twice-born monists, like his father, who needed a surrendering, comforting faith. As Perry observes, James understood the need for such a faith "from his own periodic weariness and from his sympathy with the extremity and tragic plight which is the common lot of man."[36]

In the *Varieties,* he argued that "morbid-mindedness ranges over the wider scale of experience" because it finds that "radical evil" is part of the "normal process of life," and may, "after all be the best key to life's significance, and possibly the only openers of our eyes to deepest levels of truth." He had only contempt for "your robust Philistine type of nervous system, forever offering its biceps to be felt, thumping its breast, and thanking Heaven that it hasn't a single morbid fibre in its compositions"; he much preferred the flinty character who had "some austerity and wintry negativity, some roughness, danger, stringency, and effort, some no! no! mixed in with its capacity for happiness." As Jonathan Edwards shook his parishioners by a sermon envisioning sinners in the hands of an angry God being like a loathsome spider held above a searing fire, so James aimed to shake his modern readers by pointing out to them what they tended to deny: "Here on our very hearts and in our gardens, the infernal cat plays with the panting mouse, or holds the hot bird fluttering in her jaws."[37]

The imagery and rhythm of James's example are Emersonian, and Emerson himself in "Fate" illustrates the rudeness of Providence in a Jamesian way: "The habit of snake and spider, the snap of the tiger, and other leapers and bloody jumpers, the crackle of the bones of his prey in the coil of the anaconda—these are in the system, and our habits are like theirs." (James himself gave the example of a tiger carrying off an explorer in his mouth.) Should you nod too complacently, Emerson goes alarmingly on to amplify his point by listing comets, earthquakes, slaughterhouses, scurvy at sea, cholera, smallpox, sharks, sea wolves, and other "hints of the ferocity in the interiors of nature."[38] He declares that he will not (as he sometimes may seem to have done before) dress up Providence, "that terrific benefactor, in a clean shirt and white neckcloth of a student in divinity." Even so, for Emerson this is natural history, and he opposes it to will, "the one serious and formidable thing in nature." For him there is no conflict in the will and, as a monist, he invokes and relies on "the Blessed Unity which holds nature and souls in perfect solution."[39]

On both counts, James is no Emersonian. He takes account of Emerson as a religious man for whom the question of "whether this soul of the universe be a mere quality like the eye's brilliancy or the skin's softness, or whether it be a self-conscious life like the eye's seeing or the skin's feeling, is a decision that never unmistakably appears in Emerson's pages."[40] He also cites Emerson as an example of the "sky-blue healthy-minded moralist" who thinks that "the theological problems of original sin, origin of evil, predestination, and the like," as Emerson put it, "are the soul's mumps, and measles, and whooping coughs."[41] Typically, Emerson argues in "Spiritual Laws" that Crump is not a better man, because of his "grunting resistance to all his native devils," than a soul "whose acts are regal, graceful, and pleasant as roses." "True enough," James memorably replies in a witty footnote: "Yet Crump may really be the better *Crump,* for his inner discords and second birth; and your once-born 'regal' character, though indeed always better than poor Crump, may fall far short of what he individually might be had he only some Crump-like capacity for compunction over his own peculiar diabolisms, graceful and pleasant and invariably gentlemanly as these may be."[42] It is impossible not to hear his father's scornfully humorous tone, with what his son called its "inward palpitating human quality," in this telling rejoinder.

Emerson and James had both been sick souls, but neither one converted to a traditionally pessimistic religion like Christianity. Emerson's historic "Divinity School Address" scandalized the Harvard Divinity School for over thirty years precisely because he scorned not only biblical miracles, but old revelations, the "noxious exaggeration" of the person of Jesus, and even the hope for new systems or new rites and forms. There was the Sabbath, which needed revivification, but mainly there was only the possibility of a genuine preaching, "the speech of man to men," exploring the moral nature of man with its infinite resources of "astonishment and power." The "readiness of sacrifice" was indeed a virtue but "it is in rugged crises, in unweariable endurance, and in aims which put sympathy out of question, that the angel is shown."[43]

James himself disparaged the Calvinist debates about justification, sanctification, and judgment because he thought "our modern imagination" finds it incredible that "this glorious universe, with plants and winds, and laughing sky and ocean, should have been conceived and had its beams and rafters laid in technicalities of criminality."[44] Passionate defender as he was of the believer's right to believe, in opposition to the agnostic's demand for waiting "until all the evidence is in," he himself made chary use of such a right—only enough to suggest that the higher power "might conceivably even be only a larger and more godlike self, of which the present self would then be but the mutilated expression, and the universe might conceivably be a collection of such selves, of different degrees of inclusiveness, with no absolute unity realized in it at all."[45] The idea is reminiscent of Emerson's Over-soul, but the Jamesian note is the absence of overarching unity, whether in terms of Nature or God.

The personal context of James's centenary address on Emerson is crucial for understanding what the poet meant to the philosopher. James wrote his Swiss friend, Theodore Flournoy, that he felt "very tired & unable to work this spring," that he was "reading nothing heavy, only Emerson's works again (divine things, some of them!) in order to make a 15 minute address about him on his centennial birthday." What he wanted to get to "(at last)"—"and let no interruptions interfere"—was his own " 'system' of tychistic and pluralistic 'philosophy of pure experience.' "[46] He increasingly felt that the success of his popular lecturing was keeping him from his more technical philosophical work. He needed confidence to imagine that he could pull together his insights and make a final major statement of his vision. He had already written the first sentence of his forthcoming book—"the only one yet written: 'Philosophy is a queer thing—at once the most sublime and the most contemptible of human occupations.' There is nothing like having made your start! I shouldn't be surprised if the rest were like rolling down hill."[47]

A few days later he wrote his brother Henry in a similar vein: "The reading of the divine Emerson, volume after volume, has done me a lot of good, and, strange to say, has thrown a strong practical light on my own path." What impressed James was "the incorrigible way" Emerson had "followed his own vocation, of seeing such truths as the Universal Soul vouchsafed to him from day to day and month to month, and reporting them in the right literary form, and thereafter kept his limits absolutely, refusing to be entangled with irrelevancies however urging and tempting, knowing both his strength and its limits," and clinging to the rural environment he found propitious. Emerson was in this way "a moral lesson to all men who have any genius, however small, to foster." Henry himself was sticking to his last: "You too have been living an Emersonian life—though the environment differs to suit the needs of the different psychophysical organism which you present."[48]

When he came to speak about Emerson at Concord in 1903, James declared that his "paramount impression" was of a man loyal to his own "personal type and mission," as an artist of "spiritual seeing and reporting." Not even the antislavery cause could make him desert his post, where the fight was against "imprisoned thoughts" that had no watchman but himself. This was the Emerson who could inspire James to keep to his own path. What he saw as "the hottest side" of Emerson was his "non-conformist persuasion" as the preacher of self-reliance, "a bugle blast" on behalf of "the sovereignty of the living individual." His love for the authentic was quite willing to sacrifice the past to the present decisive hour, but James emphasized that Emerson's optimism "had nothing in common with that indiscriminate hurrahing for the Universe with which Walt Whitman has made us familiar." The individual fact, moment, and person to be revered had to be "symbolic mouthpieces of the Universe's meaning." Just as Whitman had saluted Emerson as Master, so did James conclude his address by saying " ''Gainst death and all oblivious enmity, shall you pace forth,' beloved Master." Emerson would continue to cheer and strengthen human hearts, "so long as our English language lasts."[49]

William James went off to his house in the country therewith, trusting in Emerson's example to keep himself on his own path with faith in his own talent and devotion to his project. In 1900, he had first tried unsuccessfully to resign from Harvard; six years later he was arguing with himself in his diary on different days: "Resign! . . . Resign!!!! . . . Resign? Resign! . . . *Don't* resign!"[50] When he did resign in 1907, it was with a sense of "unspeakable" comfort and relief because he was free now "to be my own man, after 35 years of being owned by others."[51] This Emersonian condition of self-reliance and integrity seems to have been fostered by his preparation for the centenary. But there was an unnoticed irony involved: James's great successes were, like Emerson's, in the mode of popular lecturing, as *The Varieties of Religious Experience* had been; its success had made the idea of resigning from Harvard financially possible. But it was just such successes, James feared, that were keeping him from more technical and professionally respected philosophical work. A true Emersonian might have seen that to follow his own talent would mean accepting the lecturing mode without being intimidated by conventional academic views of what "serious" philosophical endeavor had to be like. In practice anyway, James did continue on the path of his talent, for the work he is most identified with—*Pragmatism: A New Name for Some Old Ways of Thinking* (1907)—consisted of lectures, written shortly after he had stopped teaching at Harvard, and delivered to an audience of more than a thousand people at Columbia University. James acknowledged that it was "certainly the high tide" of his existence "so far as *energizing* and being 'recognized' were concerned."[52]

James's penciled notes, written into his copies of Emerson's works while preparing for the centennial, indicate that he particularly checked or underlined passages where he felt sympathy for the emphasis on self-reliance, action, common experience, and the present. (He also underlined a wry journal entry in which Emerson wrote: "It is dainty to be sick, if you have leisure and convenience for it. One sees the colors of the carpet and the paper hangings. All the housemates have a softer, fainter look to the debilitated retina."[53] The underlining is a reminder that James had written much of the Gifford Lectures while he was in bed.) In the category of "against my philosophy," written on the inside cover of *Miscellanies,* James cites the Idealism segment of "Nature" and adds "Monism," "Superiority of what is intellectualized," "Intellectualism," and "The rationalist attitude"—all targets of Jamesian polemics.[54]

The most interesting feature of his fragmentary penciled commentary is his use of the word "pragmatism" to point to certain passages in Emerson. Thus, he hears a pragmatic note in "The American Scholar," where the world is said to be plastic in the hands of God; in "Prospects," where nature is seen as fluid; in "The Divinity School Address," where the appeal is made to obeying oneself and trusting one's heart; in "Literary Ethics," where there is a statement about the "mutual reaction of thought and life" as well as a reference to "humble commerce and humble needs of life"; and in "Lecture on the Times," where there is a passage about charting the sea by ourselves, not by loud winds or older sailors.[55] He distinctly underlined in "Experience" the long passage about the "mid-world" which scorns "disconsolate consciences," sets up "the strongest present tense," and urges: "thou, dearest scholar, stick to thy foolish task, add a line every hour, and between whiles add a line."[56] It was a prescription exactly suited to James's malady.

Rereading Emerson had a tonic effect on James's spirits. The centennial celebration itself made for "a sweet and memorable day" that "took one back to one's childhood, and made that rarely realized marriage of reality with ideality, that usually only occurs in fiction or poetry." Though he felt the lack in Emerson of "too little understanding of the morbid side of life," he also felt him "loom larger than ever" as a human being. Three months after the centenary, he told a friend: "It is pleasant to find that one's organism has such reparative capacities even after sixty years have been told out." His son notes that at the age of sixty-three James "turned to the formulation of his empirical philosophy with the eagerness of a schoolboy let out to play. Misunderstanding disturbed him only momentarily, opposition stimulated him, he rejoiced openly in the controversies which he provoked, and engaged in polemics with the good humor and vigor that were the essence of his genius."[57]

James did not derive his pragmatism from Emerson; looking back at him he could see some overlappings of his own thought with the great artist who had been a friend of the family. He had little use for Emerson's "monistic formulas" except insofar as they expressed a genuine ideal direction in things, but, he added, "his dogmatic expression of them never led him to *suppress the facts they ignored,* so no harm was done." He gave as an example the last few pages of "History," where Emerson stresses the need, as Perry has noted, to appreciate "the variety of life and nature—all that escapes the unities and generalizations of history."[58] What mattered most was the reinforcement James found in Emerson for developing the confident secular emphasis in his own thought. *Pragmatism* understands the function of religion in granting believers "a moral holiday," as it did for James's father, but the lectures treat more sympathetically the radically secular view that prefers the struggles of morality to the consolations of religion:

> For pluralistic pragmatism, truth grows up inside of all the finite experiences. They lean on each other, but the whole of them, if such whole there be, leans on nothing. All "homes" are in finite experience; finite experience as such is homeless. Nothing outside the flux secures the issue of it. It can hope salvation only from its own intrinsic promises and potencies.[59]

James, however, does not join "the tough minds in their rejection of the whole notion of a world beyond our finite experience." His pragmatism is meant to be "a mediator between tough-mindedness and tender-mindedness." He gives as an example Walt Whitman's "fine and moving poem" addressed to the reader: "To You." It can be interpreted as saying that whatever happens "inwardly you are safe"; or to say that what you deeply are "picks its way" through "possibles in the plural, genuine possibles, and it has all the restlessness of that conception." James tips his hand, however, by saying that "plainly the pluralistic way agrees with the pragmatic temper best, for it immediately suggests an infinitely larger number of the details of future experience to our mind." Healthy-minded moralists need only a world with a fighting chance for making it better without any eternal guarantees. The morbid-minded "want a universe where we can just give up, fall on our father's neck, and be absorbed into the absolute life as a drop of water melts into the river or the sea." From this point of view the alternatives are exclusive: "We could not remain healthy-minded and sick-minded in one indivisible act."[60]

Much of James's previous thinking reflects this conflicted impulse to justify both attitudes. But in *Pragmatism,* the emphasis falls—as it did to a lesser extent in his introduction to his father's *Literary Remains*—on healthy mindedness, not as a monistic positive thinking that denies evil (the invidious role it played in *The Varieties*) but rather as a buoyant acceptance of an uncertain universe in which there are genuine losses and negatives, a world in which tough-mindedness knows that "something permanently drastic and bitter always remains at the bottom of the cup." He personally is willing to give up "the claim of total reconciliation," the "prodigal-son attitude." But, he concedes at the end of the lectures that, as the author of *The Varieties of Religious Experience,* he does not believe "that our human experience is the highest form of experience extant in the universe" because, like dogs and cats in our libraries, "we are tangent to the wider life of things."[61] James says nothing more in *Pragmatism* about this transcendence of the secular. His emphasis instead is more on pragmatism's tough-minded empiricism than on its ability to mediate tender-minded religion, more on "Rocky Mountain toughs" in philosophy than on "Bostonians," as he figures the two types.

This confidence in the secular is a measure of his own sense of relief from the morbidities of his earlier life. Paradoxically, James challenged the monism he saw in both his father and Emerson, while sympathizing with his father's "tough-minded" understanding of sin, evil, and morbidity in contrast to Emerson's "tender-minded" Platonism. But, it was Emerson, unlike the elder James, who spoke for "the moral sentiment," and it was Emerson's counsel of self-reliance that inspired the philosopher to become his own man. If it is the elder Henry James, with his morbid twice-bornness, who stands behind *The Varieties,* it is Emersonian self-reliance (without Emerson's optimistic monism) that helps to animate *Pragmatism.* James may have seen Emerson's monism as a once-born philosophy, but he himself, in a struggle longer than Emerson's, had to earn his right to the confidence of self-reliance, which he celebrated in his centenary address and practiced thereafter in the development of his pragmatism.

James thought that Emerson's rival and successor was his own colleague George Santayana, but it was the difference between them that impressed him the most: "E. is receptive, expansive, as if handling life through a wide funnel with a great indraught; S. as if through a pin-point orifice that emits his cooling spray outward over the universe like a nose-disinfectant from an 'atomizer.' "[62] In the light of his own devastating metaphor, it is James himself who seems much more truly the successor of Emerson in a sense that includes overlapping, opposition, and not least the sense that Emerson was "really a crittur to be thankful for."[63]

Chapter 6

"Gentle William" and Warren's Willie

WILLIAM James saw in Emerson an intellectual godfather of his own stress on the philosophical primacy of action, but in practice James's personal "moral equivalent of war" was being hospitalized in Brazil on Agassiz's collecting expedition. It was his brother Wilkinson who was badly wounded in the doomed assault on Fort Wagner, in which the leader, Colonel Robert Gould Shaw, was killed. William's relation to the war was vicarious: he drew a sketch of the wounded Wilkie, recuperating at home, and he participated in the celebration of the unveiling in 1897 of a monument to Colonel Shaw by delivering a speech from memory to several thousand people in Boston. James praised Shaw not for military valor but for his "civic courage" in being undaunted by the prejudice against a white man commanding a black regiment.[1] It was this emphasis on the need for civic virtue that made James a "Mugwump" independent Republican, willing to bring the Democrats into power in 1885 in the hope of killing off the old guard and its "dead shibboleths."[2]

Another much more ruthless enemy of the "old guard" suggested to the poet and novelist Robert Penn Warren the pertinent figure of William James standing in the background of *All the King's Men* (1946). Warren turned to James in the midst of the Great Depression while mediating on the rise and fall of a Southern dictator, the governor or Louisiana, and writing both a verse play and a novel about him while living in Italy, where Mussolini was a dictator.

It would not be Warren's only rendezvous with Jamesian pragmatism. Reflecting on the legacy of the Civil War in 1961, he suggested that the conflict had prepared the way for the philosophy of pragmatism. The

North's criticism of slavery as a violation of a higher moral law and the South's defense of slavery as a legally justified form of property posed a conflict of absolutes. Higher law doctrine could become in the hands of some transcendentalists and abolitionists an absolute individualism that discredited not only institutions but also the very idea of society in the name of a totally uncompromising moral solution to the problem of slavery; while Southern apologists defended a closed society with little space for criticism, change, and growth. This conflict of absolutes prepared the way for pragmatism as a criticism of absolutes. Warren dedicated *The Legacy of the Civil War* to Sidney Hook, one of John Dewey's most devoted and influential students, and quoted William James twice. In victory, Warren pointed out, we have been too much "wrapped in our own righteousness" to grasp "the full implications of William James's remark that 'the victory to be philosophically prayed for is that of the more inclusive side—of the side which even in the hour of triumph will to some degree do justice to the ideals in which the vanquished interests lay.' " Something like this took place, Warren suggested, when Henry Adams used a Virginian hero in *Democracy* and Henry James a Mississippian hero in *The Bostonians* to serve as critics of the Gilded Age. For Warren the costs of victory in the Civil War also illustrated James's most un-Emersonian point in *Pragmatism:* "something permanently drastic and bitter always remains at the bottom of the cup."[3] This note of tragedy also marks Warren's novel.

Warren has insisted that *All the King's Men,* even though Huey Long was called "the Kingfish," is not the story of any actual person. He explained that "Long was but one of the figures that stood in the shadows of imagination behind Willie Stark. Another one of that company was the scholarly and benign figure of William James." Warren has never expanded on this reference, except to say in 1981 that he was trying to see "the difference between philosophical pragmatism and that unphilosophical pragmatism represented by Bolingbroke—or Huey. Or by Mussolini, who . . . regarded himself as a kind of disciple of the gentle William."[4]

To consider the Jamesian philosophical element in the making of the novel opens up windows on the international historical situation of the 1930s as well as on the philosophical "deeper concerns" in the novel that Warren has always insisted are more important than the political framework of the story. It is understandable that the novelist would want to distinguish his story from an historical account of an actual political figure. He needs to defend his freedom from literalism and freedom for invention, and Warren exercised both in setting the present time of his story in 1939, when war broke out in Europe and four years after Huey Long had been assassinated. Moreover, the novel can employ events in relationship to the unifying consciousness of a single narrator, as Warren does, whereas the process of history is more collective in its unfolding, too complex and diverse to be focused through a single mind. Furthermore, the novelist typically finds a tragic pattern in the story of the rise and fall of a hero who has insight into his tragedy, a recognition common in literature but unlikely in history, where the evidence for such self-consciousness is usually lacking.[5]

Warren helped create his distance from what actually happened to Huey Long in Louisiana by giving the central consciousness of his novel to a fictional character, Jack Burden, who had made a brief appearance in the earlier version of the story as a verse play, *Proud Flesh*. His philosophical concerns go beyond the specific events of the political narrative to encompass not only the international issue of dictatorship, but universal questions about power, ethics, and the role of the great man in history.

Warren's insistence (in his introduction to the Modern Library edition of his novel in 1953) that Willie Stark was "only himself, whatever that self turned out to be," does not do justice, however, to the way in which the fictional governor, his rhetoric, his entourage (male and female), his murder, and the political context of the state extensively overlap with historical actuality.[6] To cite just one striking (but unfamiliar) example: the dictator's assassin, Adam Stanton, is presented as an idealist unable to understand (as his name suggests) a fallen human nature. This prelapsarian Adam might seem to be a very literary and unhistorical fiction of the author's. Yet in fact, the actual assassin, also a brilliant doctor, a man with accomplishments in music, painting, and mathematics, was described by his mother in these terms: "All we know is that he took living seriously. Right with him was right. Right above everything."[7] That simple exclusive distinction is exactly what Willie Stark and his creator reject as inappropriate for understanding and influencing the political situation.

Nor does divorcing the fictional from the actual give sufficient weight to Warren's own noting of the political context in which the novel was written. Warren's verse play was started and mainly written in Italy "with the news of the war filling the papers and the boot heels of Mussolini's legionnaires clanging on the stones." He began the novel in 1943 and was finished in the summer of 1945, when "great fleets of bombers, roaring, sky-filling constellations returning from Europe and victory, shook the house."[8] In 1939, the question of dictatorship had been urgent for a reflective American, sitting in Rome and meditating on Mussolini, Machiavelli, and James—especially if he had just come from teaching at Louisiana State University, which was experiencing a burst of growth because of Huey Long's special interest in its fortunes. Warren had heard the governor dazzle an academic audience and had graded papers written by his daughter.[9]

It would be astonishing if Willie Stark were entirely fictional, as if Warren's experience had no relation whatever to his creative work. His tendency sometimes to sunder them in talking about the novel seems to be mainly a reaction to the irritating fact that "the first major review took it to be an apologia for fascism."[10] His sensitivity on this score is probably connected with his awareness, as a member of a group of Southern poet-critics called the Fugitives and the Agrarians, that many of them contributed to the *American Review,* and its editor, Seward Collins, preached a romantic reactionary monarchism that he incongruously identified with both Mussolini and Long.[11]

Warren has been more inclined recently to accept the strong connections between the novel and the historical reality. He is featured both at the beginning and ending of Ken Burns's impressive documentary film, "Huey Long." The film opens with Warren's arresting, raspy voice telling us that "if you were living in Louisiana, you knew you were living in history defining itself before your eyes and you knew that you were not seeing a half-drunken buffoon performing an old routine, but witnessing a drama which was a version of the world's drama and the drama of history too: the old drama of power and ethics."[12] The film ends with Warren intoning a passage from his novel. Introducing his film in 1986 at the annual meeting of the Organization of American Historians, the producer and director explained his point of view, which gives voice in the film both to Long's supporters and his enemies, by saying that he thought of Long "as a volcano—both beautiful and frightening."[13] The film in this sense chimes with Warren's attempt in the novel to look at Willie Stark in a way that takes account of the partial truth in what his enemies and his friends believed about him.

Yet the story does not leave the question of judgment as open as the film does. We learn about Warren's governor through the narrator Jack Burden, a former graduate student in history, who becomes one of Willie's hench-men. Burden meditates on Willie throughout the story and doesn't jell his view of him until near the end of the book. What he thinks of Willie is part of his own view of himself and his world: "The story of Willie Stark and the story of Jack Burden are, in one sense, one story."[14] Jack reflects on Willie's political role in the state as a reformer and, at a more general level, philosophizes on the role of the hero in history. These reflections show the influence of James's ideas.[15]

Warren's reference to the "scholarly and benign figure of William James" points indirectly to the paradox of Mussolini's claiming that James's pragmatism was of "great use" to him in his political career: "James taught me that an action should be judged rather by its results than by its doctrinary basis. I learnt of James that faith in action, that ardent will to live and fight, to which Fascism owes a great part of its success." There was an Italian group in Florence of Jamesian pragmatists, whom Mussolini had met, but he admitted that his "greatest debt" was to the Syndicalist advocate of violence, Georges Sorel.[16] Moreover, some of the Italian pragmatists were anti-fascists who died for their opposition to Mussolini's regime.

James's liberalism is unquestionable. He was an outspoken public critic of imperialism and materialism in this country, as well as abroad, and he urged raising the banner of "Les Intellectuels" to represent those who speak for "critical sense and judgment" against the prejudice represented by the anti-Dreyfusards in France or the Republican advocates of expan-sion at the turn of the century in this country. Though he was of the party of "pale reflection," not the party of "red blood," as he told a Harvard Graduate School audience in 1902, he believed that "the chronic fault of liberalism is its lack of speed and passion." Things get dammed up, and there is value in a leader with liberal ambitions who has "the *vis viva* of the rifle bullet" that can make a hole in the dam when necessary for "flowing water" to enlarge it—such men as Cromwell, Garibaldi, Bis-marck, and even "an adventurer like Napoleon." An "educated" country would be able "to use such men for what they are worth, and to cast them off before they victimize it."[17]

Stark's gritty political "realism" is a populistic version of James's skepti-cism about the finality of any particular social balance of conflicting ideals. Compare these two passages:

I'm not denying there's got to be a notion of right to get business done, but by God any particular notion at any particular time will sooner or later get to be just like a stopper put tight in a bottle of water and thrown in a hot stove the way we kids used to do at school to hear the bang. The steam that blows the bottle and scares the teacher to wet her drawers is just the human business that is going to get done, and it will blow anything you put in it if you seal it tight, but you put it in the right place and let it get out in a certain way and it will run a freight engine.[18]

Willie's pungent rationale is a vernacular version of James's analysis in "The Moral Philosopher and the Moral Life" of relativity in law and custom:

And yet if he be a true philosopher he must see that there is nothing final in any actually given equilibrium of human ideals, but that, as our present laws and customs have fought and conquered the other past ones, so they will in their turn be overthrown by any newly discovered order which will hush up the complaints that they still give rise to, without producing others louder still. . . . These experiments are to be judged, not a priori, but by actual finding, after the fact of their making, how much more outcry or how much appeasement comes about.[19]

Willie's feeling for the social welfare of the hill folk of his state, too long neglected by the inertia and the class bias of the ruling gentry from the Delta, gives him his mission to create a new social balance. Scorning his attorney general, who resigns for legal and moral reasons, Willie uses the Machiavellian devices of fear, favor, force, and fraud to obtain his ends. In the process, as the story shows, he becomes corrupted by an inordinate egotism, a vindictive passion for revenge, and a relentless drive for power over others—a recoil from his having once been a gullible political innocent, set up as a "fall guy" by political intriguers. (This episode has no parallel in Huey Long's case.) Warren's title refers indirectly to Humpty Dumpty's fall, and it is Stark's fall from innocence that precipitates the change from a populist reformer to a demagogic dictator.

James's analysis of the hero in history has a direct bearing on Jack Burden's meditations on Willie Stark. "Every now and then, however," James asserts, "some one is born with the right to be original, and his revolutionary thought or action may bear prosperous fruit. He may re-place old 'laws of nature' by better ones; he may, by breaking old moral rules in a certain place, bring in a total condition of things more ideal than would have followed had the rules been kept." In substance, that is Willie's justification of his own actions. The opposition claimed it was a poor state that could not stand being taxed any further. Jack remembers the Boss's telling the crowd: "There is a passel of pore folks living in it and no mistake, but the state isn't poor. It is just a question of who has got his front feet in the trough when slopping time comes. And I aim to do me some shoving and thump me some snouts."[20]

Jack has been inclined as a cynical determinist to depreciate the role of the leader in history. Listening to Willie's speeches, he wonders if the crowd had elected him "because of a complex of forces which had made them what they were or because Willie Stark could lean toward them with bulging eyes and right arm raised to Heaven." He concludes that only one thing is certain—the sound of the crowd's chant was to be "the cause of nothing, nothing at all," and he hugs that knowledge "like a precious and thorny secret, and did not think anything." It absolves him from any sense of responsibility for his own role as one of Willie's hench-men. He had previously found such comfort when he had walked out on his dissertation and on his wife and learned that, through his own nostal-gia for a vision of Anne Stanton's youthful innocence and his own journal-istic exposures, which tarnished her image of her father, she had become Willie's mistress. Burden finds consolation in the theory of mechanism, that "all life is but the dark heave of blood and the twitch of the nerve," because then "nothing was your fault or anybody's fault, for things are always as they are."[21]

James himself faced the question of naturalistic determinism when he was studying chemistry and medicine during the period of his vocational crisis, and it was an important intellectual moment for him when he discovered in Renouvier an argument for free will: he could exercise it by believing in it. In 1880, he had himself reflected on the causal role of the great man in history: "Great Men and Their Environment." Protesting against the vague determinism of Herbert Spencer's theory that "a real explanation" of the changes brought about by individual leaders "must be sought in that aggregate of conditions out of which both he and they have arisen," James conceded that the environment could adopt or reject, preserve or destroy, the great man for "a given genius may come either too early or too late." But the causes of change are "the accumulated influences of individuals, of their examples, their initiatives, and their decisions." Mugwump reformers (like James) might sigh for a leader to "preserve and adopt," but they could "neither move without him nor yet do anything to bring him forth."[22]

It was in 1943, when Warren was gestating his novel, that the pragmatist philosopher Sidney Hook published *The Hero in History* and cited James: "His recognition of the relative autonomy of the realms of nature, society, and individual personality, combined with his belief in the plurality of historical causes, carries to the heart of the problem." Hook even mentioned Huey Long in the context of arguing that if John Nance Garner instead of Franklin D. Roosevelt had been President from 1933 to 1938, many fewer New Deal measures would have been adopted, and Long would have made "great political capital" out of the "tremendous growth of indigenous Fascist sentiments and movements."[23]

But Willie and Huey cannot be entirely conflated. Vindictive and magnanimous, clownish and charismatic, puritanical and hedonistic, courageous and expedient, calculating and irrational, as Robert T. Heilman has observed of the man portrayed in T. Harry Williams's biography, Long is the hero of "ironic melodrama: the protagonist wins the battle, but at a terrible cost, here finally that of widespread bitterness and of his own life." Huey Long understood well enough that his enemies might kill him, but "he seems not to have looked at himself in the more profound way called for by the moral contradictions" in his character and program.[24]

Warren's hero, however, is more self-conscious. The story of Jack Burden is linked to Willie Stark by Jack's gradually coming to have a sense of responsibility at the same time as he comes to see that his boss is not "Cousin Willie from the country, the boy with a Christmas tie," a deluded and gulled hick. Jack realizes, as Anne Stanton has once told him, that he has never known Willie's real face, "except perhaps in those moments when it had leaned forward to the crowds and the forelock had fallen and the eyes had bulged, and the crowd had roared and I had felt the surge in me and had felt I was on the verge of the truth."[25] Burden thus comes to see that the governor's commitment to building a public hospital without any corruption of his purpose testifies to his attempt to salvage his reformer's identity from the corrupt atmosphere he has created by his Machiavellian methods. As Willie tells him: "You got to start somewhere."

Jack reflects that the state was "sure due for some change" and speculates that maybe the theory of "historical costs" and "the moral neutrality of history" meant that a man might have "to sell his soul to get the power to do good." But it is "a high historical view from a chilly pinnacle," he concedes, and "maybe it took a genius to see it" and "maybe it took a hero to act on it."[26] After Willie has been shot by the idealistic doctor, outraged by his sister's affair with the dictator, the dying governor tells Jack that "If it hadn't happened, it might—have been different—even yet." This is the scene where Willie has insight into the tragedy of how his corrupt means have endangered his ends and led to his assassination.

The closest the novel comes to an apologia for Willie is Jack's belief that "Willie Stark was a great man," no matter what happened to his greatness, even if "he spilled it on the ground the way you spill a liquid when the bottle breaks. . . . Perhaps he could not tell his greatness from ungreatness and so mixed them together that what was adulterated was lost."[27] But the novel never hides from the reader the terrible costs of Willie's methods, nor does it consider them inevitable, for it clearly shows the perversion of his character by an egotism and vindictiveness that were precipitated by his burning resentment of having been gulled in his first electoral defeat. For James, in the challenge of action, "it is simply our total character and personal genius that are on trial," revealing "our personal aptitude or incapacity for moral life."[28] Both Willie and Jack are tested in the same way: how they respond to their loss of innocence puts their characters on trial.

Jack's belief in Willie's greatness is connected with an awareness of his own guilt in its perversion, and he asserts his own responsibility at last for a link in the chain of events that led to Willie's affair with Anne and the killing of his friend Adam for assassinating the Boss. At the end of the novel Jack is prepared to become a responsible agent in history, going into politics with Hugh Miller, once attorney general under Stark. From his theorizing about "the moral neutrality of history," Burden has moved to Miller's position that "history is blind, but man is not."[29]

We may unpack this aphorism to mean that the process of history may bring good men to do evil and bad men to do good in unforeseen ways, but that irony does not absolve individuals from taking responsibility by seeking to estimate the probable consequences of their acts. That process begins with Jack Burden when he finally refuses to give Sugar-Boy, Willie's fanatically loyal chauffeur, information that would lead him to kill Tiny Duffy, the disloyal henchman who had triggered Adam Stanton's murderous act by telling him about the affair between his sister and the Boss. Jack realizes that he cannot expunge his own guilt in the process that led to the assassination by treating Duffy as a scapegoat.

Warren also incorporates into the modern story a supposedly historical episode that Jack is doing research on for his thesis. This flashback to the 1850s makes the same point about guilt and responsibility. By his affair with Duncan Trice's wife, Cass Mastern brings about the suicide of his friend, as Jack does in exposing Judge Irwin's crime of bribery, and Cass also feels complicit in the misery of slavery when the slaves' eyes are upon him. He sets his slaves free and enlists as a private in the Mississippi Rifles, refusing, however, to kill anyone and hoping for his own death as an expiation. Jack's inability to understand Cass's motivation aborts the thesis. Unlike his subject, Jack has no sense of the world being "all of one piece"; it is only a jumble of "odds and ends."

The metaphor Burden uses for Cass Mastern's understanding is that of a spider web; touched anywhere, its vibrations will alert the drowsy spider, with eyes glittering "like God's eye," to awake and then to "inject the black numbing poison under your hide." The metaphor illustrates Warren's aside in an interview that "when it comes down to Hawthorne and Emerson meeting on the woodpaths of Concord, I'm strictly for Hawthorne."[30] The idea is reminiscent, too, of James's reminder that here in our own gardens "the infernal cat plays with the panting mouse, or holds the hot bird fluttering in her jaws."[31] In another sense, Burden's metaphor is quite adverse to James because it suggests the "block universe," a thoroughly interrelated totality, seen as a whole by an omniscient eye under the aspect of eternity—precisely the absolutist standpoint that James's pluralism systematically rejected as a fiction denying time and finitude.

It is Warren's point in *The Legacy of the Civil War* that in trying to determine the limits of responsibility in experience, we must oppose the kind of historicism that envisages the North as "merely the bright surgical instrument in the hand of God, or History," making the Civil War morally inevitable.[32] Looking backward historically is always an attempt to make the past intelligible, but a retrospective intelligibility does not make the future a determined one. It might seem that Jack's reflection on how the incompleteness of Willie and of Adam, the realist and the idealist, "doomed" them to destroy each other in the "terrible division of their age" is itself a deterministic idea. But Burden contrasts such a doom with "any doom under the godhead of the Great Twitch," for they lived in "the agony of will."

Burden's point is consistent with James's argument in "The Dilemma of Determinism." *Psychologically,* as he pointed out, looking backwards tends to transform "an equivocal and double future into an inalterable and simple past" merely because decisions have granted consent to one possibility and withheld it from another in a "self-luminous and self-justifying" way.[33] In *All the King's Men,* Jack's sense that he is bound with Tiny Duffy in a "monstrous conspiracy" of guilt "under the untwinkling eye of Eternity and by the Holy Grace of the Great Twitch whom we must all adore" is only a temporary nightmare: "That was the way it was for quite a while." His next step is to break the chain of complicity by refusing to give Sugar-Boy the information that would lead to Duffy's death. The sense of guilt and the sense of responsibility together enable him now to resume his thesis because he can at last understand Cass Mastern.

James's distinction in *Pragmatism* between "the tough-minded" and "the tender-minded" philosophers is echoed in Warren's novel by the contrast between Willie as "the man of fact" and Adam Stanton as "the man of idea." James endorsed his pragmatic method as a mode of mediating between these two types in some form of reconciliation, just as Burden sees the incompleteness of Willie and Adam as "the terrible division of their age." There is some kind of mediation of these poles in both Cass Mastern's brother, Gilbert, and Jack's natural father, Judge Irwin, men who (as Cass says) "in the midst of evil retain enough of innocence and strength . . . to do a little justice in the terms of the great injustice." With this more proportioned perspective, Jack will finish the book on Cass Mastern, give up the house he acquired from the judge's estate, and enter politics with Hugh Miller. He and Anne Stanton will "go into the convulsion of the world, out of history into history and the awful responsibility of Time."[34]

Warren's narrator with his wisecracking "weary self-irony" often sounds like a Southern version of the private eye detectives created by Raymond Chandler and Ross Macdonald. The novel is a kind of detective story about a political murder, but it is much more philosophical than this melodramatic genre because Warren has been reading Machiavelli and James. Warren's luminous poetic and dramatic eye is entirely his own, and he comes naturally by a sense of history that is a hallmark of many Southern writers and scholars: his grandfather, who had a share in raising him, was a Confederate veteran "who was a great reader of history and talked it all the time."[35] Yet, the themes Warren explores in *All the King's Men,* his best known and most highly regarded novel, are remarkably tangent to those in James's philosophy. Southerners have relatives with whom they have different degrees of intimacy. In *All the King's Men,* "the gentle William," intellectually speaking, is "kissing kin."

Chapter 7

Refractions of History: Lowell's Revision of Hawthorne and Melville in *The Old Glory*

THE LITERARY sense of history is not only a Southern trait; it is also a New England one. They met in 1937 when Robert Lowell of Boston went to study at Vanderbilt University, where the Southerners Allen Tate, John Crowe Ransom, and Robert Penn Warren, had founded the *Fugitives* magazine. Lowell's interest in the South was in its influential contemporary poets and critics, not its history. When he wrote his cousin Lawrence Lowell in 1940 about having embarked on "the turbid waters of poetry and scholarship," he was confident of his knowledge of the classics, in which he had majored at Kenyon College (where Ransom had moved from Vanderbilt), and of his ability to read poetry closely in the style of the New Criticism, which he had learned from his Southern mentors; but he felt the need of a "thorough acquaintance with history, particularly with American history."[1] Many years later, one book of his poems would be called *History* and three of his plays, linked under the title *The Old Glory* (1964), would deal with American history as mediated through the fiction of Hawthorne and Melville.

Lowell went South as something of a fugitive from conflict with his family over his decision to marry Jean Stafford. He accepted a fellowship at Louisiana State University, where he could study poetry and criticism with Cleanth Brooks and Robert Penn Warren. The newly married couple moved to Huey Long's favored university, where she took a secretarial job at *The Southern Review* and Lowell studied with Brooks and Warren, coeditors of the journal. Lowell later said that he did not appreciate that he had intellectual and literary figures in his family history until he went South. He discovered himself, in the light cast by his Southern mentors, as someone having an equally legendary status: "I too was part of a legend. I was Northern, disembodied, a Platonist, a Puritan, an abolitionist."[2]

Puritans like Jonathan Edwards and antislavery men like Colonel Robert Gould Shaw and Abraham Lincoln would become subjects of Lowell's poetry when he found his distinctive voice. They entered it entangled with his radically troubled personal history and his life-long quarrel with his family and Boston. "Out of splutter and shambling comes a killing eloquence," he wrote of Tate's poetry; and his own, like Tate's, would be "terribly personal."[3] Converting to Catholicism, as his wife had previously done, was heretical for a Lowell, but his Southern intellectual mentors were sympathetic to myth and ritual (Allen Tate would convert to Catholicism in 1950). Lowell's adherence was brief but militant, ending in 1946 when he demanded a divorce from his wife. It was during the increasing troubling of his marriage that he did what he later called "the most decisive thing"[4] he ever did as a writer: he refused to be drafted in September 1943 and served a jail sentence as a conscientious objector.

Yet, he had previously registered for the draft, sought to enlist, and expected to be drafted unless he were rejected for bad eyesight. The change does not seem entirely accounted for by the legitimate political reasons he gave: the razing of Hamburg by saturation bombing and the unconditional surrender policy, which seemed to threaten Germany and Japan with "permanent destruction." There were personal matters at stake. His wife, whose health was failing badly, feared that she was "on the edge of some kind of nervous crack-up." Lowell felt that he could not resign himself to the army "with her illness still unsettled." She returned from a writer's colony to join Lowell in the same week that he refused the draft. Yet, Lowell's prison term isolated him from her, except for an hour each Saturday; and his militant religious fervor made her suspect that he was indulging himself in "the pleasurable monasticism of the penitentiary."[5] Lowell's scrupulosity must have harbored a sense of guilt for the serious damage he had done to his wife's face in a car smash while he was driving; and her own tormented drinking and nervous difficulties made her a burdensome wife. Unconsciously, he might have found a compromise solution in his penitent, self-punishing separation from her.

There is also a characteristic note in Lowell's letter to President Roosevelt, explaining his decision to reject the draft call. The letter justifies his break with family tradition by stating his fear that modern wars are "the iron gates to totalitarian slavery." Putting himself on the President's level, his letter asserts proudly that his act is particularly painful because the traditions of his own family, "like your own, have always found fulfillment in maintaining, through responsible participation in both the civil and military services, our country's freedom and honor."[6] He would later refer to himself as "a fire-breathing Catholic C.O." who made a "manic statement, telling off the state and president." Twenty years after his decision, he wryly told an interviewer: "I thought that civilization was going to break down, and instead I did."[7]

There was a paradox in his character: he was himself fascinated with Napoleon and the military men in his ancestry: the Revolutionary General John Stark, the War of 1812 Major Mordecai Myers, and the Civil War Colonel Charles Russell Lowell.[8] These figures of the past contrasted vividly with Lowell's sense of his father, whose undistinguished military career climaxed in his being second in command at Boston's Naval Shipyard. He was, in the son's contemptuous view, an ineffective, inconsequential man who failed to represent an idealized tradition of military leadership.

The son at age nineteen had knocked the father down in an argument over a girl: "How could he stand/without Mother's helmsman hand?" Lowell had also struck his wife and broken her nose, even after the accident that had first smashed it.[9] It became increasingly clear that he was victimized by a disease in which cycles of manic-depressive feelings had their own potential for violence. He had to live with a terrible awareness that he was himself a ticking bomb that might unaccountably and unpredictably go off at risk to himself and those around him. Powerful fears about war, however politically justified, were also, in this context, psychological defenses against his own dangerous tendencies, which recurrent psychiatric treatment was not able to keep entirely under control.

Given this tradition of personal and family involvement with violence, when Lowell turned in 1960–1961 to dramatizing American history, he was attracted to episodes involving violence, whether the Puritan suppression of the Merry Mount colony, the tarring and feathering of Tories in the Revolution, or a slave mutiny at sea. The writing of three plays (*The Old Glory*) followed closely upon his participation in the Boston Arts

Festival in June 1960, when he declaimed before a huge audience his best-known poem, "For the Union Dead." The occasion is reminiscent of William James's speech celebrating the St. Gaudens memorial to Colonel Robert Gould Shaw, because Lowell's poem is also a tribute to Shaw, whose sister married the brother of Lowell's great-grandfather. Lowell refers specifically to a passage of James's speech in the line "William James could almost hear the bronze Negroes breathe." In the poem, the colonel, "lean / as a compass-needle" and with "a greyhound's gentle tautness," leading his black soldiers to death, and his father's wish to have no monument, "except the ditch, / where his son's body was thrown / and lost with his 'niggers'," sharply contrast with the "savage servility" of a present in which the monument "sticks like a fishbone / in the city's throat," as the poet sees on television "the drained faces of Negro school-children rise like balloons."[10]

His idea for *The Old Glory* began in 1960 with Melville's *Benito Cereno,* and he wanted its racial conflict to speak to the present historical moment in a contemporary tone, "rather what's happening now, wrong blazing into a holocaust, no one innicent [sic]."[11] Later, he added *Endecott and the Red Cross* and *My Kinsman, Major Molineux,* his version of Hawthorne's stories. (Endecott is a variant spelling of Hawthorne's Endicott; the play, integrating Hawthorne's "The May-pole of Merry Mount" and "Endicott and the Red Cross," was not included in the original 1964 production by the American Place Theater at St. Clement's Episcopal Church in Manhattan's Hell's Kitchen, but was performed later.) In each play an issue involving violence is highlighted.

Hawthorne and Melville were two of Lowell's literary heroes. Just as Charles Ives's *Concord Sonata* is a tribute to Emerson, Hawthorne, Thoreau, and Alcott in a new medium and a personal style, so is Lowell's trilogy an original tribute in another medium to the imaginations of his two predecessors. He saw Hawthorne as "an ironical allegorist," for whom he felt "more warmth" than for "the more exemplary heroes," and Melville as "our tragic poet," no other having "more apprehensively studied the omens of our imperial fortune."[12] What Lowell saw in them is what we see in his plays.

The historical material in the plays was refracted even before Lowell revised Hawthorne and Melville. They had already made their tales twice-told stories. Hawthorne, in writing "The May-pole of Merry Mount" (1836) and "Endicott and the Red Cross" (1838), reworked material that he took mainly from John Winthrop's *Journal* and Nathaniel Morton's *New England's Memorial* (1669). Melville, in writing *Benito Cereno* (1855), reworked Captain Amasa Delano's account of his "Voyage in the Ship *Perseverance*" (1819).[13] Lowell's own reference to his sources added to the Hawthorne and Melville stories only one earlier account, *New English Canaan* (1637), by Thomas Morton, founder of the Merry Mount colony, who appears as a character in Lowell's version. This literary layering of the distance between us and the actual events to which the play refers makes it clear that Lowell, like Hawthorne and Melville, is not interested in establishing any literal truth about what actually happened, but rather is concerned to set out in a symbolic way a pattern of meaning.

But it would be equally fallacious to forget that Lowell, like his predecessors, is concerned to make his pattern germane to our understanding of ourselves as Americans and as moral agents in history. Like Hawthorne and Melville, he is interested in the then and there as an element in the here and now. The trilogy is arranged chronologically from colonial times through the Revolution to around 1800, the beginning of Jefferson's administration. The sequence serves the function of looking into the foundations of American history for recurrent issues.

Hawthorne's story of the Merry Mount Colony highlights the conflicted intermingling of old English and new Puritan elements in colonial New England. The mixture is symbolized by the May-pole wreath that is made up of English and native roses. The "gay sinners" of Thomas Morton's colony, enjoying the old English pagan custom of the May-pole festivities, contrast with the "grisly saints" of persecuting Puritanism. Morton is not present in Hawthorne's story; instead there is an English Anglican, the Reverend Mr. Blackstone, whose affinity for Morton and the Indians affronts the Puritans' belief that "the Lord hath sanctified this wilderness for his peculiar people." Blackstone performs the marriage ceremony of Edgar and Edith, the lord and lady of the May, and the Puritan leader Endicott cuts down the May-pole, arrests the priest, and, softened by the spectacle of the couple's "early love" and "early hopes," throws the wreath of roses over the heads of the couple. Hawthorne's paradox is that "the severest Puritan of all who laid the rock-foundation of New England" is the one who makes this conciliatory gesture. The intermingling of the two strains, old England and new Puritan, at the conclusion of the tale, like the wreath itself, becomes a prophetic metaphor for the mature love of Edith and Edgar as a "troubled joy" that mingles care and sorrow with the "best of their early joys."[14] It is hard to say whether the story uses history to develop this "philosophic romance," as Hawthorne calls it, or instead uses the idea of the difference between premarital and marital love to point to an historical theme about the entwining of a dominant Puritan and subordinate English strain in the culture of New England. The two themes reflect each other.

Hawthorne's story of the Red Cross involves two Salem Puritans: Roger Williams, the defender of civic toleration of religious differences, who contrasts with Endicott (not yet governor) as the militant Puritan. Williams in the tale brings a message from Governor Winthrop (who will later banish him), urging Endicott for tactical reasons to hush up rumors about the prospect of a royal governor coming to establish English Episcopacy in New England. Defying both Williams and Winthrop, Endicott gives his bombastic speech against pope and tyrant, and the narrator philosophizes that this rending of the Red Cross is the "first omen of that deliverance which our fathers consummated" more than a century later in the Revolution.[15] The brief tale suggests that Puritanism incorporated not only the repressive coercion of religious uniformity, which Williams opposed and suffered, but also the capacity, which Endicott had, to defend the New England way from being absorbed into English colonialism. Hawthorne had no intention of whitewashing the Puritans, as is shown by the "sad and quiet smile" on Williams's "mild visage" when Endicott orates about liberty of conscience and civil rights. But Hawthorne's tale also sees in Puritan defiance of royal control the seeds of American independence.

Yet, cutting the cross out of the flag suggests Williams's own repudiation of civil religion. He was a Calvinist who on principle refused (unlike the other Puritans) to consider the colonial churches as being in any way connected with the Anglican Church, and he strictly separated the "garden" of the church from the "wilderness" of the world. Endicott had once fallen briefly under Williams's potent influence. Endicott's rash action gave occasion (as Winthrop complained) for the English to think badly of colonials when a more cautious, waiting policy would better have served their interests. Both Williams and Endicott, for different reasons, threatened to incur King James's wrath; but Williams was the greater threat to the New England way because Winthrop's vision of "a city on a hill," as Michael Colacurcio has pointed out, is "quite a different thing from a separatist outpost in a spiritual wilderness."[16] Endicott's political rhetoric is entirely Hawthorne's invention, yet it accurately points forward to what New England revolutionaries would come to make of their Puritan past, seeing it (as John Adams did, for example) as transformed into a fusion of independence and civil liberty.

Lowell's play moves in a different direction by using both Morton and Blackstone as speaking characters to represent two views of the New World, each seeking to use the other. Both are Anglicans, loyal to England and opposed to the Puritans, but Morton favors intermarriage with the Indians, has been made a sachem of the Narragansett, and trades guns and liquor for their furs, while Blackstone envisages an Episcopal America, like the England of King Charles. To the Puritans, Morton's colony is a civic threat because of his Indian policy, and Governor Endicott, in an effort to stop Indians from killing Puritans, has killed the chief that made Morton a sachem.

Lowell's treatment of the governor is the most interesting feature of the play and greatly expands on Hawthorne's sketch of him. He is saddened by the death of his wife and troubled by the "hedging and compromising" entailed by his administrative tasks in a diverse and complicated world that resists his subordinate Palfrey's clear and truculent belief in "one faith and one flag." Endecott knows that to work with "merciless efficiency" is to "leave a desert." He qualifies with moderation every punishment that Palfrey suggests for the Merry Mounters and the Indians. Endecott foresees that the king one day will revoke the Massachusetts charter, and he predicts that his own speech, designed to spur his men to resist royal control, will be "half truth, half bombast."[17] Lowell supplies him with a motive for his softened attitude to the lord and lady of the May: Edith reminds him of his wife and child, buried in England, and he hopes the young woman will bear children.

Lowell's more complex Endecott opens up Hawthorne's stories to the political issues that are submerged in "The May-pole of Merry Mount," where the pagan/Puritan contrast is highlighted. They involve Morton's ties to the Indians and to Sir Fernando Gorges, which, like Blackstone's ties to the English king and bishops, are threats to the Puritan mission to build its own New England way in church and state. But while Hawthorne's tale understands that Endecott's Puritanism could build a society with a long-range destiny, as Williams's spiritual individualism or Morton's paganism could not, Lowell updates the material so as to give the

Red Cross episode a contemporary meaning. His Endecott not only
regrets his rashness (as the actual Endicott did when, after being officially
censured, he apologized and was pardoned), but he speaks the poet's own
thoughts. In the climax, the governor gives his predicted stirring speech
against kings and bishops, ordering Blackstone and Morton to be tied up
and the Red Cross to be torn out of the flag. Now he abandons moderation and orders the burning down of Merry Mount and the Indian vil-
lage. But his rueful second thoughts accuse him:

> I should ask for a day of mourning in the colony,
> or better my own day of mourning,
> for the people we have sent into misery, desperation—
> that I have sent out of life:
> my own soldiers, the turncoat Indians who served
>   our turn,
> and for the other Indians, all those who are fighting
> with unequalled ferocity, and probably
>   hopeless courage,
> because they prefer annihilation to the despair of
>   our conquest.[18]

Lowell's biographer, Ian Hamilton, points out that in the character of
Endecott, Lowell hints at his own ambivalence about the exercise of
power.[19] The point can be developed further: Endecott's reflective mono-
logue (in the revised 1968 edition of the trilogy) is actually taken, almost
word for word, from Lowell's letter to the *New York Review of Books* on 4
February 1968, where he asked for "our own day of mourning, for the
people we have sent into misery, desperation—that we have sent out of
life; for our own soldiers, for the pro-American Vietnamese, and for the
anti-American Vietnamese, those who have fought with unequaled ferocity, and probably hopeless courage, because they preferred annihilation to
the despair of an American conquest."[20]

Hawthorne's two stories encourage the reader to think about the mixture of elements that went into the making of colonial America and
prepared the way for the Revolution. Lowell's play dramatizes an irrational resort to excessive violence by a moderate and intelligent man, who
substitutes the prestige of a symbol, the flag, for more concrete goods.
Hawthorne's Endicott does "imperiously" declare the meaning of his act

in rhetoric that exceeds the actual situation and threatens the wiser, quieter policy, suggested by Governor Winthrop; and Lowell's reading of Hawthorne is insightful on this crucial point. But, by conflating Endecott with himself, Lowell moves away from Hawthorne's point about the prophetic aspect of the flag episode in terms of American independence. Lowell's trilogy instead works cumulatively to underline what he sees as a recurrent American trait in relation to violence.

In *My Kinsman, Major Molineux,* both writers speak to the issue of the Revolution, Hawthorne indirectly and Lowell explicitly, once again foregrounding the political matter. Hawthorne's story (1832) begins in the 1730s at a time of popular resentment of royal authority and invokes the later pre-Revolutionary years through Robin's dream-like encounter with a conspiratorial mob that suggests the Sons of Liberty, who tarred and feathered Tories and cast English tea into Boston Harbor. Hawthorne's mob leader has a face that is painted in two colors, like the Indian war paint used by the actual Tea Party raiders, as described in Hawthorne's "The Whole History of Grandfather's Chair," a children's story about New England history.

Hawthorne's tale, one of his earliest, is deceptively simple. Young Robin comes to Boston, looking to his eminent uncle for a patron, only to discover himself in the midst of a Revolutionary mob that tars and feathers his relative. Robin himself, while shocked by the fate of his uncle, is strangely caught up in the mob's derisive laughter, and a friendly stranger, who has been Robin's guide to witnessing the action, later suggests that he might stay on in Boston and rise in the world without the help of his kinsman. The tale reflects Hawthorne's deep knowledge of early American history and is densely compacted with subtle allusions to actual pre-Revolutionary figures, political idiom, and opposing parties, mixed in with hints of traditional English symbolism about the May Day festivity in which tarring and feathering were used to initiate a mock king in a saturnalian overturning of authority led by a Lord of Misrule.[21] The story has been explicated in recent years by psychological and historical theorizing, undertaken with all the ingenuity and scholarship of arcane biblical exegesis. Hawthorne's fusion of a boy's coming-of-age in relation to his uncle (as Hawthorne did himself under the guardianship of an uncle) with an incident of Revolutionary violence is the most artistically interesting and complex example of what Michael Kammen has shown to be a common American way of interpreting our Revolution: as a rite of passage.[22]

Hawthorne's story, in the light of earlier celebration of the Revolution, stresses instead (as Colacurcio puts it) the idea that "not only do revolutionary passions express themselves in ways that seldom accomplish God's justice, but they proceed far more intelligibly from somebody's ordinary political design than from God's special providence."[23] The story demystifies the patriot cause, which tramples on "an old man's heart," making a tragic figure out of Major Molineux, yet without politically justifying his Toryism. In this sense Lowell's version replicates Hawthorne's story very well.

Lowell's version takes place just before the Revolution. His mob leader (called Man With Mask or Colonel Greenough) also has a face that is divided in two colors with the addition that one half is pock-marked, and his face becomes all red as the Revolutionary fever comes to its climax. The imagery of illness indicates Lowell's deflationary strategy, and the divided face is made to stand for the division of political opinion in Boston. This version incorporates the dream-like dimension of Hawthorne's tale largely through Jonathan Miller's inventive staging of the play. He thought it should be "put across with scintillating artificiality," so he worked on the basic idea of an eighteenth-century political cartoon. The actors were painted grey and costumed to look "like pieces of paper cut out of a coffee-house broadsheet." Miller, an Englishman, captured Hawthorne's surreal texture by thinking about the image of Alice in Wonderland—"as if flesh and blood Deerfield boys had wandered into a dream world of sloganeering playing cards."[24]

Lowell made some inventions of his own. Robin's ferryman is a Charon, whose legendary function is to bear the newly arrived dead across the Styx, and he carries off the major's body in his boat at the end of the play. Lowell created a younger brother for Robin, and he functions, as Palfrey does in the earlier play, as a truculent voice to contrast with the more sympathetic protagonist's temper. The playwright explicitly identifies (as Hawthorne does not) the scarlet woman as a prostitute and the friendly stranger-guide as a minister. The latter considers the major his patron, but opportunistically has his ear to the ground, waiting to see how the political wind will blow. This is a modern note; historically, the so-called "black regiment" of Protestant preachers was, to the dismay of the Tories, remarkably unified in support of the patriot cause.

But the clergyman's fiery speech to the crowd, linking the Day of Judgment, "the scarlet whore," and King George is a genuinely historical touch.[25] Lowell's conception of the minister provides an opportunity for his byplay with the British and patriot flags, carrying further the flag symbolism of *Endecott and the Red Cross*.

The mob leader in Lowell is a former lawyer, taught by the major, and takes over his mansion. As a leader, the Man With Mask has Lowell's own ambivalence: he is a military man who says he hates war, "wars leave us where / they find us, don't they, boy."[26] As in Hawthorne's tale, the old citizen, presumably connected with the legislative power, for he claims to have authority, is the same pompous gentleman. In Hawthorne, however, he appears on the balcony of the mansion opposite the church (the Old North Church was opposite the balconied Town House, where the court was, as Hawthorne points out in "Grandfather's Chair"),[27] thus suggesting the old citizen's link with the legislative power that is in conflict with royal governors. In Lowell's play, he visits the prostitute and at the end holds the major's sword of office, which is only a hollow scabbard.

The major difference between the two texts is tonal: the modern version melodramatizes the action. The major grinds the Rattlesnake flag under foot; the ferry man hits him on the head with an oar; he is despoiled of his scabbard, wallet, and hat; and the masked mob leader plunges his sword into him with the anachronistic cry of John Wilkes Booth: "*Sic semper tyrranis!*" Hawthorne shows us only "a majestic person" with "a steady soul," shaken in his "tar-and-feathery dignity"[28] and subjected to the derisive laughter of the revolutionary crowd. Admittedly, the theater has to dramatize what a short story can be content to suggest; even so, Lowell's transformation tends to rob the situation of some of its imaginative power by literalizing it. Hawthorne's silent disgraced major, staring at Robin, is more evocative than the one who says to Robin: "*Et tu, Brute!*" Lowell's Robin has read Plutarch, and Caesar's famous reproach, like the Masked Man's cry of "*Sic semper tyrannis!*," tends to broaden the play's range of reference. In 1964, audiences would inevitably think of more recent assassinations. Lowell sent a signed copy of *The Old Glory* to Jackie Kennedy.[29]

Lowell was not sure how much of his play was his and how much was Hawthorne's, nor was he happy with any of his plays, read or acted; but he thought "well enough" of his version of *Benito Cereno* and was sure its "genius is Melville."[30] It was particularly hailed as "a cultural-poetic masterpiece" by Robert Brustein, and the director, Jonathan Miller, thought it had "long swells of superb verse which called for an almost operatic vocal mastery."[31] Actually, like the other two plays, it reads more like prose than verse, and Lowell himself thought of it as his best prose.[32] The theatrical need to turn everything into speech is bound to distinguish a play from a story that is narrated impersonally and includes at the end long stretches of quotation from an official account of the events previously related. But Lowell's overlaying of past with present does focus the issue of the differences between the two versions of the New England captain's original story.

Melville's tale, with its ominous early reference to "Shadows present, foreshadowing deeper shadows to come," has a prophetic purpose.[33] Melville dramatizes the prophetic aspect of the slave mutiny on Captain Delano's ship by inventing a dramatic incident. When the cable of the Spanish ship is cut, its end lashes out and whips away a canvas shroud to reveal a human skeleton of the murdered slaves' owner as a figurehead with the chalked words below: *Follow your leader.* The ship's proper figurehead was "Christopher Colon, the discoverer of the New World," and the mutiny's leader, Babo, has warned the Spanish Captain Benito Cereno that if he does not keep faith with the blacks by taking them back to Africa he will "follow your leader." Three months after the owner's bones are buried in a church, Captain Cereno, borne on a bier to a monastery on Mount Agonia, "did, indeed, follow his leader."

Melville's name for the Spanish ship, the *San Dominick,* is a link to Santo Domingo, where there was a slave revolt in the same year of the fictional Babo's mutiny—1799; and Columbus founded the island, named it for his father, and was rumored to be buried there. At the end of the story, the black leader's head, "that hive of subtlety," fixed on a pole, stares accusingly at the church and monastery where the owner and Captain Cereno, respectively, are buried. Melville's readers in the mid-1850s, when the crisis over slavery was intensely accelerated by opposition to the Kansas-Nebraska Act, the controversy that brought Lincoln into national prominence, could be counted on to know that many atrocities had been committed by black revolutionaries in Santo Domingo and Haiti. Melville's tale of black terrorism and white paternalistic racism, seen in this context, as Eric J. Sundquist has pointed out, anticipates "an explosive resolution of the conflict between American democracy, Old World despotism, and Caribbean New World revolution."[34]

Melville is devastating in presenting the sentimental primitivism and complacent paternalism of Captain Delano's racist outlook. They work, in potent combination with his republican prejudices against the Spanish captain, to prevent the Yankee from realizing that the blacks are actually holding Don Benito captive while pretending to be his slaves. Delano cannot make up his mind, until it is almost too late, if the Spaniard is an innocent lunatic, a "true hidalgo" gentleman, a "low-born adventurer," a hypochondriac, a sick man, or a "plodding pirate." Delano cannot grasp how the tables have been turned because he sees nothing but "pure tenderness and love" in the black women, considers blacks "too stupid" and docile to be capable of forming a conspiracy, and genially takes to Negroes "just as other men to Newfoundland dogs."[35] Above all, Delano is "of a singularly undistrustful good-nature," confident in a "watchful Providence," unable to imagine anything that might involve "the imputation of malign evil to man," whether in oppressor or oppressed.[36] It is characteristic of him to want to forget the whole episode after it is over, and he cannot understand why the Spaniard should still be haunted by the shadow that "the negro" has cast upon him.

Melville's readers were thus warned not to forget the past, to remember that what had happened on the *San Dominick,* or in Santo Domingo or Haiti, was a portent of what could happen wherever slaves suffered the injustice of being held in bondage by white men. The warning was particularly appropriate when in the same year and magazine in which *Benito Cereno* was published, a writer on the Kansas Question would link the issue of slavery in Kansas to the spread of slavery in Latin America and the possibility of black revolt in Cuba against Spanish rule.[37]

When Lowell was writing his version of Melville's story, sit-ins and Freedom Rides on behalf of Martin Luther King's civil rights movement were under way. Before the play was produced, King was jailed in Birmingham; some blacks rioted in retaliation for segregationist bombings, and President Kennedy ordered thousands of federal troops near the city. In August 1963, King, echoing the Gettysburg Address, stood at the Lincoln Memorial, announcing to a huge audience the need for a new birth of freedom. Campaigns of King's followers in the summer of 1963 "forced thousands of hotels, restaurants, schools, parks, and swimming pools to desegregate in 261 cities."[38] Yet, resistance was stiff, and Malcolm X was already prominent as the most stringent black critic of King's nonviolent methods and the most bitter accuser of whites. In this context, an audience would have to be asleep not to see Lowell's play as being especially pertinent in unearthing "the seeds of our present discords."[39]

It also has a prophetic cast because its portrait of a smugly confident, seemingly amiable naval officer who resorts to excessive retaliatory force in a crisis is not restricted to the racial context of the play. Lowell distinguished Melville's protagonist from his own: "My hero is a State Department autocrat, Melville's is an innocent abroad. My man is imperial, his is poignant. Mine knows everything, so steers for disaster."[40] Here are two small examples of the updating: Delano's bosun, Perkins, fearing that the Spanish won't pay for the help they have received, complains, like congressmen about foreign-aid programs: "They think America is Santa Claus." Delano justifies his sailors' shooting of the slaves with the argument used in defense of the atomic bombing of Japan: "We have saved American lives."[41]

Lowell adds touches of humor to Delano that set him off from the more puritanical and provincial bosun. The name of Delano's ship is changed from *The Bachelor's Delight* to *The President Adams,* a New England touch to counterpoint the Virginian Jefferson's recent defeat of John Adams in the election of 1800. The play preserves the theatrically effective shaving scene, with Babu (Lowell's variant of Melville's Babo) holding a razor to the throat of Don Benito, wrapped in a Spanish flag; and it incorporates as well the dramatic revelation that the ship's figurehead is really the corpse of the owner, Aranda, though in Lowell's version we learn this through Perkins and Babu rather than through the more surprising action of the cut cable's ripping off of the shroud.

Lowell also embroiders Melville's episodes involving a sailor plunging his hands into tar, a Negress sleeping with her baby, and a sailor who tosses an intricately knotted rope to Delano, as a clue to the deception being practiced on him. Lowell elaborates these incidents into a staged entertainment, presented by Babu, who shows the Yankees a sailor painting a doll with tar and cleaning it up; a black boy playing chess with a crowned doll; and a black Virgin Mary with her baby and a white Saint Joseph—the latter indicating the contrast between a white Protestant America and a Latin American Catholicism that sanctions interracial marriage. Babu's staging, however, has no credible justification in terms of the actual situation, as Melville's incidents do.

A more significant and telling variation is Lowell's expansion of Babu's role. Melville emphasizes his silence, especially after "all was over," uttering no sound, as if to say "since I cannot do deeds, I will not speak words."[42] But as Lowell well knew, the American black was notably speaking words and doing deeds in the 1960s. He takes account of this remarkable change by making Babu a more vocal and aggressive character, who finally openly scorns the Americans' insolence. He forces Don Benito to assume the chains worn by Atufal, the former African king, to kneel, to ask pardon for having enslaved fellow men, and to kiss the mouth of Aranda's skull, as Perkins is also forced to do. This is a double reversal—a slave, himself once enslaved in Africa, enslaves his master. It is a potent reminder of the dangerous potential for reversal in all master-slave relationships. Babu's last words before Delano kills him are: "Yankee Master understand me. The future is with us."[43]

The other major change, as in the other two plays, is Lowell's escalation of the violence. When Melville's Delano is jostled by a black, the captain responds with a "half-mirthful, half-menacing gesture," while Lowell's captain crudely retaliates by knocking down an old black with his fist. Melville's Yankee sailors do clash with the blacks, losing none of their own men and killing nearly a score of the slaves. But Melville cites the court record that shows Delano restraining two Spanish sailors from stabbing the shackled blacks.[44] Melville underlines the retaliatory violence by the horrific final detail of Babo's severed head on a pike, but in the last dialogue between the two captains he emphasizes the Yankee's unhistorical wish to forget the whole thing and to ignore the shadow of the Negro that has fallen on the melancholy Don Benito. Lowell's Delano, however, after the Negroes have raised the black skull and crossbones flag (another example of the recurring flag symbolism) shoots Babu dead, and "then slowly empties the remaining five barrels of his pistol into the body." The director added the final harrowing effect of having a black girl come on stage and "give a long awkward ghastly scream—like a wounded albatross."[45]

The repetition in all three plays of seemingly moderate leaders who resort in a crisis to excessive violence was especially pertinent in a prophetic way to President Johnson's conduct of the Vietnam War. Lowell consistently became a major literary spokesman against it, refusing on principle the President's offer to read at a White House Festival of the Arts in June 1965, and joining two years later with over three hundred others to raise funds for draft resisters and to participate in civil disobedience at a march on the Pentagon.

Lowell was fond of Edmund Wilson's great study of our Civil War literature, *Patriotic Gore* (1962), and the poet's complimentary letter to him cited the metaphor in Wilson's angry, mordant introduction, rather than the more nuanced texture of his sympathetic and complex portraits of individual writers and political figures. Wilson's introductory comment on American expansionism concludes by treating "our panicky pugnacity" in relation to the Soviets as "the irrational instinct" of "a sea slug of vigorous voracity in the presence of another such sea slug."[46] Lowell expressed his agreement: "The States have become a menace, sea-squids as you say, and I guess they never were too good."[47] *The Old Glory* reflects this negativity. It would be characteristic of the late 1960s, even though in 1963 he felt that the times were much different from the 1930s, when "everybody was taking sides on something, usually very violently."[48] By the time of his 1968 revision, the 1960s had become much like the 1930s in this respect.

He paid a price, however, for his inventive and pertinent updating of his literary models. Lowell gave new life to them by showing audiences their pertinence to their own public life, but he acknowledged that some critics wished that he had not "hardened and politicized."[49] The critic and director Robert Brustein hailed the trilogy as marking "an event of great moment" because *The Old Glory* is "the first American play to utilize historical materials in a compelling theatrical manner." It was Lowell's achievement, Brustein noted, to make the plays "look forward and backward at the same time."[50] That doubleness, however, is both the strength and the weakness of these versions of Hawthorne and Melville. It accounts for the impact they made on Brustein in the mid-1960s, but it also accounts for the judgment of Lowell's biographer that they are "often crudely underscored."[51]

This doubleness connects with his biographer's remark about the poet's discomfort with his own role in the controversy over Vietnam policy: "His difficulty was that his image of America was not too sharply different from his image of himself." Lowell was fearful in 1963 of an American Ahab, "the fanatical idealist who brings the world down in ruins through some sort of simplicity of mind," and he had the grace to recognize the trait not only in "our character" but also in his own "personal character." He struck his interviewer as a man of "saint-like gentleness," but Lowell knew himself better. He found, paradoxically, that in the medium of plays he could "say things that were personal," things that he couldn't say "in a confessional poem."[52] That personal note gives authority to his portrait of the psychology at work in his Endecott, Man With Mask, and Captain Delano. But it also leads the reader to suspect that some personally based conflict in the author clouds his vision of America and coarsens his revision of Hawthorne's and Melville's treatment of our history.

Chapter 8

Twain, Doctorow, and the
Anachronistic Adventures of the Arms
Mechanic and the Jazz Pianist

"THE LOCUS of fiction is the unruly jostling of all the objects of culture," as Avrom Fleishman has said, "—of the real with the illusory, the found with the imagined, the irreducible with the artificial." He notes that "it is a paradox of our time, in which "the 'fictionality' of fiction has become a watchword of literary pundits, that many currently approved fictional works have incorporated pieces of the real world in an increasingly self-assured way."[1] Indeed, one vivid literary sign of our times is the breaking down of *any* boundary between novelists and historians. On the theoretical level, it is reflected in the work of Hayden White, who has insisted that written histories presuppose certain narrative forms, derived from literature, and these are held to be built on a few basic figurative forms of language, or tropes. Among journalists, the same tendency is evident in Norman Mailer's strategy in *The Armies of the Night* (1968), his account of the March on the Pentagon in 1967, which is subtitled "History as a Novel/The Novel as History." Among novelists, John Barth in *The Sot-weed Factor* (1960) characteristically mixes real and invented documents, borrowing his title, hero, and diction from a real person, who in 1731 published a verse satire in Maryland. Barth's novel deliberately blurs the line so that "we cannot be sure when we are in touch with facts, as opposed to fictionalized versions of facts."[2]

The novelist who captured the popular imagination by this tendency to collapse history and fiction together is E. L. Doctorow. The traditional historical novel tends to keep historical persons on the margin of the fictional scene, but *Ragtime* (1975), a best-seller made into a popular movie, freely intersects the lives of historical characters with each other as well as with fictional characters. Its intention is to suppress in the reader's mind any question about "what actually happened" as a matter of detail, but at the same time to suggest to the reader something pertinent in contemporary terms about the meaning of the past. The author himself told a reporter: "If you ask me whether some things in the book 'really' happened, I can only say, 'they have now.' "[3]

Ragtime was advertised in its jacket copy as a sport: "You will never have read anything like *Ragtime* before. Nothing quite like it has ever been written before." But, in some important respects, it has at least one unnoticed classic American precursor as a speculative and satirical history: Mark Twain's *The Connecticut Yankee in King Arthur's Court* (1889). Like Twain's romance (three times made into a movie), *Ragtime* is also a time-travel story with a deliberate anachronism built into its structure, with a magician playing an important part in the plot, and with an ironic and violent climax involving military technology.

The analogy between these two comic historical romances may seem implausible. Twain's story, unlike Doctorow's, which is told by an imitation of an impersonal historian's narrating voice, is a vernacular, first-person narrative, and its material is legendary, the Arthurian Camelot, far removed from the author's own time and country, unlike Doctorow's prewar period of America. Moreover, the plot of *Ragtime* turns centrally on racial conflict, which is absent from Twain's sixth-century Britain. Yet, the more each text is read over the shoulder of the other, the more interesting correspondences do appear. Are they accidental or was Doctorow, at some level of his mind, aware of Twain's story, which he never mentions in connection with *Ragtime?* At any rate, the audience for *Ragtime* eagerly assimilated its deceptively simple declarative sentences without paying any attention to its epigraph, a warning by Scott Joplin: "It is never right to play Ragtime fast." A good way to play it slowly is to read the novel side by side with Twain's story. If *The Connecticut Yankee* is not a close relative of *Ragtime,* it is surely at least a first cousin once removed.

It is clear that Doctorow was self-consciously rewriting (though few of his readers know it) another precursor text; his hero Coalhouse Walker is an updating of the hero in Heinrich von Kleist's *Michael Kohlhaas* (1810) which is set in the time of Martin Luther but is based on an earlier medieval document. The American hero's first name, overlapping with the German hero's last name, is Doctorow's only offered clue (as he has confessed) to this "intertextual" aspect of the story. He has changed Kohlhaas's horses to an automobile, but the hero's retaliatory and escalating violent acts, done to avenge the unjust loss of his vehicle, is the pattern in both stories.[4]

Twain's romance also has its self-conscious reference to a precursor— Sir Thomas Malory's fifteenth-century version in *Morte d'Arthur* of the sixth-century Arthurian legend, a text Twain read in 1884 when George Washington Cable gave it to him while they were on tour, doing public readings on stage. Another classic, *Don Quixote,* which Twain echoed earlier in his pairing of Huck Finn and Tom Sawyer, can also be heard as a presence in the Yankee's recreation of the Quixote project to laugh away the chivalric tradition, which he believed Sir Walter Scott's *Ivanhoe* had romantically restored in antebellum Southern imaginations as a prop for slavery. The usual Cervantes polarities are reversed by the Yankee's time travel: "The past is made vividly present and the present is relegated to a visionary future."[5] It is possible that Twain knew of even another precursor for some of the ingredients of his story. Marcus Cunliffe has noted that Edward Bulwer Lytton's *The Last of the Barons* (1843), a book in Twain's library, involves three characters who are literary relatives of Twain's cast: the fifteenth-century Earl of Warwick, an inventor of a kind of steam engine, and a villain who is a friar.[6] Twain's story opens in Warwick Castle and the Warwick Arms Hotel. The point of my method, however, is not to accumulate evidence for all the possible influences on the making of a book; it is rather to put texts side by side, or back to back, to see how they illuminate each other. From this point of view, a comparison of *Ragtime* with *A Connecticut Yankee in King Arthur's Court* will have to carry its own evidence of its value.

Twain's Hank Morgan, a superintendent of a Hartford arms factory in 1879, is obviously anachronistic in Arthurian England, and he can only get there by a kind of magical time travel. The hero speaks mysteriously about the transposition of epochs and bodies. (J. P. Morgan in *Ragtime* believes in reincarnation.) He claims to have been responsible for a bullet hole in a suit of armor, on display at Warwick Castle, the costume once worn by a knight of the Round Table. From reading Malory in the Warwick Arms, the narrator turns to reading Morgan's own bizarre story of his time travel (the result of a blow on the head) to Camelot. At the end of Morgan's account, called "The Tale of the Lost Land," we learn from a postscript that Merlin, disguised as an old woman, has magically put his rival to sleep for thirteen centuries. (In *Ragtime*, Houdini disguises himself as a veiled gray-haired widow while attending seances.)

Twain's narrative technique has not only licensed his extravagant departures from realistic historical standards, but also alienated his hero. In a second postscript, this time by "M. T.," we learn how he has finished reading Morgan's manuscript and finds him in a last delerium in his bed. Twain's additional spin to the time-travel idea is to have the dying man imagine that he is back in Camelot. He speaks, in fact, as if his real home were in ancient Britain, while his nightmare is that he has been set down thirteen centuries later in the England of 1879, which "M. T." inhabits. Morgan's time-travel experience has dislocated him from both time periods so that he is a stranger when he is in Camelot and a stranger when he is in the Warwick Arms.

This ending connects with a precedent in Twain's own work, his short account of his war experience in "A Campaign That Failed," written four years earlier. In it a stranger in civilian clothes, fatally shot by Twain's band of rangers, looks at him reproachfully and mumbles, "like a dreamer in his sleep," about his wife and child; and the situation is partly replicated when "M. T." bends over another stranger, Hank Morgan, and hears him make precisely the same kind of murmur. As Justin Kaplan has pointed out about the Civil War story, "the victim is related to all the other 'strangers' who populate Mark Twain's fiction," and the biographer could have cited Hank Morgan as a highly charged example.[7]

Doctorow's narrative strategy is similar in its effect. His hero, the black jazz pianist, Coalhouse Walker, is anachronistic because he engages in confrontational violence against the establishment in a way that was characteristic of the 1960s and quite unthinkable for blacks in the ragtime era before the First World War. Moreover, *Ragtime*'s plot also begins with a magical element, a premonition that is fantastic rather than historical: a small boy mysteriously tells a magician, Harry Houdini, to "warn the Duke," and many years (and pages) later it will be the Archduke Ferdinand's assassination that triggers the First World War. Houdini is notoriously effective in exposing fraudulent mediums, and his own magic is entirely naturalistic. But *Ragtime* links him to the paranormal by portraying his love for his dead mother as a motive that drives him to visit seances in the hope of finding a genuine medium who can put him in touch with his mother.

Morgan's final homelessness is paralleled by Coalhouse Walker's displacement from the 1960s to the ragtime era. Doctorow subtly acknowledges his hero's unhistorical presence by telling us that there is no information about his parentage, no school records, no explanation for his vocabularly and manner of speaking—except perhaps "an act of will."[8] (That act, of course, is the author's decision to put him into the ragtime era.) In the end, his wife having been fatally wounded by a militia man and a Secret Service man at a public appearance of the Vice-President, the bereft Walker is suicidally prepared to be shot down when he leaves the Morgan Library, after successfully negotiating the rebuilding of his car and the escape of his terrorist band of supporters. No more than Hank Morgan does Walker have any secure place in the earlier era to which he too brings the outlook of a later one.

The climax of both stories shows an embattled hero, surrounded by a small band of youthful supporters, using modern firepower in a showdown with armed authorities. To carry the analogy even further, there is a final stroke of irony in the use of weaponry. Hank Morgan in the Battle of the Sand-belt, aided by a small band of fifty-two young boys, confronts the massed might of the Arthurian establishment and defeats the enemy by the effectiveness of his electric fence, Gatling guns, and an artificially created flood. Nevertheless, the poisonous air bred by the dead puts the victors in a trap of their own making. Similarly, one of Doctorow's major characters, Father, a flag manufacturer, goes to London on the *Lusitania* with a shipment of grenades, depth charges, and puttied nitro invented by his son, Younger Brother, and thus inadvertently contributes to the explosion that kills him when the ship is torpedoed by a German submarine.

Both Twain and Doctorow by their technique of deliberate anachronism put two eras into juxtaposition. In both books, the later one judges the earlier one. Twain's preface tips his hand, signaling his critique of the Arthurian era, by explaining that if he refers to any laws or customs that did not actually exist in the sixth century, "one is quite justified in inferring that whatever one of these laws or customs was lacking in that remote time, its place was competently filled by a worse one."[9] Doctorow is moved by a similar political indignation to subvert any sentimental nostalgia for the earlier era. He begins with the mock-historical tone of a social historian: "Patriotism was a reliable sentiment in the early 1900's." Then he shifts gears: "There were no Negroes. There were no immigrants. . . . Across America sex and death were barely distinguishable." The mention of Emma Goldman, the revolutionary anarchist, an immigrant Jew, leads him to this second thought: "Apparently there *were* Negroes. There *were* immigrants."[10] The end of chapter 6 coldly enumerates with cumulative force the oppressions suffered by miners, child workers, immigrants, and blacks, while trusts proliferate and the rich entertain themselves by playing at being poor.

Both authors underline the continuity as well as the differences in their comparison of earlier with later times. Twain's treatment of serfdom explicitly insists on its continuity with slavery in the Old South and the old regime in France. By dramatizing the racial conflict of the ragtime era through the takeover of the Morgan Library, a tactic characteristic of radical politics in the 1960s, Doctorow underlines the persistence of racial injustice. More subtly, when the conservative black leader Booker T. Washington encounters the militant Coalhouse Walker in the library, the narrator notes on the wall portraits of Martin Luther, and Washington prays that the Lord may lead his people to the promised land—a strong echo of Martin Luther King, Jr., with Walker playing the role of the radical Malcolm X.[11] Walker's supporters speak in revolutionary terms of setting up a provisional American government. At the same time the story dramatizes another aspect of the 1960s, the reluctance of the authorities to enter into, or respect, negotiations with the rebels.

What saves both books from historical smugness is their refusal to follow a traditional Whig interpretation of history with its idea of progress that congratulates the past for having led to the present. Twain judges the British past by his endorsement of the American and French revolutions. But from this point of view, his present is also criticized. When the Round Table becomes a stock exchange, wildcat manipulations (with which Twain as a heavy investor in the market was familiar) lead to warfare among the knights and the end of the Boss's new deal. He may think that his anomalous position in the kingdom makes him "a giant among pygmies, a man among children, a master intelligence among intellectual moles; by all rational measurement the one and only actually great man in that whole British world."[12] But the reader is made increasingly aware of the dark side of the Boss's project with its complacency about his own assumption of power and his addiction to a technocratic "progress" that depends heavily on weapons of destruction. His political and cultural imperialism is the other side of his role as the democratic reformer.

Similarly, Doctorow is aware of the comic absurdity in some of the radicals' 1960s-style gestures. The small isolated band of terrorist blacks speak ideologically about being "a nation," and neurotic Younger Brother, in his disgust with his father his identification with the rebels, and his obsession with violence, corks his face black the better to be one of them in their occupation of the library. He ends up, as a *villista* in Mexico, wearing cartridge belts crossed over his chest, making bombs, and leading reckless guerrilla raids for the *zapatistas*. Emma Goldman sees that this "poor dangerous boy" is like the assassin of President McKinley, Leon Czolgosz.[13] (He had heard her lecture on anarchy, and when she was falsely arrested as a coconspirator, she had insisted that he was a troubled homeless man who had acted alone. The reader of the novel in 1975 would probably think of Lee Harvey Oswald.)

Doctorow's hero is locked into an escalating confrontation with the bigoted firechief Willie Conklin, who trashed Walker's car, because each man is as intractable as the other, and their violent methods become virtually indistinguishable. Eventually, with eight people dead by his hand, Walker transforms Pierpont Morgan into his enemy, substituting for an ordinary bigot one of the most influential people of his era, and captures his library as a symbol of the white world. Struck by the arrogance of the avenger, the narrator's mock-historical voice speculates: "Or is injustice, once suffered, a mirror universe, with laws of logic and principles of reason the opposite of civilization's?"[14]

The other Morgan—Hank, not Pierpont—in his own way mirrors his rival Merlin, who exploits the credulity of the public. When the Yankee is first captured by a knight on horseback, Morgan assumes that he is someone from the circus; and Morgan later virtuously contrasts his "new deal" program of education with a violent revolution that would appeal to "the circus side" of his own nature. It constantly erupts, nevertheless, with comic effect in his various stunts to impress the populace, culminating in the liberation of the imprisoned king by five hundred knights on bicycles, "one of the gaudiest effects" Morgan ever instigated.[15] In his duel with Sagramor on behalf of "common sense and reason" the Yankee incongruously appears in flesh-colored tights and uses a lasso like a cowboy in a circus Wild West Show. It is quite in the Boss's style, foreshadowed in Dan Beard's sketch, introducing "The Tale of the Lost Land," that shows a check-suited man in a derby, looking like a carnival barker or pitchman, tickling the nose of the British lion with a straw.

Ragtime has its own strong link to show business. Evelyn Nesbit's testimony in the murder trial of Harry K. Thaw "created the first sex goddess in American history," an inspiration for "the concept of the movie star system." The Jewish immigrant Tateh's upward mobility carries him out of the labor movement into making drawings that move by flipping the pages and on to the new movie industry and a made-up identity as Baron Ashkenazy, who acquires a WASP wife and a new career as a director of popular comedies. Doctorow's impersonal historian's voice interprets this development: "Thus did the artist point his life along the lines of flow of American energy. . . . The value of the duplicatable event was everywhere perceived."[16]

Its corollary in business is Henry Ford's Model T automobile, and Doctorow pictures Ford regarding his first car on the moving assembly line: "His derby was tilted back on his head. He chewed on a piece of straw." It is uncannily like the image, sketched by Dan Beard for Twain's book, of the Yankee mechanic tickling the British lion with a straw. Ford in *Ragtime* is an evil genius because he establishes not only that the parts be interchangeable, "but that the men who build the products be themselves interchangeable parts." It is the reverse of Twain's idea of the Yankee's "man-factories," where he is going "to turn groping and grubbing automata into *men*."[17] Twain himself, however, is aware that the factory has its own automatism, and he burlesques the process of mass production in a scene where Simon Stylites, praying on his pillar, is hitched up to a sewing machine in order to use his energy to produce cheap shirts for the masses. The Yankee also shrewdly understands that the creation of wants by advertising is necessary to the economy of popular consumption, and he uses knights to advertise stove polish before there are any stoves.

Both writers are joined as well by an amusing, American talent for using vernacular culture to poke fun at more pretentious or foolish high-mindedness. They both use baseball for that purpose. The Yankee replaces the chivalric ritual of a tournament with a baseball game, in which all the players are kings, to preserve the spirit of emulation without the violence of jousting. Doctorow shows Father's disdainful surprise at finding out that ballplayers are not Yale boys, but immigrants; and he portrays J. P. Morgan's even greater disdain and surprise when, after spending a chilly, itchy night, fruitlessly awaiting revelation from Osiris, in service to his obsession with a religious belief in reincarnation, he emerges from Egypt's Great Pyramid and is stunned to see the New York Giants baseball team scrambling over the Great Sphinx. Both Twain and Doctorow see the comic possibilities in the American reversal of the profane and the sacred.

Both writers, for all their demystifying spirit, do not escape, however, some sentimentality. Twain's Yankee improbably describes his marriage with Alesande ("Sandy") in Camelot as "the dearest and perfectest comradeship that ever was," and when he is dying, he yearns for Arthurian England again because it contains "all that is dear" to him, "all that could make life worth the living!" Doctorow's story is more tough-minded and sexually explicit, in the modern manner, but it sentimentalizes Walker's beautiful wife Sarah, who is portrayed as a pure innocent "who understood nothing but goodness."[18] Nevertheless, she attempts to kill her newborn child.

The time-travel idea poses a problem for Hank Morgan's republicanism as it does for Coalhouse Walker's insistence on equality of respect, because both are obviously utopian in eras totally unprepared for them. Even the Yankee realizes that his educational work is cut out for him, and he sometimes doubts its value because "no people in the world ever did achieve their freedom by goody-goody talk and moral suasion: it being immutable law that all revolutions that will succeed must *begin* in blood, whatever may answer afterward. If history teaches anything, it teaches that."[19] He believes that a reign of terror would be necessary, as in the French Revolution, but he thinks that he is "the wrong man" for that role.

If training is everything, how can it be reversed? In the end, he discovers that it cannot be done: "The mass of the nation had swung their caps and shouted for the republic for about one day, and there an end!" When the church, the nobles, and the gentry frowned upon them, the masses like sheep had begun "to gather to the fold."[20] The Boss can only use his technological superiority to tip the balance in his favor, but it is only snatching defeat from the jaws of victory because of the ironic result of his success in extermination. Doctorow's Houdini does not have Merlin's triumph, but *Ragtime* does return to the magician after Walker, doomed by the scale of his own resistance to injustice, has been shot. On the day that the Archduke Ferdinand is assassinated, the magician, hanging up-side down in a strait-jacket during one of his daring escapes, remembers the boy, who had warned him about the event.

If we raise the question about the meaning of history in these two historical romances, we are faced with problematic answers in both cases. In the chapter "The Beginnings of Civilization," the Yankee brags that he has with his hidden program conspired to have "the civilization of the nineteenth century booming" under the nose of the kingdom, but he also calls it "as substantial a fact as any serene volcano, standing innocent with its smokeless summit in the blue sky and giving no sign of the rising hell in its bowels."[21] Morgan speaks here as if he has condemned his own project before he has accomplished it. He sounds as if he were both a character and the author's mouthpiece, though the two outlooks are not the same. Morgan's bragging is characteristic; his metaphor of the vol-cano is not; it registers the profound unstable ambivalence of Twain's own relation to the nineteenth-century civilization that is the Boss's goal. Twain's uneasiness was accentuated by his frustrating investment in the Paige typesetting machine that was too fiendishly complicated ever to function properly, "a sublime magician" that bankrupted him soon after he finished his novel.

Twain does not entirely explode the idea of progress—at least not yet for himself, whatever the modern reader may think. The American and French revolutions still make sense out of history for him in 1889, as his letters show, even after he finished the book. Dan Beard, Twain's illustra-tor, whose work much pleased the author, read the novel as a "great missionary work to bring Americans back to the safe honest and manly position, intended for them to occupy, by their ancestors when they signed the declaration of independence." Twain told Howells, who edited the novel and liked its references to the French Revolution, that "next to the 4th of July & its results, it was the noblest and the holiest thing and the most precious that ever happened in this earth. And its gracious work is not done yet—nor anywhere in the remote neighborhood of it." Twain shared Howell's lament that "an aristocracy-loving oligarchy" had re-placed "the American Republic."[22]

Yet, either Twain's hold on the Yankee as a republican slips badly at some points or else he is trying to trace a change that modifies the Yankee's outlook by Arthurian influences. Morgan falls into a didactic reformer's meditation about the power of training over originality and then incongruously adds that all he thinks about in "this plodding sad pilgrimage, this pathetic drift between the eternities, is to look out and humbly live a pure and high and blameless life." It is as if he were a monk, more influenced by the sixth century than by the nineteenth. At another point Morgan seems to lose his republican identity when he sees the crowd doing homage to the king and reflects that "really there is something peculiarly grand about the gait and bearing of a king, after all." When the Yankee learns of the king's death, he is surprised because he did not think "that any wound could be mortal to him"; he seems to have succumbed to the idea, which he has always scorned, of the divinity of kings.[23] These changes would be appropriate if Twain were bent on doing an international novel, in the mode of Henry James, with the European milieu having its forbidden attractions for the New World American, as it certainly did for Morgan's creator, who eventually resided in Vienna as if he were the American literary ambassador to Europe. Twain's Yankee has some of the same charm and naiveté of James's Christopher Newman as a fellow innocent abroad. Yet the novel cannot consistently be read in this way, even though it would make its ending more appropriate. The ending is problematic for both republicanism and feudalism. With Hank Morgan's "redoubled homelessness," as Walter Reed has called it, he becomes "exiled from the past that had previously exiled him from the present, and neither time nor place retains its identity."[24]

Morgan's showmanship is replicated in his creator's performance as a comic writer, and Morgan's conflict between Camelot and Hartford replicates his creator's life as an exile from the South, a deserter from the Confederacy, who became an admirer of General Grant, whose memoirs he published, and then an independent Republican Mugwump, who voted in 1884 for the Democrat Grover Cleveland. Dualism is built into Clemens's choice of a pen name. In a notebook entry for 1897, appropriately made while he was living in Freud's Vienna, Twain expressed his interest in Stevenson's *Dr. Jekyll and Mr. Hyde* as an attempt to account for "the presence in us of another *person*." Twain went on to argue that experiments with hypnotism show that the two persons are not known to each other. He elaborated the idea into "a dream self" who can make "immense excursions" in the role of one's "spiritualized person."[25] He humorously called his other self "Watson," rather than Mr. Hyde, but surely one of those "immense excursions" of his dream self was Hank Morgan's journey to Camelot.

Doctorow ends his story with the historical facts of the First World War and the deportation of Emma Goldman. But he also suggests the circularity of history by his last line, which refers to the murderer Harry K. Thaw, marching in the annual Armistice Day Parade, after obtaining his release from an asylum. This last note brings the music of time back to its beginning, as if none of the author's changes in the mosaic of the past has changed time's repetitious tune. Doctorow makes it explicit: "The era of Ragtime had run out, with the heavy breath of the machine, as if history were no more than a tune on a player piano."[26]

Doctorow's point of view is hard to elicit from *Ragtime* because at one point he devotes a chapter to the meditations of the boy in Father's family as a theme for the novel. The boy seems to be a mouthpiece for the author in expressing thoughts too metaphysical for a child. Listening to his grandfather, the boy learns that "the forms of life were volatile and that everything in the world could as easily be something else." The boy finds proof of this in his own experience of "the instability of both things and people," and his own self-duplication in the mirror gives him a sense of having two selves "neither of which could claim to be the real one." (Mark Twain would have no trouble understanding him.) His conclusion is simple: "It was evident to him that the world composed and recomposed itself constantly in an endless process of dissatisfaction."[27]

From this point of view, the world is pure contingency; nothing is necessary; time has no meaningful direction, and there is no place to stand from which judgments can be made. Twain himself did move towards this nihilism. With Doctorow, however, the boy's strange meditation is perhaps a rationalization for Doctorow's own playful rearrangements of history—anything might be anything else in the historical past. He has elsewhere cited the structuralist critic Roland Barthes on behalf of the proposition that historical discourse is itself "a particular form of fiction," and Doctorow concluded that fiction itself is "a kind of speculative history, perhaps a superhistory, by which the available data for the composition is seen to be greater and more various in its sources than the historian supposes."[28]

This erosion of any difference between fiction and history is too facile. It is even contradictory. The idea of a "superhistory" itself suggests some kind of referentiality, not explained by "fiction," yet it is not at all clear what constraints would discipline this new kind of history. Doctorow's byplay with historical characters, however, is not as fancy-free as it might appear at first, for it is controlled by his own considerable historical knowledge. To take what seems to be a bizarre example: Emma Goldman's orgasm-inducing massage of Evelyn Nesbit. The event never took place, but Goldman's criticisms of Nesbit's life in that scene are entirely authentic ideologically, and the erotic aspect of the moment connects with an historical fact: Goldman admitted that her friendship with Margaret Anderson, editor of the *Little Review,* had stirred feelings expressive of a "previous theoretic interest in sex variation."[29]

Doctorow himself is not prepared to question that "some facts, for instance the Nazi extermination of the Jews, are so monstrous as to seem to stand alone."[30] His example is revealing. His earlier novel *The Book of Daniel,* the strongest expression of Doctorow's historical consciousness, fictionalizes the story of the electrocuted Rosenbergs, as seen from the point of view of their children, to dramatize a larger theme involving three generations of Jewish-Americans and the defeat of their hopes for America.[31] The only non-Jew in the novel is a black janitor.

Doctorow's Jewishness is not just a fact; it is the key to his personal interpretation of the history he has fictionalized, for he orients himself in it by his concern for the Jewish immigrants, whether they be Houdini, Tateh, or Emma Goldman. His views of the three cases are pertinent: Houdini "never developed what we think of as a political consciousness" because he could not "reason from his own hurt feelings."[32] His obsession with escapes speaks to the immigrant experience of repression and to the function of show business as an opiate of the people. Tateh's upward mobility sacrifices his solidarity with the workers and compromises his artistic aspirations when he achieves affluence in making escapist movies. Emma Goldman, when arrested and asked for her views about Coalhouse Walker, simply says, "Wealth is the oppressor. Coalhouse Walker did not need Red Emma to learn that. He needed only to suffer."[33] It is a radical perspective, married (in contrast to the usual socialist realism) to a modernist interest in technique, one that calls attention to its own fictionalizing.

In an interview, Doctorow has spoken of his admiration for Goldman's prophetic kind of Jewishness and of his growing up in "a lower-middle class environment of generally enlightened, socialist sensibility," stemming from his Russian grandfather's radical humanism.[34] Indeed, *Ragtime*'s image of what historians used to call "the Progressive era" is notable for the conspicuous absence in it of persons drawn from the large, ideologically mixed group of non-immigrant native reformers, who were active in the period. Teddy Roosevelt appears in *Ragtime* only as a greedy big-game hunter, and Woodrow Wilson is seen only as a man "who wore rimless glasses and held moral views. When the Great War came he would wage it with the fury of the affronted."[35]

Ragtime's image of the past is vulnerable to John Lukacs's criticism that Doctorow's interest in America is in *"things* American—altogether on a different level from his knowledge of Jewish-American *thoughts."*[36] His remoteness from the non-Jewish characters is indicated by the fact that (except for Walker) they have no particularizing names. What is most American about *Ragtime,* Lukacs suggests, is its pictorial imagination and a rapidly moving clipped style, like the comics and the movies. Doctorow himself has spoken of his experiments in narrative discontinuity as being "akin to television—discontinuous and mind-blowing."[37] It is curious that this experimental vanguardism in technique and this radicalism in political ideology should be akin to the mode of a mass medium. It testifies to the extent to which the 1960s marked the process in which, as Gerald Graff has pointed out, "the antinomian disparagement of 'bourgeois values' is celebrated by the agencies of publicity, exploited by the manipulators of cultural fashion, and emulated in personal conduct—an additional reason why the ante of provocation and radical experiment must continually be raised if the arts are to justify their vanguard credentials. . . . The point seems to have been reached at which artistic intransigence is indistinguishable from celebration of the dynamisms of mass society."[38] *Ragtime*'s immense popularity illustrates his point.

Doctorow's sense of having a particular place to stand in Jewish-American radicalism, as a resource for his art, does not square with the boy's nihilistic metaphysical meditations in *Ragtime.* They may serve to rationalize Doctorow's fictionalizing of the historical material, but the material itself is viewed from the standpoint of the political sympathies that he acknowledges in the interview. The tension between the boy's meditations and his creator's responses in the interview defines the ambiguous quality of *Ragtime*'s point of view. It has led one perceptive critic to say that his art is "committed yet unconvinced," written out of a Jewish biblical view that "history is redemptive—and also out of Modernist doubt."[39]

Twain's conflict is analogous to Doctorow's because of the tension between his view of history as redeemed by the American and French revolutions and his despair of majority human nature on whose good judgment democratic republicanism depends. The Yankee can assure the reader at one point that "there is plenty good enough material for a republic in the most degraded people that ever existed . . . if one could but force it out of its timid and suspicious privacy," but in the end he finds that the Arthurian masses are sheep.[40] That disappointment could be explained, however, by the immense historical gap between his project and the society in which he is a stranger. But Morgan's ideological conflict intersected with his creator's self-division, the sense of having a separate "dream self." The artistic result for his novel was a lack of control reflected in its loose, rambling, repetitive, and anecdotal structure in contrast to the controlled and skillful braiding of historical and fictional lives in Doctorow's tale.

The competing elements in Hank Morgan are significant, however, because they are not just the author's. His sympathy for the oppressed majority and his deep suspicion of its judgment and ability would be competing themes as well in the Progressive movement itself, which often joined indignation against the trust, the political boss, and the sweatshop with a passion for organized efficiency.[41] Hank Morgan has the artistic burden of having to carry more meanings than Doctorow's stylized characters. The Yankee contains a multitude, incorporating the showman, inventor, rationalist, entrepreneur, democratic reformer, dictatorial imperialist, and disenchanted romantic in his identity. This amplitude of meaning, however, is also what gives a modern resonance to Twain's fantastic version of history, which might otherwise simply have been reduced to what it is in its worst stretches—a heavy-handed tedious assault on monarchy and aristocracy. It is Hank Morgan's complexity that makes it possible for a contemporary reader to think of Twain's story as the precursor of a more sophisticated and more disenchanted form of black humor.

Twain needed a successor to go beyond his own speculative history. His literary sense of America, for all its close familiarity with a rich variety of American experience, lacked any appreciation for the immense process of immigration. It is historically symbolic that the year in which Twain began writing his story about the Yankee was the year that Emma Goldman emigrated from Russia to America, her romantic imagination stirred by anarchist literature and history. When the novel was published, she was moving to New York to join the anarchist movement. One of the important literary consequences of immigration was the development after the Second World War of many influential and highly accomplished Jewish-American novelists. Doctorow's *Ragtime* is one sign of that coming-of-age; and, among the historical figures in his book, Emma Goldman is the heroine. *Ragtime* is also a sign of the extent to which a Jewish grandchild of the immigrants can become what Mark Twain was, a popular interpreter of America to itself. Hank Morgan, meet Coalhouse Walker and Emma Goldman.

Doctorow in *Ragtime* cites Freud's remark that "America is a mistake, a gigantic mistake." Another Jewish-American novelist, Saul Bellow, referred to the remark in a speech, given shortly after the publication of *Ragtime,* to the Anti-Defamation League when accepting its America's Democratic Legacy Award. (Curiously enough, Bellow's *Henderson the Rain King* seems also to be partly inspired by Twain's fable: a Connecticut pig-farmer journeys to a fabulous Africa, encounters a primitive society, and becomes involved with a king.) Bellow used the occasion to counter Freud's judgment with the philosopher Morris Cohen's belief that "the future of liberal civilization was bound up with America's survival and its ability to make use of the heritage of human rights formulated by Jefferson and Lincoln."[42] If this stirring confidence is missing from both Twain and Doctorow, it is partly explained by the difficulty in the late 1880s or in the Nixon years of hearing any trumpets sounding in the corridors of power for that great tradition. The final despair of Hank Morgan and Coalhouse Walker draws on that silence.

Chapter 9

American Dilemma:
Lincoln's Jefferson
and the Irony of History

LOWELL'S poem "For the Union Dead," memorializing Colonel Shaw's monument, which William James had helped to dedicate with his speech, connects the white churches on New England's greens, holding their air of "sparse, sincere rebellion," with the "frayed flags" that "quilt the graveyards of the Grand Army of the Republic." It is a highly condensed forging of a link between a Puritanized Revolution and the Civil War. The rhetoric of Abraham Lincoln's greatest speeches also strikes this historic note. His assassination only a few days after the surrender of Lee at Appomattox Courthouse has fixed the image of Lincoln as a martyr to the cause of the Union and obscured the extent to which his ardent response to the Revolutionary Jefferson defined Lincoln's political religion as a Republican.

Of all the American presidents, only Jefferson and Lincoln have commanded a literary style that is indisputably their own and memorable to later generations. Both men were also distinguished by their interest in ideas, and they developed and applied them with a persistence and consistency notably absent from contemporary political debate with its penchant for slogans and catchphrases. (One Republican politician, without a trace of irony, has praised his party's presidential campaign in 1988 for being so pragmatic in angling for conservative votes "that if running an ideological campaign is what they need to do to win, they'll do it."[1] So much for principles.) Jefferson and Lincoln, by contrast, not only had a touch of the poet about them; they had also a touch of the philosopher.

Their crucial roles in the great events of American history give them a common bond as interpreters of American democracy.

The connection between the two men, however, is not at all immediately evident. A recent biography of Lincoln mentions Jefferson only four times and then only as a fellow founder with Washington and Madison, whom Lincoln revered. The biographer correctly cites Henry Clay, the Whig leader, as Lincoln's "political idol."[2] He was a slaveholder who believed in gradual emancipation and colonization of the Negro, as Lincoln did. But in his eulogy for him in 1852, Lincoln also praised him for his devotion to "the white man's charter of freedom—the declaration that 'all men are created free and equal,' " unlike John C. Calhoun of South Carolina, "the first American of any note" to ridicule it.[3] Lincoln had not yet been stirred into action by the controversy over slavery precipitated two years later by the Kansas–Nebraska Act. After that, his speeches would return again and again to Jefferson's example, his phrasing in the Declaration of Independence, his condemnation of slavery in *Notes on the State of Virginia,* and his attempt to give Congress the power to prohibit it from any new territory. Jefferson would live in his imagination more intensely than any other American figure.

Jefferson's legacy that has attracted the most modern attention, because of the intense controversy over it in our pluralistic religious culture, has been his authorship of the Virginia Statute for Religious Freedom. He listed the statute, along with the Declaration of Independence and the University of Virginia, on his tombstone to mark the achievements for which he wished to be remembered. By 1947, several justices of the Supreme Court of the United States had come to read the two clauses in the First Amendment having to do with religion through the eyes of Jefferson, amalgamating them with his Virginia Statute and his letter to some of his Northern Baptist supporters, referring to the clauses as "building a wall of separation between church and State."[4] A recent wide-ranging study by many minds of the Statute's origins, nature, legacy, and significance mentions Lincoln briefly and only once, yet the reference is important because it refers to an "American creed" that includes "the Declaration of Independence and the classic documents of Abraham Lincoln or the Virginia Statute."[5] Indeed, the Statute is unified with the Declaration and the University of Virginia because they all figure in Jefferson's conception of a new republican order, as Ralph Lerner has pointed out, representing "his singular vision of what America and its people might become."[6] Lincoln as a statesman would find his inspiration in Jefferson precisely because of that political vision.

Lincoln did not speak about the Virginia Statute for Religious Freedom because he was primarily interested in another kind of threat to freedom, one posed by the institution of slavery in America. Curiously, however, Jefferson's Statute was once used in Virginia with respect to slavery when the state's high court in 1850 was hospitable to hearing a lawyer cite it on behalf of a minister, Jarvis C. Bacon, who was accused of having violated the law by speaking against the legal right to own slaves. He had said that giving the slave "nothing for his labour, except once in a while a whipping or a few stripes," was thievery. The judge thought "a humane casuist" might indeed find it worse than stealing *if* no "suitable comforts or necessaries" were given for the slave's work, such as those normally provided by slaveholders. The judge was encouraged by Jefferson's Statute to read the minister's statement in this casuistic way and therefore allowed a motion for a new trial.[7]

An historian of the making of the Statute has suggested another connection between it and slavery by noting that the mass evangelical campaigns for conversion in Virginia had threatened to loosen the planters' control over their slaves, and the opponents of Jefferson and Madison had therefore sought in the 1770s to institutionalize an ordered corporate worship in Episcopal style. Jefferson's and Madison's successful campaign against this move had institutionalized instead a rationalistic, libertarian and individualistic alternative view of religion; and it may have dampened the fear of social subversion by defining religious freedom in terms of opinion and belief, rather than in terms of social organization and relationships. With respect to them, coercion was not presumed to need new and more legitimate grounds.[8]

It was not the Statute, however, but the Declaration of Independence that was primarily the "electric cord" (in Lincoln's metaphor) linking Jefferson to his successor. The Declaration was mainly a set of charges against the king, but it was also a public philosophy: "all men are created equal" in the possession of their "inherent and inalienable rights" to "life, liberty, and the pursuit of happiness." A form of government is legitimate when it is derived from the consent of the governed and is devoted to preserving those rights. Otherwise, the people can "alter or abolish it." Much else is left unsaid: how universal is "men"? What rights are "inalienable"? How is consent obtained? Who are included in the "people"? What governmental institutions can best secure the preservation of natural rights?

Jefferson's phrasing that it is a "self-evident" truth that "all men are created equal" has had a libertarian legacy in spite of his being a slaveholder throughout his life in a state where more than half of American blacks lived. He had inherited over a hundred and thirty slaves from his father-in-law and was dependent upon them for the successful completion of his cherished, life-long project, the great house of Monticello. The expression of his remarkable artistic and mechanical talents needed the artisanship and labor of his slaves. Ironically, some of his own slaves had deserted him to gain freedom by joining the British forces in the Revolutionary War. He was well aware that the Revolution's theme of natural inalienable rights contradicted the practice of slavery. His original substitution in the Declaration of "the pursuit of happiness" for "property" in the familiar clause that includes "life" and "liberty" made it much easier to notice the contradiction and to be embarrassed by it.

The ideology of the Revolution would play its part in the growth in the number of free Negroes not only in New England and Pennsylvania, where gradual emancipation became a general policy, but even in the Upper South, where it did not.[9] His discussion of slavery in *Notes on the State of Virginia,* published in English in 1787 and originally written in answer to queries proposed by a distinguished French diplomat, was vigorously condemnatory. The institution was a combination of "unremitting despotism on the one part, and degrading submissions on the other." Children, witnessing it, are corrupted. As an English historian, J. R. Pole, has pointed out, Jefferson appreciated "rather more clearly than most of his contemporaries that Negroes were not the only victims, but that the white personality, and therefore the entire Republic, were among the casualties of black slavery."[10] Jefferson feared in his darkest moments that a just God would wreak His wrath by kindling a slave revolt in which He would not take sides with the planters. Jefferson was usually sanguine, however, and he looked optimistically forward instead to "a total emancipation" with "the consent of the masters, rather than by their extirpation."[11]

Yet Jefferson envisaged no future except exportation for freed slaves. *Notes on the State of Virginia* revealed Jefferson's inability to think consistently about slaves as having been created equal. He was unusually willing to make "great allowance" for circumstances in evaluating the potentiality of Indians, and he saw no reason to think that they were not "formed in mind as well as in body, on the same module with the 'Homo sapiens Europaeus.' "[12] But with blacks it was quite another matter. Their color seemed to him an "immoveable veil" making for "eternal monotony" in the visible signs of their emotional life, which lacked "a tender delicate mixture of sentiment and sensation."[13] Jefferson in one passage unhesitatingly declares them inferior in reason and imagination; in another, he cautions that this judgment "must be hazarded with great diffidence," not only because of the difficulty of making one on such a complex issue, but because his conclusion would "degrade a whole race of men from the rank in the scale of beings which their Creator may perhaps have given them."[14]

The firm assertion he made in the Declaration of "self-evident" truths has given away to a tentative "perhaps," and his conclusion is that "the blacks, whether originally a distinct race, or made distinct by time and circumstances, are inferior to the whites in the endowments both of body and mind." True, as "a lover of natural history," Jefferson would speculate with scientific caution, advancing his theme of inferiority "as a suspicion only"; nevertheless, he had no hesitation in assuming that while the freed Roman slave "might mix with, without staining the blood of, his master," the American slave when freed "is to be removed beyond the reach of mixture."[15] Indeed, Jefferson's unsuccessful plans for freeing the slaves always entailed their colonization elsewhere, because he feared that a host of reasons, including "the real distinctions which nature has made," would produce political "convulsions which will probably never end but in the extermination of the one or the other race."[16]

Notes on the State of Virginia joins the hope for a gradual emancipation of the slaves by slaveholders with a colonization policy for freed Negroes that is based on the terrible fear of a bloody race war. God could not sympathize with the planters in such a war, Jefferson believed, yet nature's "real distinctions" and other circumstances would have produced it. The Declaration spoke of the "laws of nature and of nature's God" as if they were harmonious in entitling the colonies to a "separate & equal station" among the powers of the earth.[17] In *Notes on the State of Virginia* the pressure of Jefferson's dilemma threatens to rend asunder God and nature. Ironically, the phrase "separate & equal" would in the next century have a long constitutional life in legally justifying the racism that troubled Jefferson's struggle with the problem of slavery.

Yet, it is too easily overlooked that Jefferson's racism did not deny to blacks either "the endowments" of the heart or attribute to them "any depravity of the moral sense," and he did not begrudge petty thievery by slaves since masters should ask themselves "whether the slave may not as justifiably take a little from one, who has taken all from him, as he may slay one who would slay him?"[18] Jefferson's speculations about inferiority, moreover, were not designed to justify slavery, but rather to explain his policy of exportation for freed slaves.[19] When Benjamin Banneker sent him an almanac as an example of black intellectual capability, Jefferson sent it on to Condorcet in Paris because "our black brethren" had "a right for their justification against the doubts which have been entertained of them."[20] Jefferson's devotion to an aristocracy of talent and virtue (rather than of property or descent) in the future might have to make room for some black members. He could not rule it out because his political theory, as such, idealized "the small but independent farmer in a real republic of equals."[21] Only his practice as a slaveholder denied that equality.

His attempts to get rid of slavery have impressed recent historians as being either ineffective or timid. The failure of some of his early efforts, as in his rejected draft for a Virginia Constitution, persuaded him that his peers would never look kindly on this aspect of his reform-program. Even so, he freed no slaves in his lifetime and only five in his will. When one of his young supporters, Edward Coles, decided to take his slaves into free territory and urged his hero to lead an emancipation movement, Jefferson pleaded that prayers were "the only weapons of an old man," while counseling Coles to stay in the South: "I hope . . . you will reconcile yourself to your country and its unfortunate condition; that you will not lessen its stock of sound disposition by withdrawing your portion from the mass." Coles ignored the advice, settled seventeen former slaves as farmers in Illinois, and led the forces in 1824 fighting against a pro-slavery amendment to the state constitution.[22]

Nevertheless, Jefferson once came close to a major victory in the anti-slavery struggle. His draft of the Ordinance of 1784 prohibited slavery in all the territories of the United States; if passed, it would have excluded slavery from the Great Lakes to the Gulf of Mexico. It failed by one vote. (The Ordinance of 1787, the successor to Jefferson's proposal, prohibited slavery only from the territory north of the Ohio River.) Jefferson, relating that the fate of his draft hung on a single vote, lamented that "Heaven was silent in that awful moment!" He hoped it would not always be silent, so that "the friends of human nature will in the end prevail."[23] That was written in 1786; the purchase of Louisiana in 1803, however, not only doubled the area of the new country and removed a French threat to closing the Mississippi to Western commerce, it also added more slave territory to the United States.

"Jefferson began his career as a Virginian," John Chester Miller has pointed out; "he became an American; and in his old age he was in the process of becoming a Southern nationalist."[24] The political controversy over the Missouri question revealed Jefferson to be no longer a believer in federal responsibility for regulating slavery. Northern Jeffersonian Republicans unsuccessfully promoted the Tallmadge Amendment, requiring Missouri to provide for gradual emancipation and to bar further slave admissions, and they cited Jefferson's words in the Declaration of Independence about equality. He was convinced however, that the Northern Republicans were playing politics to dominate the South, and he now began to emphasize that regulating slavery should be "the exclusive right of every State, which nothing in the constitution has taken from them and given to the General Government." He was driven by his fear that the Missouri question was, "like a fire bell in the night," a terrible portent of "the knell of the Union." The terms of the Missouri Compromise, drawing a sectional line with respect to slavery, filled him with terror because "a geographical line [36° 30'], coinciding with a marked principle, moral and political, once conceived and held up to the angry passions of men, will never be obliterated; and every new irritation will mark it deeper and deeper."

The moment was a tragic one for him because he thought he might die in the belief that the sacrifices of "the generation of 1776" would be useless and its attempt to "acquire self-government and happiness to their country" would be defeated by "the unwise and unworthy passions of their sons."[25] His only compensation was that he thought "emancipation & deportation" were now more likely to be seen as a necessary solution, with Europe ("which has forced this evil on us") and the Eastern states ("who have been its chief instruments of importation") making charitable contributions towards the expense to supplement the proceeds derived from the federal sale of lands.[26] Jefferson's finger pointing at Europe and the Eastern states was consistent with his original phrasing in the Declaration of Independence (which Congress struck out), condemning George

III for violating the "sacred rights of life and liberty" by carrying African slaves into another hemisphere; and his *Autobiography,* explaining the omission, noted that "our northern brethren," though having few slaves, "had been pretty considerable carriers of them to others."[27]

Jefferson was also consistent after 1784 in his reliance, as he wrote a French correspondent two years later, not on political means but rather on "the workings of an overruling providence" to prepare the deliverance of "our suffering brethren" whose "groans" will awaken "a god of justice" to their distress and "by diffusing light & liberality among their oppressors, or at length by his exterminating thunder" will in either case not leave them "to the guidance of a blind fatality."[28] This politically utopian invocation of an Old Testament, interventionist God is hard to reconcile with Jefferson's skepticism about all the miraculous sections of the Bible and his rationalist objections to Calvinism, but John Adams reported that Jefferson's design for the Great Seal of the United States had on one side "The Children of Israel in the Wilderness, led by a Cloud by day, and a Pillar of Fire by night." In his second inaugural address he invoked the Being "who led our fathers, as Israel of old," to the promised land.[29] The idiom of promise left the future open for continuing revelations and dispensations of freedom. He was deeply committed to the idea that American republicanism was "the world's best hope," as he put it in his first inaugural address, "a chosen country," where an "overruling Providence" proves by its dispensations that it "delights in the happiness of man here" as well as in the hereafter.[30]

Jefferson thus provided a national myth for the new country, a myth that much later historians, borrowing from Marxist terminology, would condemn as a form of "exceptionalism." Certainly, it can often be only a smug rationalization for American arrogance and complacency, a cover for illusions of omniscience and omnipotence about the world. But with Jefferson, as later with Lincoln, it was something quite different—a burden of responsibility to explain to the American people the meaning of the national covenants and to persuade them to accept the onerous duties involved in making good on the covenantal promises. If leaders and led failed to understand correctly and to act appropriately, the nation would lose its special meaning in history.[31] There was nothing automatic, passive, or inevitable about keeping national integrity.

Only the persistence of slavery, the threat of sectional disunion, the danger of a large-scale slave revolt (as in Santo Domingo), or the intermixture of freed slaves with whites could threaten this Jeffersonian version of the national mythos. His hope for a scheme of emancipation and deportation, however, was less pressing than his fear that the current danger to "the principles of '76" was "founded on banking institutions, and moneyed incorporations under the guise and cloak of their favored branches of manufactures, commerce and navigation, riding and ruling over the plundered ploughman and beggared yeomanry."[32] This republican agrarianism was increasingly becoming sectional and committed to slavery. In his last letter on the subject of slavery he conceded that any basic change would take a "revolution in public opinion," one not to be expected "perhaps in an age."[33]

A month later, refusing for reasons of illness an invitation to join in a celebration of the fiftieth anniversary of American independence, he memorably expressed his Revolutionary faith in the Declaration of Independence: "May it be to the world, what I believe it will be, (to some parts sooner, to others later, but finally to all,) the signal of arousing men . . . to assume the blessings and security of self-government." He saw a general spread of light illuminating "the palpable truth, that the mass of mankind has not been born with saddles on their backs, nor a favored few booted and spurred, ready to ride them legitimately by the grace of God. These are grounds of hope for others."[34] He spoke of arousing people to "burst the chains" of monkish ignorance and superstition," but he said nothing about the chains of slavery. He had come to keep silent in public about slavery, he explained, unless he could foresee some favorable effect from speaking. His silence was not surprising. Increasingly in the South, with the flourishing of the interstate slave trade in which Virginia played a vital role, there would be many who indeed did believe that they were a favored few, ordained to ride those born with saddles on their back.

In Robert Penn Warren's narrative poem, *Brother to Dragons,* about the butchering of a slave in Kentucky by one of Jefferson's nephews, the poet imagines a Jefferson whose pride in his earlier "identity with the definition of man" has been profoundly shaken by news of the terrible event. He comes to a new conclusion about the future:

> It will be forged beneath the hammer of truth
> On the anvil of our anguish. We shall be forged
> Beneath the hammer of truth on the anvil of anguish.[35]

There is no historical evidence for Jefferson's response to this tragedy, but his complicity with an institution he could not justify was given an ironic twist by an earlier event that also dramatized the human capacity for aggression and its entanglement with the slave problem. His revered teacher and friend, George Wythe, one of Virginia's most admired judges, was poisoned to death, along with a black boy whom he had freed and educated, by his sister's grandson, who had forged his granduncle's name on checks. Strong evidence against the murderer could not be used to convict him because it came from Negro servants, who were not legally entitled in Virginia to testify in court against a white man.

Jefferson could have reflected (whether he did or not) on the disquieting fact that he had been responsible for the section on the government of slaves in the revisal of Virginia's laws.[36] In any case, his last letter about the principles of 1776 is unshaken in expressing his confidence in them. Whatever anguish Jefferson must have felt about his entanglement in an institution that his principles could not justify, he felt even more strongly a fear of civil war over the meaning of a union that contained such a glaring contradiction as slavery. Nevertheless, in seeing the Declaration as dynamic in its capacity for pointing to future fulfillment, Jefferson was prophetic of the way in which a great Northerner, who presided over the Civil War, would come to understand a great Southerner's ideals.

It was the early Jefferson that Lincoln invoked, the Jefferson of the Declaration of Independence, the *Notes on the State of Virginia,* and the proposed Ordinance of 1784 for the settlement of future states. Lincoln's first great speech, in 1854 at Peoria, Illinois, laid out all the elements of his Republican position in a reply to Senator Stephen A. Douglas. In it Lincoln saluted Jefferson, "who was, is, and perhaps will continue to be, the most distinguished politician of our history."[37] Lincoln noted that Jefferson conceived the germ of the Ordinance of 1787 that kept slavery out of the Northwestern Territory, thus establishing congressional responsibility for regulating the question of slavery in the territories. It was an important part of Lincoln's historical argument that Chief Justice Roger Taney and his supporters were quite wrong in their assumption that the founding fathers had no qualms whatever in making slaves property and never intended the Declaration of Independence to include black men. The Constitution had recognized slavery from necessity, but it had not sanctioned it by using the word "slavery" anywhere in the document; where it alluded to slavery, the term "person," not "property," was used instead.

Lincoln was passionately devoted to being worthy of his exalted vision of the Revolutionary generation. For him nothing was more truly Jeffersonian than his hero's remark in the last year of his life that the Declaration of Independence would be "grounds of hope for others." It was meant to be, Lincoln argued, "a standard maxim for free society" to be "constantly approximated" in the future.[38] Against Douglas, Lincoln ridiculed the absurdity that it could be reduced to meaning only that "all British subjects who were on this continent eighty-one years ago, were created equal to all British subjects born and then residing in Great Britain."[39] Lincoln knew how to make political capital out of this reductionism when he spoke in Chicago about the German, Irish, French, and Scandinavian immigrants who cannot by ancestry "carry themselves back into that glorious epoch" of 1776 and "make themselves feel that they are part of us," but can discover their moral relation to those men through the moral sentiment of the Declaration's self-evident truths, "as though they were blood of the blood, and flesh of the flesh, of the men who wrote that Declaration, and so they are."[40] Jefferson's ideas linked them like "an electric cord."

Lincoln went further in his application of the Declaration by arguing that "no man is good enough to govern another man without that other's consent," and this "sheet-anchor of American republicanism" he found expressed in the Declaration's assertion that governments derive "their just powers from the consent of the governed." Slavery was "a total violation of this principle."[41] This move was audacious because his opponent Douglas would use the consent principle to justify his position that the territorial question of slavery should be left up to each territory's inhabitants by popular vote. Douglas might have appealed to the Declaration too, though he did not; it became Lincoln's standard by posing the "truth" of equality as a limit on popular sovereignty. Jefferson in his first inaugural address had endorsed "absolute acquiescence in the decisions of the majority" as "the vital principle of republics," but this characteristically sweeping phrase was balanced earlier in the same address by a characteristic qualification that while it is a "sacred principle, that though the will of the majority is in all cases to prevail, that will to be rightful must be reasonable; that the minority possess their equal rights, which equal law must protect, and to violate would be oppression."[42] Lincoln's history-making modification of Jefferson was to apply this Jeffersonian idea to the issue of slavery in a political context and contest. Lincoln did not deny that the concern of the nation's fathers for the right of states to regulate their own domestic concerns had some reference to the existence of slavery among them. He did deny that their concern had reference to the carrying of slavery into new territories.

Writing to a group of Boston Republicans who had organized a meeting to honor Jefferson, Lincoln pointed out that the two parties had changed places with respect to Jefferson, who, like the Republicans, stressed "*personal* rights" rather than property rights, which were favored by the Douglas Democrats. The parties were like two drunken men who had each "fought himself *out* of his own coat and *into* that of the other." For Lincoln "the principles of Jefferson are the definitions and axioms of free society."[43]

Jefferson also came to his aid in his dispute with Douglas about Chief Justice Taney's Dred Scott decision, defining slaves as the inalienable property of their owners. Lincoln saw in it not only the practical denial of the right of a territory to prohibit slavery, supposedly guaranteed by Douglas's Kansas-Nebraska principle of popular sovereignty, but also a hypothetical danger, pointing towards a future decision that might make it impossible even for a state to prohibit slavery. Douglas reasonably considered this possibility spurious as a practical matter, but he demagogically went further by trying to make Lincoln appear to be a lawless man who refused to respect the high court's judgment. Lincoln was able to cite Jefferson's refusal to let the United States Supreme Court be the last word on constitutionality, and he asserted the right of Republicans to regard Taney's argument as lacking legitimacy and therefore entitling voters and officials to support political measures that were not congruent with it, though they did not constitute civil disobedience.

Lincoln's opposition to slavery was not radical, as Abolitionist criticism and action often were. He accepted the legality of slavery where it existed in the states, agreed to the Fugitive Slave Law (though he found it distasteful to do so), accepted the provision that Utah and New Mexico could choose whether they would come into the union as slave or free states, because it had been so agreed in Henry Clay's Compromise of 1850, and attacked the Kansas-Nebraska Act mainly because it had reversed the Missouri Compromise of 1820, which he wanted to have restored as a basis for future settlement of the territories. His whole aim, he said, was to put slavery back to where it had been in the minds of the most liberal founders: not a permanent institution, but one slated for "ultimate extinction," even though "ultimate" might mean for Lincoln a hundred years in the future.

While his position was certainly a moderate one, Lord Charnwood has perceptively remarked that it was "a deadly moderation," knowing exactly and in detail where and why it stood where it did, and it would not compromise one iota on essential principles.[44] Moreover, as J. R. Pole has pointed out, Lincoln's moderation arose from his observing not only "the moral scandal of slavery, but also the historical depth of the institution and the appalling complexity of the problem it presented."[45] What is remarkable about his role in the debates with Douglas is not so much his eloquence, which is occasional, but rather his close historical reasoning and his persistent appeal to sober judgment and humane feeling. Lord Charnwood has also put his finger on what is distinguished and rare in Lincoln as a speaker, a respect for argument that must strike us as a lost art among politicians: "He put himself in a position in which if his argument were not sound nothing could save his speech from failure as a speech."[46] (Radio and television would make that standard increasingly rare.)

True, from a modern point of view about racial equality, Lincoln shares much of Jefferson's prejudice about race. Like most of their contemporaries, they accepted the idea of white superiority and opposed amalgamation. Pressed by Douglas, who racially taunted Lincoln and his supporters by calling them "Black Republicans," Lincoln conceded that no more than Jefferson did he advocate political or social equality between blacks and whites; and he was equally devoted to a separation of the races. In a polemical reply to Douglas's alarms about racial mixture, Lincoln wrily said: "Why, Judge, if we do not let them get together in the Territories, they won't mix there. I should say at least that that is a self-evident truth."[47] He wanted the new territories to be open to settlement by poor white people, including those from slave states.

No more than Jefferson, whom he quoted on "emancipation and deportation," did he (until 1863) have any policy except colonization for free blacks. Even so, though he did not make an issue out of racial discrimination against them, he did not follow Jefferson in meditating on their supposed natural inferiority. Lincoln's concessions to Douglas's racist tauntings were at the level of political and social institutions (the state and the family).[48]

What then gives meaning to Lincoln's use of the theme of equality in the Declaration of Independence? Free blacks exist, he strongly insisted in his first major speech on slavery, because their owners have realized that "the poor Negro has some natural right to himself—that those who deny it and make mere merchandise of him deserve kickings, contempt, and death."[49] Hence, the prejudice even among Southerners against the slave dealer. Ending the debates with Douglas, Lincoln put his case for Negro equality by defining slavery as the spirit that says, "You toil and work and earn bread, and I'll eat it." Just as the Declaration had identified the king as the political evil to be resisted, so did Lincoln make the spirit of slavery an analogue of a king's claim "to bestride the people of his own nation and live by the fruit of their labor."[50] Refuting the demagogic charge that if he did not want a black woman for a slave, he must necessarily believe in racial mixture and therefore want her for a wife, Lincoln used a Lockean standard: "In some respects she certainly is not my equal; but in her natural right to eat the bread she earns with her own hands without asking leave of any one else, she is my equal, and the equal of all others."[51]

In practice, however, until 1863, Lincoln's condemnation of slavery issued in a containment policy that worked within constitutional limits by focusing on prohibiting the expansion of slavery into any new territory. That, he believed, would put slavery on the road to ultimate extinction by reinstating the principle of the Missouri Compromise that had previously kept it south of the 36—30 line. Like so many of the leaders of the American Revolution, he created a radically new historical situation by advocating a policy that was based on a conservative feeling for satisfactions already enjoyed—in his case a respect for Henry Clay's Compromise of 1820 and a reverence for the principles of Jefferson's Declaration of Independence. In time, his policy seemed radical enough from the South's point of view to warrant secession.

He was firm in maintaining a refusal to compromise his containment principle, even after seven states had seceded and made actual Jefferson's darkest fear of what the future might bring. The Virginian had seen in the line marking off slave from free territory in 1820 a source of perpetual antagonism; by 1854, however, it seemed to Lincoln that its restoration was the only way to restore sectional peace. By 1860, it was clear that no widely accepted solution could be found for solving the problem of slavery in the territories or in the Union.

After his election, by a plurality of the popular vote in a four-way contest that gave him not a single Southern electoral vote, but a decisive electoral majority, Lincoln journeyed to Washington, giving speeches along the way. Nothing could be more appropriate than his speaking at Philadelphia in Independence Hall. He was much moved and extravagantly proclaimed that he had never had any political feeling that did not "spring from the sentiments embodied in the Declaration of Independence." The statment ignored his earlier career as a follower of Henry Clay, but it pointed to what had become the major issue between Douglas and himself about the interpretation of the Declaration in relation to slavery. He said he hoped the country could be saved by his democratic reading of what Jefferson had meant—a principle "which gave promise that in due time the weights should be lifted from the shoulders of all men, and that *all* should have an equal choice." He had already been informed of a plot against his life, and he ominously remarked that if the country could not be saved on that basis, he would "rather be assassinated on the spot than to surrender it."[52]

Lincoln was moved by events to a more radical position. Already in his annual message to Congress in December 1862, he had eloquently defined the need for Americans to "think anew and act anew" in order to "rise with the occasion" in bearing an historic responsibility, in "the fiery trial through which we pass," either to "nobly save or meanly lose the last, best hope of earth." (Jefferson's phrase, "best hope," was less desperate.) The specific context of his rhetoric was a plan, addressed largely to the border states, for federally compensated emancipation to be voluntarily carried out at the state level sometime before the end of the century. The plan had no takers, but Lincoln stated then a rationale that the Emancipation Proclamation would make explicit and official a month later: "In giving freedom to the slave, we assure freedom to the free— honorable alike in what we give and what we preserve."[53] After the Proclamation, "an act of justice" executed by executive authority as a military measure, Lincoln immediately encouraged the use of blacks in the Northern armies. He wrote Andrew Johnson, the military governor of Tennessee, that the "colored population is the great available and yet unavailed force for restoring the Union."[54] No longer did he propose plans for colonizing free Negroes.

His memorable eloquence at Gettysburg asserted that the dead would not have died in vain if the living were "dedicated" to "a new birth of freedom." Lincoln's use of "proposition" and "dedication" for Jefferson's "We hold these truths to be self-evident," points to the dynamic element in Lincoln's revision of the traditional theme. Equality is a task, not just an axiom or premise. To see it that way is to see how the Declaration of Independence can be regenerated.[55]

Lincoln, in his debates with Douglas, had cited Jefferson's confession (in *Notes on the State of Virginia*) that "he trembled for his country when he remembered that God was just."[56] Increasingly, in his reflections on the meaning of the Civil War, Lincoln resorted to similar biblical idiom. It seemed to him that God must have willed the contest and willed it to continue for his own reasons. Perhaps this idea helped diminish his sense of his own responsibility for consolidating sectional division over the territorial question of slavery. At any rate, the idea did not diminish the vigor of Lincoln's practical, political, and successful efforts to use his canniness to lobby for the Thirteenth Amendment, making the end of slavery a constitutional matter. He took pride in the fact that some one hundred and thirty thousand black soldiers fought for the Union cause, as the eventual result of the Emancipation Proclamation, but he also knew that he did not control events as much as they controlled him. Responding in a letter to a Kentuckian, who was indignant that slaves should serve in the armed forces, Lincoln pointed to the irony of history. No party or person had anticipated the nation's new condition: "God alone can claim it." If God willed that both sides should pay "for our complicity" in the wrong of slavery, then it was new evidence for "the justice and goodness of God."[57]

Lincoln struck this religious note more poetically, more elaborately, and more solemnly almost a year later in his second inaugural address, the best expression of his political religion. In it Lincoln finds it strange that any Confederates should have prayed to God for help in "wringing their bread from the sweat of other men's faces," but the prayers of neither side have been fully answered, for "the Almighty has His own purposes." Yet, if we supposed that slavery was an offense, paid for by the application of "this terrible war," the accounting would still be the righteous judgment of a just God. That would be true, Lincoln asserted, indicating the enormity that faith would require us to believe, even if He willed the war to continue until the wealth lost would be equal to the bondsman's two hundred and fifty years of "unrequited toil," or until every drop of blood drawn by whipping slaves would be paid for by another "drawn with the sword." With this utterly chilling possibility dealt with, Lincoln turned to encourage his listeners to finish the work, with charity and firmness, and "to bind up the nation's wounds."[58]

"Lacking Jefferson's education," Robert N. Bellah has written about Lincoln, "he was more deeply educated. His three greatest teachers were the two texts that shaped the consciousness of Americans in those days, the Bible and Shakespeare, and Jefferson himself."[59] The rhetoric of the great Bach-like coda to Lincoln's second inaugural address is in some respects reminiscent of Jefferson's rhetoric in his letter to a French correspondent, advising him how to write about the failure of Virginia to include provision for gradual emancipation, at a time when Jefferson was absent on the legation to France. His advice used the religious language of a patient awaiting of an "overruling providence" to deliver "our suffering brethren" when "the measure of their tears shall be full, when their groans shall have involved heaven itself in darkness." Then "a god of justice will awaken to their distress" either by "diffusing light & liberality among their oppressors, or at length by his exterminating thunder" show his attention to "things of this world."[60]

Jefferson, with his sanguine temperament, was more inclined to imagine the former alternative, but Lincoln, with his melancholic temperament, was less inclined to think that slaveholders would respond to light and liberality. He did overestimate their Union sentiment and also their willingness in the border states to emancipate during the war. But events taught him more harshly than they did Jefferson, who died shortly before the hardening of the sectional antagonism. Jefferson could not know that the "exterminating thunder" would be the Civil War, which Lincoln finally came to diagnose, as in a glass darkly, through the idiom of the Presbyterian church where he often attended. It was a divine affliction for the offense of slavery. Jefferson had been inclined to fear that the convulsion would be a race war between slaves and masters.

Lincoln's Jefferson was edited for Lincoln's political purposes. It was the exact opposite of the scurrilous forgery (which he exposed) of his supposed speech ridiculing Jefferson as a statesman who "dreampt of freedom in a slave's embrace."[61] Lincoln's version of Jefferson left out the Virginian who in his draft of the Kentucky Resolutions in 1798 wrote that "every State has a natural right" to be the judge "in the last resort" of the powers exercised under the "compact" among the "co-States" and in the case where "powers are assumed which have not been delegated, a nullification of the act is the rightful remedy."[62] Jefferson's nullifying ordinance, later to be tempered by Madison's Virginia Resolutions, was developed as a protest against the repressive legislation of the Alien and Sedition Laws, Federalist measures violating freedom of speech and immigration. When South Carolina led the movement for secession, based on the theory of state sovereignty, however, it did so because of the election of a President whose opinions and purposes, it protested, were hostile to slavery. Jefferson's tactics and constitutional theory were thus deployed against a President for whom Jefferson's idealism had always been a source of inspiration in the campaign to contain slavery and set it on the long road to extinction.

As a result of South Carolina's expansion of the nullifying principle into secession, Lincoln became the major opponent of Jefferson's constitutional theory. Lincoln would insist as President that the Union is "perpetual" and is "much older than the Constitution," being formed in 1774 when the Continental Congress pledged to cease all importations from and exportations to Britain, to institute nonconsumption of British products, and to discontinue the slave trade. It followed from his nationalist's view that "no State upon its own mere motion can lawfully get out of the Union."[63]

Jefferson might well have been astonished to discover his greatest legatee in this wartime role. Jefferson did not rule out a state deciding "*to stand to our arms*" against the federal government if it should act without any limitation on its powers, but would he have seen what South Carolina saw in the election of the man who venerated Jefferson's name? Jefferson in 1825, at least, was willing to use the amending process so that Congress could have the right "to make roads and canals of intercommunication between the States," precisely the program that Lincoln's Whig mentor Henry Clay called "the American system."[64] How far Jefferson's practical acquiescence in the Southern slave system would have taken him thirty years later, when Lincoln became his champion as an antislavery Republican, is impossible to know.

What Lincoln made of Jefferson, however, is surely one of the most remarkable relationships in American culture between one man and his hero. Ironically, it was the man who revered Jefferson as the source of his own political idealism who would preside over the sectional war that his hero feared, the liberation of the slaves, and the end of the policy of deportation (which he, like Jefferson, had formerly endorsed). No wonder that Lincoln, looking the irony of history full in the face, could say of the War's outcome: "Only God can claim it."

Chapter 10

"Working on the Circumstances": Twain's Huck, Faulkner's Chick, and the Negro

HOWELLS wrote a campaign biography of Lincoln, and the novelist's highest praise for his friend Mark Twain was to call him "the Lincoln of our literature." A more appropriate title might have been "the Franklin of our literature," but the highest tribute was paid by William Faulkner. "In my opinion," Faulkner said, "Mark Twain was the first truly American writer, and all of us since are his heirs; we descended from him."[1] Faulkner would prove it in his own case by writing a novel in which Twain's masterpiece would be the point of departure.

Lincoln spoke of the printing shop as "the poor man's college," and Twain shared that education with Benjamin Franklin, with whom he felt an affinity, disguised by humor. Twain's career as a humorist began with his first after-dinner speech, given in 1856 at a printers' banquet celebrating Franklin's 150th anniversary. Like Franklin, Twain worked for his brother in editing a newspaper and, chafing at his situation, left home at approximately the same age as Franklin did. Twain's brother Orion was a devotee of Franklin's memoir, and he sprinkled his maxims throughout his newspaper. Twain ridiculed both his brother and the adages, but his comic sketch "The Late Benjamin Franklin," while complaining that his maxims were "calculated to inflict suffering upon the rising generation of all subsequent ages," also makes an audacious link between Franklin and himself. Making fun of the conflicting claims about Franklin's birthplace in Boston, Twain's sketch begins: "He was twins, being born simultaneously in two different houses in the city of Boston." Twinning is built into the Twain pseudonym and the themes of many of his stories, and he makes the connection explicit in the last line of his sketch. Complaining that his father made his son do everything "just as Franklin did, in the solemn hope" that he "would be a Franklin some day," Twain ends his piece by saying: "And here I am."[2] Like Franklin, Twain was hostile to Protestant sectarianism, endorsed republicanism, and was fascinated with technology. He also much enjoyed living in Europe and nevertheless became, like Franklin, a representative culture hero in the American grain. The biographer of Twain's Hannibal years fittingly concludes by observing that if Twain's wit could be as corrosive and alienated as Jonathan Swift's, Twain's humor could be as sympathetic and homely as Franklin's. The man from Missouri "partook of both natures."[3]

Franklin's innovative contribution to American writing is marked by his thoroughly secular form of memoir. Twain's distinctive achievement is the tour de force of a novel written entirely and consistently in the autobiographical vernacular voice of a lower-class, unrespectable orphan, who is as humorously candid as he is sensitive to sorrow and suffering. Faulkner was himself close to Twain's Southwestern tradition of humor. Very early in his career, Faulkner asserted that "we have one priceless universal trait, we Americans. That trait is our humor. What a pity it is that it is not more prevalent in our art."[4] When asked by a student many years later to name the greatest American novel, Faulkner mentioned both *Moby Dick* and *Huckleberry Finn,* the first being "an attempt that didn't quite come off," because it was so ambitious, the latter being "a complete controlled effort."[5]

During the writing of *Huckleberry Finn,* Twain conceived of a plot in which Jim would be falsely accused of a crime and later cleared. Twain later elaborated the idea in his unfinished manuscript, "Tom Sawyer's Conspiracy."[6] A variation of this conceit was the germ of Faulkner's *Intruder in the Dust* (1948). Explaining that he had been thinking about detective stories, he added: "And I thought of an idea for one would be a man in jail about to be hung would have to be his own detective, he couldn't get anybody to help him. Then the next thought was, the man for that would be a Negro."[7] Moreover, shortly before he began writing *Intruder in the Dust* Faulkner was outlining an idea for another story involving a young boy, a white man, an old black servant, and a stolen race horse. It would be, he said, "a sort of Huck Finn."[8] (The story was delayed until in 1962 he published *The Reivers.*) The boy, the old man, and a horse are recombined, however, for *Intruder in the Dust,* and it reads like an updating of Twain's greatest novel.[9] In both stories, which draw on the detective-story form, a white boy helps a black man to escape from being unjustly punished by the law. In both tales, the boy heroes come to act against their received prejudices about blacks. As is usual in updating, Faulkner's novel, however, is revisionary of Twain's classic in both form and content.

Twain's structure is loosely strung out in space, defined by the vicissitudes of a river journey and the alternation between events on the shore and on the river, to which the escaping boy and Negro return again and again, until their escape is finally grounded at the Phelps farm in southern Arkansas. The element of time enters into the novel in terms of its authentic historical setting, sometime between 1835 and 1845. Huck himself, however, is oriented toward the present moment as a matter of survival. The widow Douglas, who adopted Huck, in reading to him about Moses may possibly compare herself to Pharaoh's daughter, who discovered Moses as a baby floating on the Nile in a basket of bulrushes, but Huck himself characteristically loses all interest when he discovered that Moses has been dead "a considerable long time," for Huck "don't take no stock in dead people." He wants to know who shot the man he and Jim find in the abandoned boat (Jim doesn't tell him until almost the end of the book that it's Huck's father, pap), but his curiosity doesn't go further back than his own adventures.

His future has only a slightly further horizon, being defined by their need to get to the free states "and then be out of trouble," but once they drift past Cairo in the fog this goal becomes unrealizable as they move deeper into slave territory. At the end of the novel, when Jim has been set free by Miss Watson in her will, making Tom's fantastic "evasion" plan even more absurd than it has already seemed, Huck's future is very short-range. It is formed by his willingness to be complicit with Tom's romantic idea of going "for howling adventures amongst the Injuns, over in the Territory, for a couple of weeks or two." That future looks even less defined or promising when Huck's aversion to Aunt Sally's plan to adopt and civilize him persuades him that he must "light out for the Territory ahead of the rest."

Nothing he has shown us about the hypocrisy, violence, sentimentality, and cruelty of life along the shore, however, gives us any basis for criticizing his decision. His only regret about leaving shore life is felt when he sees the flash of Mary Jane Wilks's light in her window, spied as he is running away, and his heart "swelled up sudden, like to bust." Huck says he won't again tackle the trouble of writing a book, and it is hard to imagine what sort of story he could have to tell. When his creator tried to tell it in "Huck Finn and Tom Sawyer among the Indians," he never finished the manuscript. Probably he recognized that it is an unpromising sequel. It is almost entirely lacking in the rich humor of *Huckleberry Finn*, and the sequel's view of the Indians is melodramatically simplistic and prejudiced in contrast to the novel's more complex portrait of Jim.[10]

The figure of Jim owes a debt to the minstrel tradition, as Ralph Ellison has pointed out, and it is from "behind this stereotype mask that we see Jim's dignity and human capacity— and Twain's complexity— emerge."[11] The character oscillates between having adult capacities for intelligence, self-respect, parental caring, and courage, on the one hand, while seeming, on the other hand, even more comically ignorant and superstitious than Huck. This problem merges with the much-discussed issue of the ending with Tom Sawyer's bookishly derived, humiliating, and cruel scheme for "freeing" Jim at the Phelps farm, when Tom knows that Miss Watson has already freed him in her will. How do we explain Huck's acquiescence in this absurdity when he has earlier come to see Jim as a beloved friend? In the great scene of his crisis of conscience Huck has even been willing to be damned, as his Southern conscience tells him he will be, for helping a fugitive slave. And how can we account for Jim's enthusiastic praise, in retrospect, for Tom's "beautiful" and "splendid" plan of "freeing" him by victimizing him?

One critic has gone to the extent of rewriting the story to take account of the critics' objections, making the lower-class characters more credibly profane, giving Huck sexual feelings, and changing the ending: Jim, escaping from the Phelps to whom he has been sold, drowns with the weight of his chains, as Huck fails to paddle to him in time to rescue him. Tom and his plan are omitted and Huck is finally left bereft on the river, not much caring "if the goddamn sun never come up again." It sounds more like Hemingway than Twain—including this possible allusion to *The Sun Also Rises*. John Seelye himself acknowledges the drawbacks of his revision, which is impressive in its linguistic rendering of Huck's character, when in his introduction he has Huck say that this version is "for crickits. And now that they've got *their* book, maybe they'll leave the other alone."[12] Comedy's idea of a return to prosaic muddle is better served by the ending of the original version; and Twain's calling Tom's scheme an "evasion" has the virtue of being a figure for what was happening nationally in the 1880s to black freedom. The Supreme Court of the United States was well on its way to emasculating by racist interpretation the three Civil War amendments that promised new freedoms to the blacks. Tom's idea of "freeing" an already "freed" black man suggests how much genuine freedom has been evaded by the victory of the North.

Faulkner, in talking about J. D. Salinger's *Catcher in the Rye* as a sort of contemporary *Huckleberry Finn,* spoke of Huck in 1958 as "another youth already father to what will some day soon now be a man." Faulkner believed that in time Huck would be "as big as any man he had to cope with"; the human race "was accepting him already; all he needed was just to grow up in it." By contrast, Salinger's character was contemporary in being compelled to exist in isolation, "not to pursue in myriad company the anguishes and hopes of all human hearts in a world of a few simple comprehensible truths and moral principles, but to exist alone inside a vacuum of facts which he did not choose and cannot cope with and cannot escape from like a fly inside an inverted tumbler."[13]

Faulkner's description of Huck tells us more about the protagonist of *Intruder in the Dust,* Charles (Chick) Mallison, than it does about Huck. In the same year that Faulkner published *Intruder,* Lionel Trilling wrote an introduction to *Huckleberry Finn,* arguing in terms similar to Faulkner's that Huck is "involved in civilization up to his ears" and that "responsibility is the very essence of his character," so that it is pertinent that the original of Huck, Tom Blankenship, grew up to become a justice of the peace in Montana, a good and respected citizen. Huck's adventures are entwined with civilization and his warm-hearted sympathies frequently do put him "in a sweat" about the predicament of other people, whether they are friends or enemies. Even so, Huck illustrates better Trilling's quite different point, made three years later, that while Huck in his "isolate freedom" sees much of ordinary life, including its seamy side, and can judge and even forgive it, he "can never be part of it." Indeed, Huck in this sense has come to represent Trilling's theory about "desocialized" American literature, just as Kipling's Kim, for whom ancestry represents destiny and who gladly works for the Indian Secret Service, represents by contrast the English social novel, which takes it for granted that becoming a member of society is "possible, fascinating, and desirable."[14]

Faulkner's young hero in *Intruder* is much closer to Kim and to Faulkner's idea of Huck than he is to Twain's character. Faulkner makes the contrast with Huck almost explicit by speaking about Chick's checking his "first instinctive impulse" to flee, to jump on his horse and ride "as the crow flies into the last stagger of exhaustion," because he was a person "who now simply because he happened not to be an orphan had not even that escape." By exposing the town's inclination to lynch an innocent black, Chick had "brought into the light and glare of day something shocking and shameful out of the whole white foundation of the county," but he knew that it is a shame "he himself must partake of too since he was bred of it." Chick realizes that his criticism of the local people's intolerance is all the sharper "since they were his own and he wanted no more save to stand with them unalterable and impregnable: one shame if shame must be . . . one heart one land." He sees himself as a product of his ancestry, having been shaped for six generations into "a specific man" with the "specific passions and hopes and convictions and ways of thinking and acting of a specific kind and even race"—a process that even includes "whatever it was that had compelled him to stop and listen to a damned highnosed impudent Negro."[15]

This self-conscious awareness of his Southern past and of his voluntary identification with the Southern people is quite different from Huck's involuntary unself-conscious reflection of his region's racial prejudices. Precocious in Chick, such awareness is, of course, a profound trait of Faulkner himself, and we are thus reminded by this difference between the two fictional characters of the difference between the two creators. Twain deserted the Confederacy after two weeks in the militia and fled to the Territories, where he became secretary to his brother, and never returned to live in Missouri. Faulkner, however, devoted his mature life to living in Oxford, Mississippi, and made of his "little postage stamp of native soil" an inexhaustible resource, as he memorably put it, for "sublimating the actual into the apocryphal."[16]

This sense of regional identity in Faulkner's hero is inextricably linked with an historical consciousness entirely lacking in Huck. By the third paragraph of Faulkner's story we are moved back four years, when Chick was rescued by Lucas from drowning in the river and given the hospitality of a dinner. It engenders in Chick a troubling sense of indebtedness to a black man who is too proud to let the boy repay him in any way. The proud independence of Lucas, so unlike most local blacks, threatens Chick's sense of his "masculinity and his white blood," and the burdensome obligation eventually drives him to accept Lucas's request to prove false the murder charge against him by engaging in a highly dangerous violation of a white man's grave. We are also privy to Chick's imagining himself and Lucas in the far future as "old men meeting" and recalling the long-ago scene of embarrassment when Lucas refused the boy's money. Chick imagines that he has turned the other cheek by forgetting his anguished need for "reaffirmation of his masculinity and his white blood," that Lucas has accepted the gesture, and that now Chick is free of the debt.[17] Chick's consciousness thus extends much further backwards and forwards in time than Huck's does.

The techniques of the two novels reflect this difference. Twain's achievement is stunning in creating the sound of Huck's voice and in generating the story out of it and the boy's vision of things. That is why Hemingway and Faulkner have saluted Twain. Faulkner's novel is narrated by an authorial voice, though it only relates events that Chick experiences or has heard about. If we are given, for example, a dramatized event that demonstrates Lucas's pride in being the grandson of a white McCaslin, an old family, rather than descending from the "new folks," the Edmonds, we are told that it is a local story, which Chick heard. But the vocabulary and rhetoric of this narrator are Faulkner's, because the syntax is much too complicated and the words often too abstract to be credible as Chick's. Even though we can believe that Chick's embarrassment at Lucas's refusal of Chick's coins could become for him a symbol, "fixed at last forever in the black vault of his anguish like the last dead and waneless moon and himself, his own puny shadow gesticulant and tiny against it in frantic and vain eclipse," we cannot believe in his use of that language.[18]

Sometimes the famous Faulkner parentheses will interrupt a single sentence for two full pages; sometimes there will be parentheses within parentheses. The simplicity and directness of Huck's narrating are conspicuously absent. Sometimes Faulkner's parentheses, however, serve his remarkable sense of the past, as when Chick and his uncle are led by the jailor who is about to open a heavy oak door. Before he can do so a parenthesis intervenes to tell us that it has a modern padlock but handwrought iron bars and hinges that are over a hundred years old. Their antiquity occasions a page of parenthesis about an incident when a drunk visitor from New York drives through a window, is jailed at his own request, and then goes to extraordinary lengths to try to buy the jail's door. Faulkner only then completes the sentence about opening the door.

This parenthetical comedy is a reminder of the mixture of present and past in the town itself and in the larger story that the novel is telling; and the fascination of the Northern outsider with the Southern past is relevant to a much later discussion between Chick and his uncle about the sectional differences between North and South. The Northerner perceives the Southerner as a kind of quaint relic, a museum piece rather than the member of a living community.

Chick has the advantage over Huck not only of having civilized parents, but also of having a mentor in Gavin Stevens, a bachelor lawyer with degrees from Harvard and Heidelberg. Huck's father is a vicious bigoted drunk, and his son fakes his own murder to escape him. The only thing he ever learned from his father, Huck tells us, is that "the best way to get along with his kind of people is to let them have their own way."[19] Tom Sawyer can only initiate Huck into a grotesquely Quixotic style of juvenile adventures. It is left to Jim to teach Huck that people who try to make a fool of a friend with a lie, as Huck once did to Jim, are "trash." Throughout the story, Huck keeps assuming different names as a disguise, but there's some identity confusion in this habit, for when Mrs. Phelps mistakes him for Tom Sawyer, Huck says: "It was like being born again, I was so glad to find out who I was."[20]

Chick's sense of self is sponsored by his mentor. Ever since the boy can remember, he had felt "a blind and absolute attachment to his mother's only brother," for whom he does errands as "an intimation of his willingness to carry some of his own weight." It is his uncle who tells him about moral values: "Some things you must never stop refusing to bear. Injustice and outrage and dishonor and shame." Stevens also inculcates a Southern consciousness in his nephew by reminding him that the moment before Pickett's doomed charge on Cemetery Ridge in July 1863 at Gettysburg is still recallable to any Southern boy, as if it has not yet happened and might even this time be successful, because "It's all *now* you see."[21] Faulkner's historical sense is singular because it tends to dissolve the differences between all the tenses. As he once explained: "That time *is,* and if there's no such thing as *was,* then there is no such thing as *will be.*"[22]

Despite these profound differences between Chick and Huck, the similarity of their nicknames is not misleading, for their stories do overlap. There is a lynch mob in both novels as well as a mystery about a murdered man (pap and Vinson Gowrie); and just as Tom joins Huck in the "evasion" scheme of "freeing" Jim, Chick has a companion in the black boy Aleck Sander for the grave-digging adventure on Lucas's behalf. More importantly, the two white boys are linked by their coming to understand the humanity of the black men whom they undertake to defend. When his uncle tells him that Lucas lost his wife Molly a year ago, Chick with surprise realizes then, as he had not before, that Lucas was grieving then on the day of the rescue and *"you don't have to not be a nigger in order to grieve."*[23] Similarly, Huck is surprised to discover that Jim is homesick for his wife and children, grieving "just as much for his people as white folks does for their'n." Just as Huck can express pity even for the rapacious king and duke when they are being tarred and feathered, so can Chick recognize that even "a violent foulmouthed godless old man" whose son has been murdered can be grieving.

Twain's novel tends to see the corruption of natural feelings in the influence of civilization, though he notably does not sentimentally stack the cards by ignoring or slighting either the river's harsh dangers or the mean corruption in his low-caste characters—pap, the duke, and the king. Faulkner's version of this suspicion of culture is to make it clear that Chick and Aleck can find an ally only in an old white woman, Miss Habersham, born in the same week as Lucas's Molly and suckled with her at her mother's breast. Miss Habersham explains that "Lucas knew it would take a child—or an old woman like me: someone not concerned with probability, with evidence," to believe the improbable assertion that it was not Lucas's pistol that had killed Vinson Gowrie. The menfolks, as old Ephraim explains, aren't suited for *"something outside the common run"* because *"they works on the rules and the cases,"* while the women and children *"works on the circumstances."*[24] Their more intuitive responses can prove Lucas innocent.

A curious overlap between the two books is that both have aroused much criticism for their endings. There is nothing in Faulkner's book like the absurdity of Tom's "evasion" plan; Chick's adventure pays off in proving that Lucas is innocent of the murder and by leading to the discovery of the fratricide. The problem with *Intruder in the Dust* has to do with the space given to Gavin Stevens's political harangues about the contemporary race problem in relation to sectional division in America. To some critics it turns Stevens into Faulkner's mouthpiece for a self-serving propagandistic sectionalism, like the "Dixiecrat" ideology that led governor Strom Thurmond and others to bolt the Democratic Party

Convention in 1948 because of its strong stand on civil rights. Stevens is certainly long-winded and tendentious, sometimes just pompously didactic. But it is a mistake to see his rationale as simply Dixiecrat; though it overlaps in some respect with that ideology, it also is sharply different from it. Moreover, Chick resists some of his uncle's theorizing, and Faulkner himself has made it clear, outside his novel, that he does not always endorse Stevens, even though there is some agreement between them.

Faulkner said about him: "Well, he had got out of his depth. . . . When he had to deal with people, he was an amateur, he was—at times he had a good deal less judgment than his nephew did."[25] When Chick's uncle rambles on about how the American loves nothing but his automobile, which has become a national sex symbol, American wives having projected their libido on to it because it will not get them sweaty, Chick simply says: "That's not true." When his uncle elaborates further, saying few of the women he has known were interested in love or sex, his nephew again sensibly replies: "I still don't believe it." His uncle then changes his tune: "That's right. Don't. And even when you are fifty and plus, still refuse to believe it."[26]

It is quite another matter, however, with respect to the uncle's views on sectional, as opposed to sexual, matters. He is Dixiecrat in rejecting Northern interference in the South through federal legislation on civil rights, but his reasons are his creator's not those of Governor Strom Thurmond and others who walked out of the convention. Stevens does talk about the virtues of homogeneity, but he grants them to the blacks as well. He proposes a utopian and partisan solution in which blacks and whites would "confederate": The white would give the black long-overdue economic and political rights in return for "the reversion of his capacity to wait and endure and survive. Then we would prevail; together we would dominate the United States."[27] Chick himself is described as sharing with his uncle a lack of kinship with the North because of its eagerness "to believe anything about the South not even provided it be derogatory but merely bizarre enough and strange enough." His uncle concedes (in spite of using the denigrating stereotype) that he does not "*know Sambo well,*" but he claims to know that the white man in the South and elsewhere as well will, when faced with federal intervention, "*grasp this opportunity to vent on Sambo the whole sum of their ancestral horror and scorn and fear of Indian and Chinese and Mexican and Carib and Jew.*" He portentously warns‘ *"History is showing us that the anteroom to dissolution is division."*[28] There is no indication that Chick does not swallow this gospel whole, because he has said about his uncle's sense of yesterday, today, and tomorrow being indivisible that in this too his mentor had anticipated Chick's own conclusion, as "his uncle had everything else which as he himself became more and more a man he had found to be true."[29]

His uncle engages in moral casuistry with Chick when the boy is overwhelmed with shame at the mob's running away when they realized that a white brother has killed his brother. Shame at almost lynching an innocent Negro had nothing to do with it. Stevens lectures Chick on the mob's running from its shame, much as Colonel Sherburn lectures the crowd in *Huckleberry Finn.* Chick finds it too legalistic and accuses his uncle of making excuses for the community's legal defenselessness against lynching, but his uncle explains that he is defending "Sambo" from the legalistic outlanders who fail to realize that the South must expiate and abolish its own injustice itself without any help or advice from outlanders.

But this solution is quite inconvincing. Stevens himself later points out that it was the unlikely and unusual coalition of Chick, Aleck Sander, and Miss Hasbersham, who were "willing to be more than grieved and shamed," that took concrete and dangerous steps to act on the belief in Lucas's innocence.[30] Faulkner's plot tends to subvert the uncle's ideology, as national events soon would do as well. Faulkner himself, speaking in 1958, conceded that "the Negro is now in motion toward more equality and he's got a lot of white folks and government bureaus and courts behind him . . . outside forces helping him move forward." Southerners would have to "either use it, direct it, or let it run over" them.[31] Faulkner had a lot of trouble choosing the first word of his novel's title. Perhaps he settled on *intruder* because it expressed his fear of those "outside forces," proposing a federal antilynching law, that would in time help the black move forward. Chick violated the sanctity of a grave in a good cause; so would the North intrude on the South.

Twain's emphasis on space over time in his best book did not prevent him from memorably exploring the American race problem in its historical context, specifically in its antebellum phase and metaphorically by implication in its postbellum phase. His next major work combined travel in space and time by sending a Yankee from Connecticut back into sixth-century England. In the end, however, his hero Hank Morgan has no more home in any territory, ancient or modern, than his author could imagine for Huck in Indian Territory. That is why Faulkner's historically self-conscious revision of Twain is much to the point—not only because it respects the Southern past (without being uncritical about it), but because it makes room for a hero with a possible responsible future. In actuality, the Southern future would not be what Chick's fancifully speculative uncle envisioned, and by 1958 Faulkner himself understood that "outside forces" were helping the black move toward more equality. But Chick knew, as Huck did not, that he would be a Southerner who someday would have to play a man's part in dealing with the injustice of American race relations.

Chapter 11

Invisible Men and Native
Sons in Wright and Ellison

IN OUR modern literature, the painfully acute sense of the contrast between the ideals of Jefferson and Lincoln, on the one hand, and the realities of race relations, on the other, finds its most moving voices among black writers. We have in the Negro, as Richard Wright put it, "the embodiment of a past tragic enough to appease the spiritual hunger of even a James; and we have in the oppression of the Negro a shadow athwart our national life dense and heavy enough to satisfy even the gloomy broodings of a Hawthorne."[1] Among our classic nineteenth-century writers, Harriet Beecher Stowe, Melville, and Twain appreciated the truth of Wright's observation. Just after the turn of the century a pioneer Negro novelist, Charles Waddell Chesnutt, in *The Marrow of Tradition,* cast a shadow forward to more modern writers on race relations by his dramatization of the humiliating impact of Jim Crow laws on a middle-class black family and his exposure of the politics behind an actual race riot, instigated in 1898 by white supremacists, in Wilmington, North Carolina. Even more prophetically, Chesnutt drew a portrait of a defiant and proud working-class black man, Josh Green, who takes revenge at the price of his own death for the racially motivated murder of his father. Chesnutt's novel, though praised by Howells, failed economically—not surprisingly, for it was published in 1901 when President Roosevelt created a furor by inviting Booker T. Washington to the White House.

Richard Wright's *Native Son* and his autobiography *Black Boy* found in the 1940s the first wide and respectful national audience for a black writer. His success was followed early in the next decade by Ralph Ellison, a beneficiary of Wright's friendship and sponsorship. The complex affinities and differences between *Native Son* and Ellison's *Invisible Man* parallel the strong crosscurrents in their personal relationship. It has been difficult to see them in perspective because Ellison, until recently, has strongly emphasized the differences between them, and black politics has also tended to make an invidious distinction in reverse between them. A poll of black writers in 1968, for example, cited Wright as the most important black American writer and put Ellison in fourth place—a ranking that no literary analysis by itself could sustain.[2] Ellison was, unfortunately, either suspected or stridently scorned by militant black separatists in the 1960s, until the man who led the charge against him reversed his field at the beginning of the next decade and rediscovered Ellison as the author of "one of the world's most successful 'political' novels."[3]

Ellison's entrance into our literary life, as he has readily acknowledged, was enabled by the generosity of Wright. Ellison's reading of a poem by Wright in the *New Masses* led him to search out Wright in New York, and a meeting was arranged in 1937 through the help of the black poet Langston Hughes. Ellison was privileged to read Wright's stories in his *Daily Worker* office before they were published and was encouraged by Wright to publish a book review and a short story in *New Challenge,* a short-lived black journal, which Wright edited. (Ellison was also best man at the wedding for Wright's equally short-lived first marriage in 1939 to a dancer of Russian-Jewish background). Both men participated in the Federal Writers Project. "Richard Wright's Blues," Ellison's review of Wright's autobiography, paid him tribute in 1945 by lamenting the absence in America of any "social or political action based upon the solid realities of Negro life depicted in *Black Boy*."[4]

In a debate with Irving Howe in *The New Leader* nearly a decade later, however, Ellison tensely expressed resentment of Howe's idea that Wright's "harsh naturalism" had by its courageous anger enabled Ellison and James Baldwin to move toward "more supple forms of fiction."[5] Ellison insisted that he had his own anger and his own way of expressing it, and he did not want to be stretched upon Howe's Procrustean bed of a certain kind of "clenched-fist" militancy. Ellison was then anxious to insist that Wright was "no spiritual father" of his and that instead he had "simply stepped around him." The stepping was rather like a boxer's footwork, however, for Ellison also insisted that his own stories and essays were "implicitly, criticisms of Wright's; just as all novels of a given historical moment form an argument over the nature of reality and are, to an extent, criticisms each of the other."[6]

Wright educated himself in modernist writers—Proust, Joyce, Faulkner, Stein, Cummings, Eliot—but it was reading Sinclair Lewis and Theodore Dreiser that moved him to reflect: "All my life had shaped me for the realism, the naturalism of the modern novel, and I could not read enough of them."[7] Ellison's sense of literary kinship, by contrast, is with classic and modern symbolists. When Ellison accepted the National Book Award in 1953, he identified his novel's significance as representing both an "experimental attitude" and an attempt "to return to the mood of personal moral responsibility for democracy which typified the best of our nineteenth-century fiction."[8] The novel's epigraphs, one from T.S. Eliot's *Family Reunion* and the other from Melville's *Benito Cereno,* make his double-barrelled point.

Yet *Invisible Man* shares with Wright's *Native Son* (as well as with Melville's *Benito Cereno*) the central metaphor of black invisibility. Wright's antihero, Bigger Thomas, accidentally kills a white girl in the presence of her blind mother. Their name is Dalton, and Daltonism, as a medical term, is a kind of color blindness. Thinking in jail of his coming execution for the murder, Thomas tells his lawyer: "I'll be feeling and thinking that they didn't see me and I didn't see them."[9] Ellison's novel also is linked to Wright's (as well as to Dostoevsky's *Notes from Underground*) by the common use of another racial metaphor, the underground man, with its subversive associations to the slaves' Underground Railway and the modern ghetto with its underclass. Wright's story "The Man Who Lived Underground" (1942, 1944) foreshadows the final vantage point of Ellison's invisible man, who takes refuge, during a riot, under the streets. Wright's figure in the sewer has nightmare visions, papers his walls with money, and decorates them with stolen goods, until he is shot by the police. The tale's surreal texture is closer to Ellison's mode than it is to anything in Lewis or Dreiser.[10]

Both *Native Son* and *Invisible Man* by their absorption in the social destinies of their protagonists refute the Tocquevillean prophecy, so popular with critics in the 1940s and 1950s, that American literature would focus not on man in society but on "man himself, not tied to time or place, but face to face with nature and God." Yet, both novels also vividly illustrate Tocqueville's emphasis on mythicizing and symbolizing, which those critics found in our classic writing. Even though

Wright's story has a basis in the actual case of Robert Nixon in Chicago, the setting of the story is not memorably particularized. Like Poe's Gothicism—not the terror of Germany, but of the soul—Wright's novel focuses on Thomas as a symbol of insurgency against Jim Crow laws and of the dangerous potential in the black slums for totalitarian impulses present in the vast upheavals of Russia and Germany. Three years before publishing *Native Son,* Wright had written of the "body of [black] folk-lore, living and powerful, which rose out of a unified sense of common life and a common fate," and he had criticized any "simple literary realism" that would ignore the "revolutionary significance of these [black] nationalist tendencies."[11] The protagonist's life, however, is not shaped by these tendencies but rather by three abstract themes, used as headings to structure the novel: Fear, Flight, and Fate.

Ellison's story moves from a Southern college to Harlem, but the journey is a highly condensed and symbolic version of black history in America from the schools organized by white philanthropists during Reconstruction to the black exodus from the South after the First World War, from the black nationalism of Marcus Garvey in the 1920s to the depression of the 1930s, and on to the race riots during the Second World War. His hero's representative status is reflected in his lack of an individual name.

At a conference on Wright, held in 1971 at the University of Iowa, Ellison evaluated Wright much more positively than he had seven years earlier in his debate with Howe. No longer caught up in polemics, instigated by Howe's invidious comparisons, Ellison acknowledged that sharing his interests with Wright had been an exciting and inspiring experience, producing "something of that sense of self-discovery and exaltation which is implicit in the Negro church and in good jazz." Ellison indirectly acknowledged his kinship to Wright by placing him in Ellison's own tradition. He paid Wright his highest praise by situating him in a central American tradition of "nineteenth-century rhetoric with its emphasis upon freedom and individual responsibility, a rhetorical style which gave us Lincoln, Harriet Tubman, Harriet Beecher Stowe, . . . Frederick Douglass and John Jasper. . . . Richard Wright was a possessor of that tradition. It is resonant in his fiction and it was a factor in his eager acceptance of social responsibility." Ellison had told Howe that Wright had failed to show in his novel how black life could have produced a Richard Wright; but he asserted in 1971 that *Native*

Son was "one of the major literary events in the history of American literature."[12]

It was difficult earlier for Ellison to acknowledge his indebtedness to Wright when tendentious critics invidiously compared them at Ellison's expense, accusing him of aesthetic withdrawal from the racial struggle.[13] His articulate candor and clarity about who he is, artistically and personally, his sophisticated range of reference in both foreign and American literature, and his admirably stubborn refusal to jump on any band wagon, radical or conservative, made him suspect to blacks for whom militant separatism and a stress on the African cultural legacy were the only politically "correct" positions. Ironically, Wright escaped this suspicion and has been celebrated for the harshness of his portrait of white oppression, yet it was Wright (as Ellison pointed out) who condemned as shallow, hollow, unstable, and timid whatever he had seen in black culture of kindness, tenderness, passion, or joy.[14] He was a homeless radical and felt from inside his description of Bigger Thomas's fate as being "estranged from the religion and the folk culture of his race."[15] Wright's self-exile to Paris (where he was made an honorary citizen) and his journeys to other countries never healed the estrangement: "I have no race except that which is forced upon me. I have no country except that to which I'm obliged to belong. I have no traditions."[16]

Wright was in this way an invisible man, refusing to be defined by color, culture, or nation, while Ellison is a person with a deep sense of tradition that includes both blacks and whites—and their cultural interaction. It derives its strength from his profound and simple sense of being a native son: "I've been reading the classics of European and American literature since childhood, was born to the American tongue and to the language of the Bible and the Constitution; these, for better or worse, shaped my thoughts and attitudes and pointed the direction of my talent long before I became a conscious writer."[17] Ellison, contrasting himself with Wright, has spoken of having a "peripheral vision" that enables him to look at nonpolitical aspects of racial and national identity, such as sports, to appreciate "the changing nature of social hierarchy, and . . . the role which individual skill and excellence can play in creating social change."[18] His reading in Eliot and Pound had led him to see a connection between jazz and modern poetry. A jazz trumpeter himself, he points out that Wright (like his novel's protagonist Bigger Thomas) had no feel for black jazz, dance, or churches, the crucial keys for opening the gates into black culture. Ellison proudly identified himself with it in his unfashionable way when he said: "I also inherited a group style originated by a 'black' people, but it is Negro American, not African."[19]

Ellison acknowledged that geography made for a significant difference between himself and Wright, whose childhood was in Mississippi. Ellison's was in Oklahoma, which had no indigenous tradition of chattel slavery and "lacked many of the intensities of customs, traditions, and manners which 'colored' the institutions of the Old South, and which were important in shaping Wright's point of view."[20] Both Wright and Ellison lost their fathers early in life, but Wright's deserted his family. Wright's account of his personal experience is overwhelmingly bleak. The horror in his Gothic fictional scene of Bigger Thomas burning in the furnace Mary Dalton's decapitated corpse echoes the role of fire in Wright's own grim childhood. Imagery of burning dominates *Black Boy,* whether in the metaphorical meaning of sexual passion, destruction, punishment, or ambition. When at the age of four he attempted to burn down his grandmother's house, he was beaten nearly to death by his mother. Ellison, who had once clerked for the psychiatrist Harry Stack Sullivan, shrewdly noticed in Wright's autobiography a rejection of both his grandmother and his aunt, who might otherwise have compensated, in a matriarchal system, for the distrust that he felt for his invalided mother. "It was as though the mother's milk had turned acid, and with it the whole pattern of life."[21]

Ellison was able to take advantage of his background. His positive feelings left him with the ordinary American's distaste for "works of art that would strip human experience—especially American experience—of its wonder and stubborn complexity."[22] Ellison's narrator suggests Huck Finn in his vernacular vividness, candid innocence, and essential decency. Like Huck, he tells us that he has written this story that we are reading. Ellison has noted that the territory to which Huck was going to "light out" was Indian Territory, where fugitive slaves often went and which would become part of Oklahoma, where Ellison grew up. When he was presented in 1979 with the portrait of Dr. Inman E. Page, the first Afro-American to graduate from Brown University and later Ellison's high school principal, he remembered that he first met Page in Oklahoma Territory and became a pupil of his daughter, who taught classical music and owned a Negro theater, where Ellison learned about the vernacular tradition of Negro spirituals, jazz, and the blues.[23] Oklahoma's racial segregation did not prevent him from getting an education in the inter-mingling of classical and vernacular art.

These differences between Wright and Ellison have artistic conse-quences. Both *Native Son* and *Invisible Man* take as their premise the problem of transplanting the folk Negro to an urban industrial setting. But only Ellison extensively uses black Southern folklore as a resource for his hero's sense of identity.[24] A crucial example is when his emigrant from the South is being subjected to a kind of shock treatment in the factory hospital, a metaphor for the impact of rapid social change in the migration from the agrarian South to the urban industrial North. In a brilliant essay on Harlem's Lafargue Psychiatric Clinic, written in 1948, Ellison located the Harlem riots of 1935 and 1943 in the "free-floating hostility" generated in migrant blacks whose psychological character "arises from the impact between urban slum conditions and folk sensibili-ties." To live in Harlem is to live "in the very bowels of the city," a ruin often "indistinguishable from the distorted images that appear in dreams, and which, like muggers haunting a lonely hall, quiver in the waking mind with hidden and threatening significance." Surreal fantasies are acted out on the streets, yet if Harlem is "the scene of the folk-Negro's death agony, it is also the setting of his transcendence."[25] The essay says in prose what the novel dramatizes and elaborates in a symbolic way.

When the invisible man is grilled about his knowledge of Buckeye and Brer Rabbit, his "doctors" are pleased when he gives no outward sign of recognizing the references. They think he has been successfully brain-washed, but his tactical silence in response to their queries is one of the ways he preserves this memory of his childhood and his ties to his South-ern past as a basis for his identity. His transition to Harlem is mediated by the kindness of a familiar kind of black woman, Mary Rambo: "Nor did I think of Mary as a 'friend'; she was something more—a force, a stable, familiar force like something out of my past which kept me from whirling off into some unknown which I dared not face."[26] Later, when he is part of the radical Marxist Brotherhood in Harlem, a political colleague tries to dissuade him from his passionate defense of an evicted old couple, whose agrarian style of religion has made them familiar to him: "History has passed them by. . . . You have not completely shed that self, that old agrarian self, but it's dead and you will throw it off completely and emerge something new. *History* has been born in your brain."[27] But the hero's problem is to make the transition to a new state without repudiating in shame his Southern past, and the Brotherhood has no wisdom about how to negotiate that tricky turn in the road. Its leaders make fun of the hero's taste in food and music as signs of "Southern backwardness."

Native Son and *Invisible Man* are affiliated by a common theme—the struggle for a sense of identity, a selfhood closely related to an idea of freedom and culminating in a kind of second birth—an individual, existentialist version of the theme that Lincoln applied historically to the nation in his Gettysburg Address. Bigger Thomas experiences his second birth through his acceptance of responsibility for the murder of the white girl, thus turning what was actually an accident, stemming from his attempt to silence the girl when her mother appeared, into someting voluntary. Otherwise his life would only be that of a rat in a trap. What prevents the novel from succumbing to the threat of becoming a piece of journalistic sensationalism is its provocative and unconventional ending in which Bigger's Communist friends are baffled by his second birth.

He gains "a new sense of the value of himself" from talking with his Jewish lawyer, Max, who wants to know how Thomas interprets his crime and his fate. If Max can see "the man in him beneath those wild and cruel acts of his," Bigger reflects on their conversation, then Max could share Bigger's hate and he would no longer be an *isolato*. He has a momentary vision of standing in the midst of a crowd with the sun's rays melting away the many differences and drawing "what was common and good upward toward the sun." If he "reached out with his hands and touched other people," he wonders, "would there be a reply, a shock?"[28]

The ideology of his Communist friends, however, compels them to see him as a mere product of capitalist oppression. In his anxiety to stress the role of past history and present environment in the inevitable making of Bigger's hate, the lawyer (Max) at one point even drops into the same stereotyping that dominates the newspaper reports about Bigger. Max portrays him as an animal that "creeps from its lair and steals toward the settlements of civilization!" Yet at the same time, he argues that Bigger's acceptance of the crime as his own "made him free, gave him the possibility of choice, of action, the opportunity to act and to feel that his actions carried weight." In this observation he grasps Bigger's own new sense of himself, but Max also tries to convince the jury that Bigger's actions in killing the two women were "as instinctive and inevitable as breathing or blinking one's eyes," the inevitable consequence of fear and hate produced by white oppression.[29] In effect, he treats the white stereotype of "the bad nigger" as an historical reality, and the irony is compounded by the fact that it is the patronizing, amiable believers in crossing the color line, the Daltons, who have led him into the tangle of events that culminate in his killing of the daughter. "The irony is reduplicated," as Marcus Klein has said, "in the fact that this bad nigger is said to be a native son."[30]

In his last conversation with his client, Max loses his own sense of fellow feeling for Bigger when he expresses his new understanding of his act: "But what I killed for, I *am*! It must have been pretty deep in me to make me kill!"[31] Max, his eyes "full of terror," refuses to touch Bigger, who no longer has the status of an inevitable victim of amoral forces, as prescribed by Marxian dialectic. Given this turn in the story, it is not surprising that Wright would one day become a friend of the existentialist philosopher Jean Paul Sartre and write an explicitly existentialist novel, *The Outsider;* but in making its hero's color irrelevant, as Dan McCall has pointed out, he denied him "any cultural reality or individual coherence."[32]

The ending of *Native Son* reflects the ambivalence of Wright's own relationship to his party. The Communists are the only friends that Bigger has, but they do not really understand him as a person. Wright's artistic individualism made him persona non grata with the Communists, who in 1936 physically ejected him from a May Day parade. In *American Hunger,* his narrative of his troubles with the party (which was set in proof by 1944 but not fully published, for politicial reasons, until 1977), Wright's painful story makes it clear that it was the callous and bureaucratic disciplining of artists and intellectuals that led him regretfully to resign. He cited as party taboos not only the "heritage of free thought," but also the "Protestant ethic" of self-redemption for the believer "through his own acts." Yet, he was still under the spell of the Communist vision enough to think that the future of mankind would be marked by "the spirit of self-sacrifice" that he saw in one Communist believer who, in a local version of the Moscow Trials, pleaded guilty, for the sake of his political religion, to false accusations of disloyalty.[33]

Wright spoke in his introduction to *Native Son* about his having tried to imply the existence of some buried sense in Bigger Thomas of both an inarticulate black nationalism, and a taken-for-granted American idealism about the Constitution and the Bill of Rights. But Bigger's consciousness is much too primitive to communicate any real sense of this complexity. Wright leaves that work to the Communist lawyer's advocacy in court. He invokes Jefferson's language in the Declaration of Independence to indicate what American blacks are struggling for, but their exclusion from the achievement of liberty and happiness has made them, Max tells the jury, as necessarily subversive and threatening as Bigger himself.[34]

Ellison's hero might seem to make the same point in remembering his grandfather's deathbed advice to "overcome 'em with yeses, undermine 'em with grins, agree 'em to death and destruction, let 'em swoller you till they vomit or bust wide open." In the epilogue, however, the hero speculates about what his grandfather must have meant: "Could he have meant . . . that we were to affirm the principle on which the country was built . . . which they had violated and compromised to the point of absurdity even in their own corrupt minds . . . because we were the heirs who must use the principle because no other fitted our needs?"[35] Ellison's novelistic version of the tension between his hero and his Communist friends is a close cousin of Wright's example, but the upshot of the conflict is significantly different. The invisible man discovers that the Brotherhood, led by a man with a glass eye, has manipulated a black riot in order to get the black nationalist leader, Ras, blamed for it. The hero discards his Brotherhood identity as only the most recent of the many masks he has voluntarily put on during his odyssey, even though they all reflect somebody else's idea of him. The narrator comes instead to accept what the makers of his masks cannot recognize: "the beautiful absurdity of their American identity and mine."[36] He is really a native son.

The gap in understanding between the lawyer and his client is the "absurdity" in Wright's novel. Up until then, it has kept the liberal reader on familiar ground by making a case for the guilt of the white establishment in its eagerness to punish Bigger as a monster; and the liberal reader can appreciate the grim irony that Bigger is charged for a rape that he did not commit and a murder that he did not intend to do, while his rape and murder of a black girl go legally unrecognized. In this sense, he is truly an invisible man. The reader is likely to be as startled, puzzled, and dismayed as Max is, however, by Bigger's identification with his act and his refusal to plead innocent on the grounds of its being an unintended accident. That is his only way of becoming visible to himself.

Ellison has his own version of Bigger's existentialist idea. It is expressed in the scene on the bus going North when a veteran, hospitalized for manic-depression and speaking in his role as Shakespearean clown and fool, tells the invisible man that "there's always an element of crime in freedom." Significantly, the veteran is the one who advises him to "play the game, but play it your own way" and "remember, the world is possibility if only you'll discover it."[37] These are the lessons that the narrator only comes to learn when he looks back in the epilogue on his recurring experience of having been taken in by appearances and his repeated failure to play the game on his own terms.

Ellison's critics have complained that he leaves his narrator paralyzed in confused ambivalence: "I condemn and affirm, say no and say yes, say yes and say no."[38] That is Ellison's way of responding to both the ideal of the Declaration of Independence and the fact of its contradiction: "In the beginning was not only the word but its contradiction; sometimes we approach life out of a tragic sense of necessity, and again with its denial."[39] It is easy to read Ellison's ending as a kind of withdrawal from history because his narrator in the novel identifies history with a particular (Marxist) version of it, one which the narrator comes to reject.

The invisible man is inclined to think that his life in the Brotherhood is "the only historically meaningful life" that he could live. But he eventually discovers that when class categories are absolute, as in principle (though not always in practice) they are in Communism, they leave no room for the reality of ethnic categories. History is then reduced to the Marxist vision that "freedom is the recognition of necessity" by those who plan its course. The hero eventually takes his inspiration instead from Rinehart, a black numbers runner, a womanizer, and bogus reverend, whose many roles negatively reveal his cynicism but positively suggest to the narrator the alternative idea that history might be "not only the recognition of necessity, it was the recognition of possibility." From this perspective (which William James called "tychism") the invisible man can find a basis for his earlier intuition that three zoot-suited young blacks whom he saw in the subway were potentially "the bearers of something precious" who might someday be history's "ace in the hole."[40] Clio, in this light, is more of a gambler, like Rinehart, than she is a political philosopher or scientist, in love with the idea of necessity.

The book ends with the narrator once again encountering, as he had in the beginning, a white man who does not recognize him. "Responsibility rests upon recognition," he had said in the prologue, "and recognition is a form of agreement."[41] The invisible man has been in hibernation, like Jack the Bear, as he puts it, because there has been no such public form of recognition and agreement. Therefore, there is no socially responsible current role for the narrator to play, as he shakes off his old skin and emerges from his hole, except to tell his story. But the strong implication is that, given mutual recognition by whites and blacks, the narrator would certainly become a visible man with a role to play. As a condensed history of black experience in America, Ellison's novel points toward the event that two years later in 1954 would represent a crucial national step in bringing about that mutual recognition: the historic decision of the Supreme Court of the United States to declare unconstitutional compulsory segregation by race in American public schools.

Even so, there is no *dramatization* of a responsible role for the invisible man any more than there is for Bigger Thomas, and they are both *isolatos* at the end with only a visionary hope of a better prospect in some unspecified future. In this respect, they are kin to Hester Prynne, Ishmael, and Huck Finn; but as an English critic, C. W. E. Bigsby, has remarked, "to be outside society is not to be immune to its claims. The special plight of the *isolato* is to be fully accountable to the world which excludes him."[42]

Bigger Thomas's wistful last word to his lawyer is "Tell Jan hello." Ellison's narrator, however, has no such comradely final feeling for any members of the Brotherhood, except for Brother Clifton, who by rejecting the Brotherhood has, like the subway zoot-suiters, plunged "outside of historical time." Yet the narrator retains his connection with historical time in an ideal form by grounding his hope as a native son on the principle of equality in the Declaration of Independence.

Ellison's novel moves beyond the limits of *Native Son* by making a positive use of black folklore in a poeticized, picaresque way and by making a decisive break with a color-blind form of political radicalism. Ellison also goes beyond Wright in creating a black protagonist who can tell his own story and interpret his own fate. These differences in technique and outlook are highly visible, but Ellison highlighted a subtle affinity between Wright and himself when he linked his predecessor, friend, and benefactor to the theme of individual responsibility. Though he did not spell it out in relation to *Native Son*, Ellison's point implicitly defines a way of reading it that, in spite of Wright's bitter exile, joins it to *Invisible Man* in a common American tradition. It is Ellison, of course, who is the reverent native son and the highly visible man, but his handsome tribute to Wright in 1971 repays a literary father by making a native son, in effect, out of Wright's terrifying portrait of Bigger Thomas's bloody second birth. "The central theme of black writing," as Bigsby has said, "is the recreation of the self and the community, the rebirth of the black Lazarus."[43]

Ellison in 1948 perceptively criticized Gunnar Myrdal's classic analysis of our race relations, *An American Dilemma,* for seeing American blacks too much as the creation of white men: "Men have made a way of life in caves and upon cliffs, why cannot Negroes have made a life upon the horns of the white man's dilemma?"[44] Black and white historians would much later come to see the force of Ellison's question, but it would be the civil rights movement that would dramatize it more forcefully than anything in *Invisible Man.* The novel could only define the problem of invisibility and the conditions for its becoming visibility. The movement would make the American black visible not as Wright's version of the stereotypical "bad nigger," but as Ellison's version of the native son.

Chapter 12

The Wise Man (Niebuhr), the Prophet (King), and Civil Disobedience

"IN THE beginning was not only the word," as Ellison has remarked in a discussion of the novel, "but the contradiction of the word." The great nineteenth-century novels of Hawthorne, Melville, James, and Twain, as Ellison read them, make it evident that "the moral imperatives of American life" are implicit in the Declaration of Independence, the Constitution, and the Bill of Rights. G. K. Chesterton, in a famous phrase for a similar point, referred to America as "a nation with the soul of a church." He recognized that the style of American nationality in principle emphasized ideological belief in the Constitution and the Bill of Rights as the mark of citizenship, even though blacks and women were effectively excluded until our century. This believers' style is analogous to the practice of the colonial Puritan churches in New England, who made membership depend upon the ability to give a persuasive account to the congregation of one's conversion experience. In these early American stories, as Patricia Caldwell has sensitively read them, the question of conversion is mixed up with the experience of migration, and they often express a sense of unexpected and troubling disappointment in the experience for finding themselves in "a strange foggy limbo of broken promises, where the human heart was felt to be 'dead and dull' "—a far cry from the biblical Promised Land that their preachers had taught them to expect.[1]

The Puritan confessions of conversion experience, as Caldwell observes, were not of value and efficacy in themselves, for these qualities were "not in the speech nor even in the speaker but in the joint action of speaker and audience—that is, in the words being spoken, heard, *and believed.*"² Since accepted accounts of conversion gained their narrators access not only to church membership but also to voting power in the politics of the Massachusetts Bay Colony, there was a political meaning to this joint action. Near the mid-eighteenth century a merger of religion and politics was eloquently exemplified in another way by the pietistic sermons of the Calvinist preachers in the Great Awakening. They spoke arousingly to large congregations in the building of a popular movement that nurtured lay people's power in the churches, Protestant pluralism of sects, and, eventually, the historic alliance contracted in Virginia between New Light pietistic Calvinists, whether Baptists or Presbyterians, and the rationalist republican leaders, Jefferson and Madison. Their joint efforts resulted by 1785 in the landmark Virginia Statute for Religious Freedom, legally separating the churches from their legal privileges. Paradoxically, for a purpose that would surprise and baffle contemporary American evangelicals, it took a long-fought political battle, endorsed by minority religious believers of a Calvinist persuasion, to make the rights of citizenship common to all sorts of religious believers and, in principle, to nonbelievers as well.³

The modern equivalent of the Great Awakening's emphasis on verbal expression and joint action of speaker and audience was the civil rights movement led by the Reverend Martin Luther King, Jr. On 28 August 1963, he stood with his back to the Jefferson and Lincoln memorials, facing the largest crowd ever assembled in Washington, and in the tone and temper of a pastor of the black Baptist church, evoking ardent vocal responses from his hearers, drew on the rhetoric of Jefferson, Lincoln, and the Bible on behalf of the rights of the black to full citizenship. It was one of the most memorably symbolic political moments in American history. While it did not have much impact on the legislative movement for a civil rights bill, nor deter President Kennedy's strategy of delaying debate on the bill until after the presidential election, the March on Washington involved leaders of the white churches in the cause, thus making a continuing and effective lobby for the bill. The remarkable dignity and discipline of the occasion helped allay the fears generated by the violent opposition to earlier protests of civil disobedience led by King.⁴

He was created politically by the movement before he helped to create it. As King's biographer David J. Garrow points out, the Montgomery boycott, the Atlanta sit-ins, and the Freedom Rides were alike in not being actions that King "sought out, not a protest he had instigated or planned, not an event that he was eager to be involved in."⁵ He simply accepted the burden of leadership that was thrust upon him because of his oratorical gifts and his intelligence. Moreover, the idea of civil disobedience as a strategy for American blacks was worked out, in principle but not in practice, many years before him by one of the American preachers who was most crucial to King's theological education: Reinhold Niebuhr.

Niebuhr was also a passionate preacher who applied his ideas to politics and whose pulpit oratory was intensely dramatic and stirring for his hearers. Both men had been enthralled by their fathers' service in the ministry, and they both grew up in religion without any wrenching crisis of disbelief or belief. "I have never experienced the so-called 'crisis moment,' " King remarked in a paper written for one of his teachers at Crozer Theological Seminary. "Religion has just been something that I grew up in. . . . The church has always been a second home for me." Niebuhr once told an interviewer: "I was thrilled by my father's sermons and regarded him as the most interesting man in our town. So what should I do but be a minister, in his image?"⁶ Their mutual scorn for the kind of religion that rationalized political complacency also linked them together. When President Nixon in 1969 invited the conservative revivalist Billy Graham to the White House Sunday services, Niebuhr compared the evangelist to Amaziah, the biblical king's chaplain who scorned the radicalism of Amos. Noting that Amos was King's favorite prophet, Niebuhr regretted that King was not alive to be invited to the White House, though he suspected that the FBI, which had spied on him, had the same opinion of him as Amaziah had of Amos. The pertinence of Niebuhr's cutting reference to the biblical story was ironically underscored when Nixon's aide, John Ehrlichman, thereupon asked the FBI for a report on Niebuhr.⁷

King was ill at ease with his middle-class privileges, celebrity, and public acclaim; and he struggled with a sense of inner conflict, which included his sexual infidelities.⁸ His recurring exhaustion and depression from his demanding political burdens paralleled Niebuhr's recurring anxiety and depressions, precipitated by a stroke suffered in 1952 that lamed his left side. Slowed down from his previous standard of vigorous political activity as a reformer, he was embarrassed that he could not live up to his widely cited prayer to be granted the serenity "to accept what cannot be changed," and at seventy-five he spoke of feeling instead an "anxious preoccupation with real or imagined future perils." He felt unworthy of his first biographer's praise and uneasy with the public adulation of him as a cultural sage: "I should have been allowed to end my days without anyone trying to make a 'prophet' out of me."[9]

Niebuhr had prophetically concluded in 1932 that "there is no problem of political life to which religious imagination can make a larger contribution than this problem of developing non-violent resistance." Secular imagination could not muster "the sublime madness which disregards immediate appearances and emphasizes profound and ultimate unities." These passages, looked at in retrospect, seem uncannily like a call for the Reverend Martin Luther King, Jr., who was then only three years old. Over thirty years later Niebuhr would declare: "The Negro church in the person of Dr. Martin Luther King has validated itself in the life of the Negroes and of the nation."[10] Niebuhr's prophecy was only a speculation; King carried it out in the dust and heat of political conflict and on a quite different basis: a comprehensive religious version of nonviolence as a way of life.

Niebuhr was a sympathetic but skeptical witness to the playing out in American history of this relationship between them. Their only recorded personal encounter was when King asked Niebuhr in 1957 to sign a petition for presidential intervention to carry out the Supreme Court's desegregation decisions, and Niebuhr, concerned about the role of moderate opinion in a resistant South, demurred on tactical grounds, believing that a visit of Southern preachers to President Eisenhower would be more effective.[11] This tactical difference was indicative of a deeper difference in their perspectives on the same problem of race in America.

Their contrast in age (Niebuhr was thirty-seven when King was born in 1929) and in personal history nurtured distinctive attitudes towards the strategy of nonviolent resistance as a remedy for the American dilemma. Niebuhr moved gradually away from pacificism and socialism, as he responded to the threat of fascism and came by 1940 to endorse both the New Deal and American intervention in the Second World War. For him nonviolent resistance was justified only in certain circumstances for secular and pragmatic political reasons. King, on the other hand, made the reverse journey. While at first reluctant to lead the Montgomery bus boycott, he became increasingly committed to a philosophy of nonviolence and a program that eventually included opposition to the Vietnam War and endorsement of a socialistic program of domestic reform. Given their different trajectories, it is not so surprising as it seems at first that there should have been no discussion between them on the subject of civil disobedience.

Niebuhr began as a child of the social gospel in his Evangelical Reformed parish in Detroit, where he had paralleled the career of the Baptist preacher and theologian of the social gospel, Walter Rauschenbusch. He had linked up the Reformation tradition of the millennial Kingdom of God with the growth of political democracy, the labor movement, and socialism. Rauschenbusch realistically understood that workers would necessarily use political leverage, group selfishness, and angry coercion in their struggles, yet he subordinated such realistic insights to an idealization of the home as the incarnation of the social ethic. His *A Theology for the Social Gospel* (1917) asserted (in the midst of war) that "the social gospel is based on the belief that love is the only true working principle of human society."[12]

Before he moved to Union Theological Seminary, Niebuhr had no basic quarrels with Rauschenbusch's tradition. When he left Detroit, his leaving was lamented by black leaders because he had greatly expanded his largely German-American congregation at Bethel Evangelical Church as a champion of progressive ideals. His "mentor and guide" in his Detroit years, as he later acknowledged, was the social-gospel Episcopal Bishop, Charles Williams, "a lonely, dissenting, religious voice in the religious complacency of the city." Niebuhr also learned much from the example of a Jewish friend and political colleague, Fred Butzel, with his "capacity for magnanimity and social shrewdness."[13] He worked with Niebuhr when the mayor appointed both to the city's Interracial Committee after Niebuhr's much-publicized sermon against Protestant bigotry and the Ku Klux Klan's support of the mayor's political opponent in an election.[14] When Niebuhr's crusading successor as pastor of the Bethel Church tried to gain admission for two black parishioners in 1929, Niebuhr supported the church council's opposition to the minister's militant tactics in the hope that the council would be able to do what the congregation was too prejudiced to concede. He was dismayed to find, however, as he later angrily wrote the council, that "prominent members of the church did everything in their power to fan latent race prejudices into a hot flame."[15] The congregation voted to bar the two Negroes and to fire Niebuhr's successor. Niebhur knew from his own experience what he would often point out some thirty years later: The most racially segregated institution in America was the church in contrast to the sporting field, the performing arts, and many unions.

Niebuhr conceded in 1928, however, that he had been "more sane than Christian" as a preacher in Detroit because in his creed "the divine madness of a gospel of love is qualified by considerations of moderation," which he called Aristotelian, "but which an unfriendly critic might call opportunistic." Otherwise, the Christian ethic would become "useless for any direction of the affairs of a larger society."[16] This "Aristotelian" reservation was predictive of the direction of his future intellectual and political career.

Niebuhr, in his notebook of his Detroit days as a young preacher, penned a meditation on the cross "as a symbol of ultimate reality." It had its central place in history because "life is tragic and the most perfect type of moral beauty inevitably has at least a touch of the tragic in it." There might be "a foolish and futile aspect to love's quest," Niebuhr conceded, "which gives it the note of tragedy," but it also could be redemptive when it "becomes the occasion for new moral striving."[17] His tragic sense was stimulated at Union Theological Seminary by responding to the European existentialist Protestant theology of Søren Kierkegaard, Paul Tillich, and Emil Brunner. Niebuhr as a Christian apologist sought to recover in modern terms the pertinent truths in the Christian myths of original sin, Christ's atonement, and divine judgment.

His primary political focus was never on civil rights. His radicalism in the early 1930s was on behalf of the industrial factory worker and was framed in terms of Marxist class categories. His critique of pacifism was based, first, on his appreciation of labor's need to have coercive weapons in its collective bargaining with powerfully organized employers, and later, on the need for the use of military force to stop Hitler's conquest of Europe. In these historical circumstances, the gospel of love as a political weapon was utopian and self-defeating. His major theological opus, *The Nature and Destiny of Man* (1941, 1943), published in the war years, was an attempt, as he later put it, to give "a theological frame to the now pervasive realism."[18]

But the early Niebuhr did deal with the problem of the American black in a remarkable (and surprisingly neglected) section of his first major work of political philosophy, *Moral Man and Immoral Society* (1932). In political terms, the book is mainly a discussion of the specific virtues and limitations of all attempts—national, legal, moral, religious, and revolutionary—to achieve justice; but its preferred solution is Marxist socialism, either revolutionary or evolutionary, depending on the national circumstances. In the midst of the Great Depression he was attracted to religious and political apocalypticism as "a splendid incentive to heroic action," but he also knew that it was "a dangerous guide in immediate and concrete situations."[19]

In an attempt to do justice to moralists as well as to realists in the struggle for freedom and equality, he analyzed Gandhi's movement for nonviolent resistance. Niebuhr pointed out that its tactics of noncooperation, boycott, or strike are not absolutely different from violent coercion because they also may result in damage both to property values and even to life, as well as injury to innocents. Gandhi contributed to the common confusion of nonviolent resistance with passive nonresistance, though in practice he recognized that "considerations of political efficacy partly determine his policies and qualify the purity of the doctrine of 'ahimsa' to which he is committed." Niebuhr also recognized and admired in Gandhi's movement the use of a noncoercive, educational appeal to the reason and goodwill of an opponent as a matter of temper and spirit, rather than of technique. Deliberately submitting cheerfully to the penalty for noncooperation with the law was "one of the great triumphs of his method." Even violence might sometimes proceed from moral goodwill, as in Gandhi's justification of his support of England during the First World War. But resentment also has its value: "A Negro who resents the injustice done his race makes a larger contribution to its ultimate emancipation than one who suffers injustice without any emotional reactions." Even so, the temper and method of nonviolence are crucially valuable (with respect to the imponderables of social conflict) because "they rob the opponent of the moral conceit by which he identifies his interest with the peace and order of society."[20]

Niebuhr's close and discriminating analysis paid tribute to nonviolent methods, but his characteristic contribution was to insist that "they must be pragmatically considered in the light of circumstances." On this basis he made a prescient prophecy: "The emancipation of the Negro race in America probably waits upon the adequate development of this kind of social and political strategy. It is hopeless for the Negro to expect complete emancipation from the menial social and economic position into which the white man has forced him, merely by trusting in the moral sense of the white race. It is equally hopeless to attempt emancipation through violent rebellion." On this basis, Niebuhr recommended boycotts against banks, stores, and public service corporations that discriminate against blacks and nonpayment of taxes to states that spend far more on educating white children than they do for black schools. What was mainly needed was a black leadership that would "fuse the aggressiveness of the new and young Negro with the patience and forbearance of the old Negro, to rob the former of its vindictiveness and the latter of its lethargy."[21]

In the year following this remarkable forecast of the kind of leader that King would represent, Niebuhr broke with the pacifism of the Fellow-ship of Reconciliation, and two years later in his journal *Radical Religion* he set forth a new agenda of "defending democratic institutions, however corrupted, against the peril of fascism."[22] Niebuhr's primary political concern became the conduct of America's role in international affairs. His long controversy with liberal Protestants had schooled him to be on guard against their perfectionist tendencies with their self-righteous cloak-ing of an irresponsible isolationism in the moralistic garb of disinterested virtue, a self-deception that prized clean hands above taking on the gritty burdens of responsibility. By 1948, when King entered Crozer Theologi-cal Seminary in Pennsylvania, Niebuhr's espousal of a tragic sense of life and of historical responsibility was enough in tune with the new Cold War containment policies of the postwar world to put him on the cover of *Time* magazine and in State Department offices as an occasional consul-tant. No other Protestant pastor and theologian in America had such prestige and influence among intellectuals and political policy makers.

King first encountered the ideas of Niebuhr at Crozer and later at Boston University, where King earned a Ph.D. in theology. In the year that Niebuhr published *The Irony of American History* (1952) King wrote a paper on "Reinhold Niebuhr's Ethical Dualism" for his teacher, Dr. L. Harold DeWolf, who would later deliver a eulogy at King's funeral. King summarized Niebuhr's theme in *Moral Man and Immoral Society* as the contrast between the "the goodness of the individual man in his immedi-ate relationships" and the disappearance of that goodness "when he acts as a member of a group." In complex social relations love had to be translated into justice by meeting "mind with mind and power with power." The student was impressed by Niebuhr's "critique of the easy conscience and complacency of some forms of perfectionism" and by his "analysis of the complexity of the social situation." But Niebuhr left unexplained, King declared, "how the immanence of *Agape* is to be concretely conceived in human nature and history" as well as "how one can develop spiritually." King quoted Dean Walter Muelder's "personalist" critique of Niebuhr for neglecting the kind of "Christian assurance which releases creative energy into the world and which in actual fellowship rises above the conflicts of individual and collective egoism."[23] In retrospect, these criticisms seem to point forward to King's career as a leader of the civil rights movement, but his papers make no reference to the race problem as a political issue.

King also reflected the influence of Boston University Personalism by cogently objecting in another paper on Niebuhr that he simply begged the metaphysical question by putting "at the disposal of so-called Biblical presuppositions" the categories of "self, consciousness, transcendence, self-transcendence, freedom, will, and personality," categories that were derived from "the very idealism he rejects." King's other objections were more conventional: Niebuhr's focus on myths and symbols in Christian doctrine was so thoroughgoing that "hardly any denotative meaning is possible." Moreover, his "extreme agnosticism as to the God concept is far from Biblical religion."[24] In another paper, "How Modern Christians Should Think of Man," praised by his teacher for its balance, King confessed to a tension in his mind between "a mild neoorthodox view of man" and "a liberal view of man." The former position seemed to "root back to certain experiences" that he had in the South "with a vicious race problem." The latter position derived from "gradual improvements" of this problem and was related to the "noble possibilities in human nature," to the "great imprint that many liberal theologians" had left upon him, and to his "ever present desire to be optimistic about human nature." He was drawn to liberal theology, with its emphasis on freedom and responsibility, rather than to the "needless paradoxes" of Calvinism or neoorthodoxy, but he had to admit that Niebuhr had pointed out "with great illumination how men sin through intellectual and spiritual pride," needing forgiveness, repentance, and conversion in a continuous process.[25]

King struggled to balance Niebuhrian "Christian realism" with a basic commitment to the liberal social gospel, which he had memorably encountered at Crozer in Walter Rauschenbusch's classic of the social gospel, *Christianity and the Social Crisis* (1907). King confessed later that it had "left an indelible imprint" on his thinking and his "sense of social responsibility." When he was "a thorough-going liberal" in his senior year at Crozer in 1950, however, Niebuhr's work had made him aware of "the reality of sin on every level of man's existence" and "the glaring reality of collective evil." King wanted somehow to synthesize these two major influences on his theology by seeing "a partial truth" in each.[26] This quasi-Hegelian dialectical method was essentially Niebuhr's own tactic in presenting his Hebraic, dramatic version of historical Christianity as the resolution of the opposition between naturalism and idealism.[27]

It is noteworthy that in his student papers King makes no mention of Niebuhr's prophetic analysis of nonviolent resistance. Yet, in his first speech to a mass meeting as leader of the Montgomery boycott movement, King paraphrased one of Niebuhr's favorite distinctions by telling the crowd that "justice is really love in calculation." Niebuhr defined love as a heedlessness without calculation, in contrast to justice, which is dependent upon the calculation of interests and rights; his emphasis in *Moral Man and Immoral Society* was on the inevitable tension between justice and love. The former is pertinent to political life, the latter is relevant to more intimate small groups, such as family and church.

King in this dramatic moment, creating his first remarkable rapport with his audience, took a leaf from Niebuhr's realism, or tamed cynicism, about nonviolent resistance: "Not only are we using the tools of persuasion—but we've got to use the tools of coercion."[28] Yet, during the boycott he confusingly spoke to a Brooklyn Baptist church about using Gandhi's "passive resistance," while to a black reporter he claimed that "this business of passive resistance and nonviolence is the gospel of Jesus."[29] In 1960, a week before the passage of the first Civil Rights Bill since Reconstruction, King looked back on his own "Pilgrimage to Nonviolence" and credited Gandhi for making it clear that love could be an appropriate ideal for large-scale groups, as it had been for the bus boycott: "Christ furnished the spirit and motivation, while Gandhi furnished the method." Whatever intellectual doubts King had had about nonviolent resistance, the issues were "now solved in the sphere of practical action." Having recently returned from a visit to India, King felt that the success of the boycott warranted his commitment to Gandhi's method as "a commitment to a way of life," not just to a strategy. This resolution was accompanied by a recent religious experience: "Whatever the cause, God has been profoundly real to me in recent months. . . . This God evokes and answers prayers." He was characteristically hopeful that "in a dark, confused world the spirit of God may yet reign supreme."[30]

King's reference to Gandhi tended to obscure the American roots of King's "realistic pacifism." The Southern Christian Leadership Conference, under King's leadership, brought to bear on American history the liberal Protestantism from which Niebuhr had also started; most of the board members were well-educated Baptist ministers, like King. In Montgomery, Alabama, where King in 1955 was drafted into leadership of the bus boycott, two of his closest advisers (Bayard Rustin and Glenn Smiley) had been conscientious objectors during the Second World War and were members of the pacifist Fellowship of Reconciliation, from which Niebuhr had resigned in the early 1930s. They counseled King to become an exponent of the philosophy and practice of nonviolent resistance.[31] King, who had earlier declined the presidency of the local NAACP to concentrate on his pastoral duties, gradually became converted to their advice during the course of the boycott.

In his account of the boycott, *Stride Toward Freedom* (1958), King claimed that Niebuhr's analysis of pacifism interpreted it as "a sort of passive nonresistance to evil expressing naive trust in the power of love." True pacifism, King countered, was instead Gandhi's "nonviolent resistance to evil," seeking to develop "a sense of shame in the opponent, and thereby bring about a transformation and change of heart."[32] Actually, Niebuhr himself had made the distinction in 1932—and always maintained it—between passive nonresistance and nonviolent resistance. He had also affirmed that the "social and moral effects" of civil disobedience when it offered "proofs of moral goodwill are tremendous."[33]

In the very year of the Montgomery boycott, Niebuhr stressed that "calculation" is the "very genius of justice," even within the family, in contrast to love's heedlessness; and he described the boycott as a "nonviolent form of coercion." Brotherhood and justice needed Christian piety and a spirit of relative disinterestedness, which King provided, but they also needed "a high type of discriminating intelligence to determine in what contingent situation this or that form of power may and can be applied, and this or that interest must be affirmed in favor of some other interest." Such prudence, he noted, is not part of the Christian ethic, but "perhaps there ought also to be a Christian witness of integrity and courage whenever fears prompt cruelty and oppression as they do today in some communities."[34] Niebuhr's analysis was entirely compatible with King's *practice*. There was in Niebuhr's view, however, biblical sanction only for nonresistance, none at all for nonviolent resistance, which only secular judgment could validate. Niebuhr's deflation of Gandhi defined the difference: "He made the pretensions of sainthood into an instrument of political power. That may have seemed plausible in the environment of India, but it must be ultimately intolerable anywhere."[35]

King's accounts of nonviolence blurred Niebuhr's important distinctions. In the spring of 1956, Niebuhr endorsed the boycott in Montgomery with an important qualification: "But one cannot help but question the definition of the boycott as 'the way of love.' Love is a motive and not a method." Even so, King's form of pacifism was impressive, Niebuhr conceded, because it sought justice and was not obsessed with being guiltless or with contracting out of society for perfectionist reasons. When Niebuhr appeared with James Baldwin on a television program, in September 1963, the preacher chided the novelist for blurring this distinction when Baldwin deprecated as a form of weakness King's preaching of nonviolence. Niebuhr pointed out that the essential ethical divide was between "people who want to be pure and those who want to be responsible. And I think King has shown this difference."[36] For that reason, this trenchant critic of pacifism could, on his own terms, support a religious pacifist because the moral scruples of King and his followers, unlike those of the old isolationists, were not based on "patriotic complacency or irresponsibility towards the ills of a poor world."[37] It was for Niebuhr a crucial distinction. The movement was demanding justice with a good conscience as a minority that had been denied the promises of American life that were so eloquently enshrined in Jefferson's and Lincoln's rhetoric.

Even so, Niebuhr's realism cautioned him that race prejudice was more stubborn than class prejudice, particularly within the churches themselves. Moreover, blacks, in spite of the success in Montgomery of the bus boycott, in general lacked the kind of economic power that had enabled workers to better their position through collective bargaining. Too many demonstrations, he thought, expressed general resentment against injustice rather than "clarifying concrete resentments and specifying particular injustices." Niebuhr had more confidence in the remedy of exerting federal power against states that denied the black the right to vote. The dimensions of the racial crisis seemed to him larger than any "we have confronted since the Civil War" and he foresaw no end to it.[38]

King for the first time noted in his book *Where Do We Go From Here?*

Chaos or Community (1967) that Niebuhr in 1932 had anticipated the movement's tactic of the black boycott against banks, businesses, and public service corporations. He said nothing about the wider context of Niebuhr's analysis and ended his book in un-Niebuhrian fashion by a utopian call for "an all-embracing and unconditional love for all men" as an "absolute necessity for the survival of man."[39] This static in their relationship was evidenced on Niebuhr's side also two years earlier. In a chapter on the race problem in *Man's Nature and His Communities,* he mentioned the role of Jews, Catholics, white Protestants, and the federal government in acting for "a new national consensus" against racism; and he mentioned the role of Thurgood Marshall as a black lawyer in persuading the Supreme Court to make its desegregation decisions. Yet, Niebuhr strangely said nothing about the historic role of King and his black followers in taking their struggle for equality courageously into their own hands.[40]

This critical distance between King and Niebuhr is in part explained by the man who came between them—Abraham Lincoln, a fellow midwesterner who most fully captured Niebuhr's political and religious imagination. In the collection of his college and university sermons, published in 1937 as *Beyond Tragedy,* he compared Lincoln with the biblical David in their rare capacity to formulate "a religion in which the ark has not been removed from the temple, but in which the temple is more than the ark."[41] In the winter of 1965, when King was discussing the need for voting-rights legislation with the Johnson administration, a reader of *The Christian Century* might have expected to find Niebuhr celebrating the political religion of King. Instead, he would have found an article saluting "The Religion of Abraham Lincoln."

Niebuhr pointed out that Lincoln's moral abhorrence of slavery and his "Jeffersonian belief in the mission of the new nation to initiate, extend and preserve democratic self-government" were linked to a sense of providence ambiguous and skeptical enough "to cast doubt on the intentions of both sides," as he did in the second inaugural address. Niebuhr acknowledged Lincoln's compromise with equality in terms of his limiting it to the right of the fruits of one's own labor, because he was "not a moral prophet but a responsible statesman." Justice had to take "an uneasy second place behind that of internal order." Lincoln's moral ambiguity about slavery was "limited to the field of tactics," prompted by the diversity of opinion on the issue. "But the ambiguity ends in the strategy"—the emancipation of the slaves, called for in his 1862 message to Congress: "In giving freedom to the slave we assure freedom to the free—honorable alike in what we give and what we preserve." The message, Niebuhr believed, "throws light not only on the moral problems of politics in general but on our current integration problems."

Even so, he appealed to Lincoln's moral superiority not primarily because of his responsible statesmanship but rather for his "religious sense of the meaning of the drama of human history" because it freed him from self-righteousness and vindictiveness. Niebuhr thought that these sentiments had made for "the consequent horrors of Reconstruction," with its modern legacy of Southern resentment against Northern interference. Abolitionists did not understand that good men may become "the bearers of social evil, even though their own consciences may be not perverse but merely conventional."[42]

"I might have been a historian," Niebuhr told an interviewer in the year following the Lincoln essay, "because I'm interested in history; but my critical daughter says, 'Daddy, you're not enough of an empiricist to be a good historian.' "[43] He told the story because he suspected that she was right. His portrait of Lincoln is authentic, but Niebuhr drew it because he saw in the great speeches important elements of his own Christian realism in theology and political temper. His conventional invoking of the "horrors of Reconstruction" owed more to Southern myth, as it has influenced earlier historians, than to the work of modern historians, who have largely rehabilitated the radical reforms of Reconstruction, especially in the light of modern attempts to resolve racial problems. Lincoln's pertinence to the civil rights movement, moreover, was sharply limited by its policy of civil disobedience, which was closer to the ideology of abolitionists. King's movement took the risk of inviting violence for the sake of dramatizing social conflict over segregation and discrimination, or to underline the repressive biased role of the law and the police in the deep South. The moving chant of the movement, "We Shall Overcome," even became part of our national political oratory when President Johnson, speaking on national television (in the month following Niebuhr's essay on Lincoln), quoted the refrain on behalf of his voting-rights bill.

None of Niebuhr's journalism endorsing the civil rights movement captures its extraordinary fervor, courage under fire, and biracial cooperation in risk taking (six white movement members were killed in action).[44] This deficiency in Niebuhr's writing reflects a general trait noted by Martin E. Marty: "He was quite uninterested in idiosyncratic or exceptional experience. . . . He lacked the historian's taste for surprise and serendipity. People were expected to act in certain ways depending upon their situation and classes. They had to be able to be counted on almost as if they existed for the interpretations Niebuhr would provide." Routinely socioeconomic in his social categories, Niebuhr gave surprisingly little attention to lower-class churches of any kind and "treated the black churches almost only in contexts where he was chastising whites for discrimination."[45]

Niebuhr was a connoisseur of irony; in his *The Irony of American History* he made a deliberate attempt to apply his own theological definition of the concept to the major events of the American past, as the idea had meaning for the current American conflict with the Soviet Union in the Cold War.[46] But he never noted the irony in the relation between himself and King. He predicted that the application of civil disobedience to the race problem would require a religious leader's "sublime madness which disregards immediate appearances and emphasises profound and ultimate unities," as Gandhi and King did. When such a leader appeared, Niebuhr was troubled that civil disobedience might become divorced from the pragmatic and circumstantial thinking that alone could validate it. "Christian realism" required a blend of the Christian dove and the secular serpent, a perilous balance that Neibuhr himself was always struggling to achieve, but his analysis of nonviolent resistance was much more oriented to the serpent than to the dove.

King's movement seemed in many ways to have turned Neibuhr's distinction between moral man and immoral society on its head.[47] Regardless of King's troubled consciousness of personal sin, the public actions of his movement were collective forms of virtue. Though it was challenged by the strident proponents of a separatist form of "Black Power," it was in the South itself a form of black power, creating circumstances through the black churches in which blacks entered the public arena and took responsibility for their own attempts to secure justice from their society.

King's power, unlike Niebuhr's, did not derive from dialectics. He spoke to his congregation in the biblical idiom of a black folk religion that drew on the myth of Exodus and put God directly into history:

For I can look out and see a great number, as John saw, marching into the great eternity, because God is working in this world and at this hour and at this moment. And God grants that we will get on board and start marching with God. . . . And we will be in Canaan's freedom land. Moses might not get to see Canaan, but his children will see it.

The most memorable phrases in his "I Have a Dream" speech at the March on Washington in 1963 were departures from the duller written text, his extemporizing preaching drawing on his experience as a Southern Baptist pastor of a black church for which the singing of spirituals was a beloved ritual. His oratory paradoxically became canonical for Americans, as Taylor Branch has pointed out, when he set aside his formal text "to let loose and jam, as he did regularly from two hundred podiums a year."[48]

Niebuhr also failed to credit sufficiently King's pragmatism, which enabled him to lead the movement so as to wrangle the necessary legislative support of Presidents and Congress. His oratorical national appeals, furthermore, invoked a civil tradition in Jefferson and Lincoln that was not specifically Protestant, Catholic, or Jewish. In his "Letter from the Birmingham Jail," he linked "the sacred heritage of our nation and the eternal will of God," "the best in the American dream and the most sacred values in our Judeo-Christian heritage," to the political moment when "these disinherited children of God sat down at lunch counters."[49] For this reason, he could provoke President Kennedy to respond in similar terms by making a televised extemporaneous address in which he joined King by asserting:

We are confronted primarily with a moral issue. It is as old as the Scriptures and is as clear as the American Constitution. The heart of the question is whether all Americans are to be afforded equal rights and equal opportunities, whether we are going to treat our fellow Americans as we want to be treated. . . . Now the time has come for this nation to fulfill its promise.[50]

But Niebuhr was right to think that there were limits to King's ideology, and they were dramatized as the movement, amid bitter disputes among black organizations, moved North to the urban ghettos. One of his closest white advisers, Stanley D. Levison, made the crucial political point. The wide support that King had found for the movement's actions in Montgomery and Selma, Levison warned, was "a coalition for moderate change, for gradual improvements which are to be attained without excessive upheavals as it gently alters old patterns. *It is militant only against shocking violence and gross injustice.* It is not for deep radical change." The movement would "head into a cul-de-sac if it can see no real progress without radical alteration of the nation."[51]

Levison was prescient. King, nevertheless, came to insist that the movement should be a social revolution, designed to bring about certain basic structural changes in the architecture of American society, but he was unable to find workable specific issues for this grand purpose. (Ironically, Levison, a radical who had done much to give financial aid to the Communist party during the period of its prosecution under the Smith Act, was considered by the FBI and the Kennedys to be the evil Svengali behind King!) After coming out against the Vietnam War, King proclaimed: "But after Selma and the voting rights bill we moved into a new era, which must be an era of revolution. I think we must see the great distinction here between a reform movement and a revolutionary movement. . . . We must see now that the evils of racism, economic exploitation, and militarism are all tied together," King told his staff, "and you really can't get rid of one without getting rid of the others."[52]

King had moved closer to a political position that Niebuhr had occupied in the early 1930s when he was most under Marxian influence. Niebuhr joined King in opposing the war in Vietnam, supporting Clergy and Laymen Concerned About Vietnam, of which King became cochairman. But where King held to a utopian moralism ("war is wrong . . . we must disarm the whole world . . . total disarmament is the only answer"), Niebuhr cogently analyzed the conflict politically: the American intervention was militarily doomed and strategically unwise, costly in terms of loss of moral prestige, because of the unpopular and unviable regime in South Vietnam, and based on the error of regarding the issue as "the containment of Communism, when we are in fact dealing with the nationalism of a small nation of Asia."[53]

Increasingly, King's sense of his religious commitment became more sacrificial, alarming his advisers about his possibly having a morbid state of mind. Speaking to his Atlanta congregation about the discouragements of his Chicago campaign, King said he was prepared to suffer, sacrifice, and even die for the disinherited because he had chosen to identify with them: "If it means dying for them, I'm going that way, because I heard a voice saying, 'Do something for others.' "[54] On 3 April 1968, the day before his martyrdom by a rifle bullet in Memphis, he invoked the familiar biblical metaphor of the Promised Land and the words of the "Battle Hymn of the Republic": "Mine eyes have seen the glory of the coming of the Lord." He rightly intuited that he would not accompany his followers to that great day, but he was still trying "to carve a tunnel of hope from a mountain of despair."[55]

Even in his Detroit years Niebuhr had declared with characteristic humility that he could not follow the logic of Christian nonresistance: "I am too cautious to be a Christian." He was on guard against the tendency to absolutize his own equilibrium "between moral adventure and necessary caution," between "Christ and Aristotle." It was best to be charitable with those who made their adjustments to the right and left of his position. In his notebook for 1928, he put his finger on what would turn out many years later to be a crucial difference between himself and King:

> Philosophers are not usually prophets. They are too reasonable and circumspect to create or preserve the prophetic vision. The wise man is too capable of balancing the truth, to which he ought to be loyal, with some other truth with which it is in conflict. Thus he involves himself in the endless antinomies of intellectualism.[56]

Niebuhr's strength as an analyst was precisely his involvement with those antinomies. But he was also detached physically by the illnesses of old age from the concrete drama of the movement, forced (as he put it) into "a view of life from the sidelines,"[57] no longer the busy circuit rider to colleges and liberal political organizations.

In theology, Niebuhr's debt to Continental thinkers was profound, but he also called himself a legatee of William James: "I stand in the William James tradition. He was both an empiricist and a religious man, and his faith was both the consequence and the presupposition of his pragmatism."[58] In an introduction to *The Varieties of Religious Experience*, Niebuhr praised James mainly for sharing with Marx and Kierkegaard a rejection of Hegel. Niebuhr criticized James's "obvious sympathy" for "the Religion of Healthy-mindedness," which did not do justice to the Reformation's emphasis on the "ambiguity of good and evil" in "all human striving." Niebuhr failed to recognize, however, James's own attack on the "sky-blue" optimism of the "once-born" souls, who lacked a sense of the "radical evil" that was inherent in the nature of things and recognized by the "twice-born sick souls." Niebuhr marked his distance from James by contrasting his own emphasis on "collective destiny" and "the meaning of history" with James's sympathy for mysticism and focus on religion at the level of personal existence.[59]

Niebuhr did not notice, however, that James also made a pragmatic critique of pacifism by pointing out in *The Varieties of Religious Experience* that "reasonable arguments, challenges to magnanimity, and appeals to sympathy or justice, are folly when we are dealing with human crocodiles and boa-constrictors." He also anticipated Niebuhr's favorite argument about democratic justice as the balancing of powers and interests by adding: "The whole history of constitutional government is a commentary on the excellence of resisting evil, and when one cheek is smitten, of smiting back and not turning the other cheek also." James was also aware, however, that in some circumstance unusual charity could be "a genuinely creative social force, tending to make real a degree of virtue which it alone is ready to assume as possible." This was the same "power of redemptive love" that King admired in Lincoln's magnanimity towards his enemies.[60]

James appreciated the symbolism of the cross for its heroic meaning. "The folly of the cross," James wrote, "so inexplicable by the intellect, has yet its indestructible vital meaning." Sorrow and suffering are, in his view, the soul's "heroic resources" in dealing with the "tragic mystery" of life. That is why heroes are so important to us: "We tolerate no one who has no capacity whatever for it in any direction. On the other hand, no matter what a man's frailties otherwise may be, if he be willing to risk death, and still more if he suffer it heroically, in the service he has chosen, the fact consecrates him forever."[61] Niebuhr had his reasons for agreeing more with Lincoln the politician than with either King the prophet or James the philosopher, but both the politician and the prophet fulfilled in our history the philosopher's idea of consecration.

Chapter 13

"I, Too, Sing America": Alice Walker's Visible Woman, Meridian

THE PREVIOUS chapters have shown various illustrations of a recurring sort of event in literary history. It has been described by a contemporary poet and novelist, Alice Walker, in these terms: "One way of looking at history (whether oral or written) is as a method that records characteristics and vibrations of our helpers, whose spirits we may feel but of whose objective reality as people who once lived we may not know." Some of my examples have known each other personally (as in chapter 4); some are contemporaries who did not (as in the previous chapter); most of my examples knew of an earlier writer only through the traces of earlier texts. These variations do not modify the pertinence of Alice Walker's statement. She tells us of her own sense of kinship with an antebellum abolitionist and advocate of women's rights, Sojourner Truth, a former slave whose name vibrates with her own: *Alice* derives from old Greek for *truth* and a sojourner is also a walker. This kinship is more than a matter of color and names: "We are both as concerned about the rights of women as the rights of men," and "we share a certain 'mystical' bent." It is for her an example of "one of those 'synchronicities' (some might say conceits)" of empowering and "reassuring proportions."[1]

But (as the case of Twain and Doctorow demonstrates in chapter 8) some connections between authors and texts are links perceived by the critic rather than by the conscious mind of the author. They point toward the possibility of tradition being formed by what might be called a "cunning of reason," to use a famous Hegelian metaphor, that seems to operate for its own ends over the heads of the agents themselves. Is forging such links forgery in the bad sense? A good test case is the question of Alice Walker's literary "synchronicity' with other black writers. She wrote in her journal that she was satisfied with the work she had done before she was forty because it carried forward the thoughts that her ancestors were trying to help her pass on. "In every generation someone (or two or three) is chosen for this work." She cited Ernest Gaines, Margaret Walker, Langston Hughes, Zora Neale Hurston (a collection of whose work she has edited), and Jean Toomer as black literary predecessors.[2] The list notably does not mention Ralph Ellison.

Perhaps the omission is partly a matter of timing. The 1960s were over before Ellison came back into the good graces of black critics, who, in the spirit of militant separatism or black nationalism, had considered him a bourgeois, aesthetic individualist. (Ironically, the man who had led the charge against him, Larry Neal, later led the move to rehabilitate him as a political novelist of black folk culture.[3]) Moreover, Alice Walker seems to be a radically different case from Ellison. She is a contemporary ideological mix of feminism (which she prefers to call "womanism"), environmentalism, socialism, and the counterculture with an enthusiastic sympathy for the cults of long hair, John Lennon's and Bob Marly's music, vegetarianism, astrology, and the alternative sexual "life-styles" that are common in San Francisco, where the former Georgian lives. There is even something redolent of California culture in her confession: "Aquarians, they say, can tolerate anything but being thought narrow-minded. In my case, this is certainly true."[4]

Sometimes she speaks of America with left-wing hyperbole, as in her pseudo-historical remark that the country "has been led—in every period of its brief and troubled history—by someone who might be called Younger Brother (after the character in E. L. Doctorow's *Ragtime* set in turn-of-the-century America), who occasionally blunders into good and useful deeds, but on the whole never escapes from the white Victorian house of racist and sexist oppression, puritanism, and greed."[5] Led in *every* period? By someone like Younger Brother? The reference is wildly inappropriate: He is an anchronistic character, drawn from the 1960s—a romanticizing neurotic who succumbs to radical chic, harbors a love of violence, and ends up being ambushed with Mexican revolutionaries by federal troops. On occasion, her political judgment can collapse into a banal sentimental belief that "war will stop when we no longer praise it" and peace will come "wherever it is sincerely invited."[6] There is abundant evidence for this partial portrait in her recent collection of essays, *Living by the Word* (1988).

My brief sketch, however, leaves out her appealing humor, self-irony, and willingness to notice uncomfortable facts that do not fit well with her public political gestures. She observes, for example, the irony that there were proportionately far more blacks among the Army men she and her fellow protestors were opposing, in a demonstration against shipping arms to Central America, than there were among the demonstrators themselves.[7] Above all, my previous sketch of her leaves out a paradoxical and unusual truth about this very contemporary person—her deep feeling for tradition, a trait not at all characteristic of most other political children of the 1960s. (She was in her mid-twenties when the decade ended.) This variation from type is what especially makes her intellectually and artistically interesting.

The variation suggests a missed opportunity for a mutual recognition of "synchronicity" by Alice Walker and Ralph Ellison. He, too, is aware of "the magic in naming," for "our names, being the gift of others, must be made our own." He confessed in 1964 that one of the burdens of his being linked to Emerson by their common middle name of Waldo was not being able to "escape the obligation of attempting to achieve some of the things which he asked of the American writer."[8] The suppressed middle name, which made him so uncomfortable as a child, is a key to Ellison's literary consciousness of being a legatee of the classic American writers of the nineteenth century, especially Hawthorne, Melville, James, and Twain.

Ellison is a respectful legatee as well of the American "ideas that draw their power from the Declaration of Independence, the Constitution, and the Bill of Rights."[9] By contrast, however, Alice Walker's heroine in *Meridian,* while speaking at a high school recitation, stumbles and fails to complete a speech extolling the virtues of the Constitution and the American Way of Life because she begins to pay attention to her words and is distracted by the revelation that she does not believe what she is saying.[10] It would not be Ellison's style to make her dismissive reference to "the Indian killers and slave owners Washington and Jefferson and the like."[11] He refused to join in the intellectuals' boycott of President Lyndon Johnson's National Festival of the Arts in 1965 and explained to a group of young black writers that Johnson, without any hedging or "escape clauses," had "spelled out the meaning of full integration for Negroes in a way that no one, no President, not Abraham Lincoln nor Franklin Roosevelt, no matter how much we loved and respected them, has ever done before."[12] It is hard to imagine him, with his bitter experience of Communist party machinations in Harlem, listening to her introduce a socialist-sponsored benefit performance in 1984 of the movie *Seeing Red,* a documentary celebrating American Communists.

Yet, he shares her belief that "folklore is at the heart of self-expression and therefore at the heart of self-acceptance," and he would find entirely congenial the major portion of her introduction to *Seeing Red*—an historical sketch of Benjamin Banneker, the free black surveyor who had sent Jefferson an almanac and impressed him with his intellectual ability. Accounts of Banneker and his English grandmother, an indentured servant who married a slave whom she had bought, confirmed the novelist in her belief that "more and more the America that really exists and the Americans that really were and are will be acknowledged and studied. . . . I, too, sing America."[13] Walker and Ellison are alike (and unfashionable) in being much more interested in their American than in their African cultural ancestry. She was particularly upset that in the 1960s black people skipped over their own families to celebrate African values and ancestors: "The loss of Black American traditions can be seen not only in terms of the loss of our literary and cultural heritage but, more insidiously, in terms of the loss of ourselves."[14]

Walker's sense of America, like Ellison's, is multiracial. In Mississippi, she met the white Jewish lawyer whom she married, made a father, and divorced. Her mother's grandmother was mostly Cherokee. Though she knew no Indians when she wrote *Meridian,* she decorates her walls with portraits of Indians, carries arrowheads on her person, and has acquired friends in the American Indian Movement.[15] She also emphasizes that blacks are not only the descendants of slaves but of slave owners, both in this country and in Africa: "Our white great-grandfathers abused and sold us *here,* and our black great-grandfathers abused and sold us *there.*" She even wrote a poem about her white great-great-grandfather, a slave owner and rapist, who seemed to her to be asking to be let into her consciousness of her self:

> I could be a liberal
> And admit one of his children;
> Or be a radical and permit two.

> But it is *he* asking
> To be let in, alas.[16]

It is her pluralism that infuriates black separatists who accuse her (as she notes) of "twisted pathology" and "queer bourgeois Liberal affectations"; but her consciousness is deeper than factional politics because it is historical: "We are the African and the trader. We are the Indian and the settler. We are the slaver and the enslaved. We are oppressor and oppressed." She wants to let into herself, as she puts it, "all of what being in America means, and not to exclude any part of it." The effort is comparable to Ellison's steady refusal "to strip human experience—especially American experience—of its wonder and stubborn complexity."[17]

Meridian and *Invisible Man* provide evidence for a meaning of tradition in which analogies of theme and technique, their common qualities of joining the marvelous with the terrible, the humorous with the grim, in a poetic way enable the critic to establish a connection, a resonance, that is not an "influence." Their resonance is more than a deeply felt relationship to a culture that is both black and American, or African-American in the currently favored idiom. What makes the relationship between *Invisible Man* and *Meridian* striking, if they are read back to back, is the "synchronicity" of the literary sensibilities at work in both books—in spite of the differences in gender and age of the authors. It suggests the presence of continuities that exist through the exercise of the artistic imagination and its capacity to bridge differences that much contemporary propaganda tends to treat as insurmountable, as if everyone were a monad, locked forever into a gender and a generation. The proof of this continuity must come from listening for the harmonious reverberations emanating from the two novels, the resonant echoes each sets up in the other.

It is no accident that both writers admire the black painter Romare Bearden, who designed the Martin Luther King poster "I Have Seen the Mountaintop." Ellison's introduction to a book of Bearden's paintings and collages found in them an "ambiguity of vision" that would "convey something of the depth and wonder of the Negro American's stubborn humanity"; and he saw the painter's Harlem (like his own novelistic Harlem) to be "a place composed of visual puns and artistic illusions and where the sacred and profane, reality and dream are ambiguously mingled." Bearden's technique (like that of *Invisible Man*) marries meaning and method in being "eloquent of the sharp breaks, leaps in consciousness, distortions, paradoxes, reversals, telescoping of time and surreal blending of styles, values, hopes, and dreams which characterize much of Negro American history."[18] Similarly, Walker describes the form of *Meridian* as a "crazy-quilt story," one that "can jump back and forth in time, work on many levels, and one that can include myths. . . . It's like the work of one of my favorite artists, Romare Bearden. In some ways *Meridian* is like a collage."[19]

Both novels begin in the present and flash back to a much earlier time, returning to the present at the end. Their ends are new beginnings. These are quest-stories with the protagonists struggling to create new patterns without losing all touch with the old ones. Walker, however, transforms Ellison's primarily man-centered story into a woman-centered one. Only Mary Rambo, the blues-singing woman from the South ("I'm in New York but New York ain't in me") plays an important female part in Ellison's novel by reminding the hero that "It's the ones from the South"—the ones who 'knows the fire and ain't forgot how it burns' "—who won't "forgits the ones on the bottom."[20] She is presented as "a stable familiar force," and for many black feminists she is only evidence of the insidious power of stereotyping.[21]

Walker's story takes up historically where Ellison left off in the sense that his hero, living before the Supreme Court's desegregation decision of 1954, has no civil rights movements to give him a responsible part to play, while her heroine moves from her Georgia town to a black college in Atlanta, where she participates in the drive for black voter registration in the deep South—as the author herself had done. Invisible Man, a figure for the symbolically condensed history of the black in America, becomes, a quarter of a century later, visible woman, a symbolically condensed, partly autobiographical account, based on her own participation in the civil rights movement. Her novel is dedicated to both a black (John Lewis) and a white (Staughton Lynd), leaders of the civil rights movement.

Meridian is introduced by a long dictionary definition of the various meanings of its title, which include: the South, the highest apparent point reached by a heavenly body, a distinctive character, and a line from which other guiding lines may be constructed. These meanings celebrate the movement as well as the heroine, Meridian Hill, and give her a symbolic status, just as the title of Ellison's novel does for its hero. We are shown her distinctive character early, a decade after the main events of the novel, as she leads a crowd of poor children, mostly black, to see a circus wagon with a freak show, the supposed mummy of a woman who has been dead for twenty-five years and celebrated stereotypically as "Obedient Daughter," "Devoted Wife," "Adoring Mother," and "Gone Wrong." It is not the day in that small southern town when blacks are permitted to see the exhibit, but Meridian believes the civil rights movement has changed all that and is not deterred even by the presence of a tank with its muzzle pointing to her chest. She thinks it is a useful lesson for the children to discover that the mummy is a fake. Later, falling down from a psychosomatic paralysis, she is carried home by some men who were looking out for her.

The narrative then flashes back to a decade earlier when she is participating in the movement. A group of protestors in New York has told her that to join she must make a declaration of her willingness not only to die for the revolution, but to kill for it. It is the day of Black Power, not of King's nonviolent resistance, but she is keeping his faith. Her close college friend, Anne-Marion Coles, is particularly insistent; nevertheless, Meridian cannot bring herself to make the declaration because she "alone was holding on to something the others had let go." She was "*held* by something in the past: by the memory of old black men in the South" who stared directly back, without shifting, into the eye of a camera and of young girls in a country choir, singing with a purity of soul. If she committed murder in the name of the revolution, she wonders "*what would the music be like?*"[22] Similarly, she had not been able to accept her mother's pressure on her to be converted, to accept Jesus as her Savior. She responds emotionally instead to the example of her withdrawn father, who has a deep feeling for the lives of the Indians, long ago driven from Georgia. He teaches history in school.

Meridian's vision of her mother is that her independence was sapped by motherhood, and Meridian feels guilty for "stealing her mother's serenity, for shattering her mother's emerging self." At college, she finds a kind of substitute mother in the school's organist, Miss Winter, one of the few black teachers, an independent spirit from Meridian's hometown, and a teacher of jazz, spirituals, and blues. When Meridian dreams ambivalently about her mother holding her over the railing of a ship but refusing to let her go, Miss Winter, "as if Meridian were her own child," tells her: "I forgive you."[23] Miss Winter's role parallels that of blues-singing, Southern-born, maternally concerned Mary Rambo in relation to Invisible Man.

But Meridian's strongest feminine identification is with her father's grandmother, Feather Mae, who experienced an esctatic and sensual religious feeling as she basked in the sun while standing in the center of an Indian burial mound. Fondly remembering her, Meridian and her father "rejoiced over so tangible a connection to their past."[24] The reader of *Invisible Man* will be reminded of the important analogical role the grandfather's advice plays in orienting the hero's life.

Meridian's unusual sense of the American past is also at work in her when she first becomes aware of the wider world, after the bombing of a voting-registration center in 1960. Deserted as a teenage mother by her feckless husband, she gives up her baby to the care of another woman, accepts a scholarship at Saxon College, where she is subsidized by a liberal white Connecticut family who had endowed it for three generations, and joins Atlanta's civil rights movement. Meridian is determined to avoid the domestic fate of her mother, who did not live in "the age of choice," but the daughter also remembers with shame that enslaved women had been made miserable by the sale of their children and found the blessing of freedom in being able to keep their own children. It is analogous to Invisible Man's eventual realization that his slave grandfather did not have to speak about being "made more human" by modern times because "he never had any doubts about his humanity—that was left to his 'free' offspring."[25]

Walker heads one chapter with the names of political figures killed in the 1960s—including Medger Evers, John Kennedy, Malcolm X, Martin Luther King, Robert Kennedy, Che Guevara, Patrice Lamumba, George Jackson, and five women civil rights workers. She follows it with an appropriately bizarre and funereal tale about Saxon College's legendary Sojourner tree, planted by a slave who buried her tongue there when it was cut out for telling folk tales that scared a white child to death. Slaves believed the tree could talk, make music, was sacred to birds, and could keep a hidden slave from being seen. Another college legend centered on a student, Fast Mary, who had killed her child, been imprisoned, and hanged herself. She is commemorated on May Day by a dance, in which all the girls were considered equal, around the sacred tree. When the college president forbids their holding a funeral in the chapel for an abandoned wild child, who has been befriended by the students, they put the girl's casket under the tree and sing the "We shall overcome" refrain. That night, the students riot for the first time, but, to Meridian's horror, instead of attacking the president's house, "in a fury of confusion and frustration" they saw down "the ancient, sheltering music tree."[26] This microcosmic example of the irrational and self-defeating element in the rebels of the 1960s also resonates with Ellison's dramatization of the riot at the end of his novel. The hero at first celebrates it for its demonstration of black initiative and then is disillusioned to discover that it is self-defeating, for it has been manipulated by the Brotherhood for its own ends.

Ellison's hero is kept running as "a nigger boy" and finds himself the desired object of white women's sexual fantasies about blacks, myths created by racial taboos. Sexual politics across the color line takes a feminist turn in *Meridian,* for it is the heroine's fate to have men like Truman Held treat her only as a sex object and potential mother. (His failure to use contraception leads to her grim abortion without anaesthesia.) Lynne, a Jewish woman alienated from her family and romanticizing black people, marries Held, but the new ideology of black separatism makes her position in the movement precarious. She is raped by Tommy Olds, who has been rendered bitter and brutal by losing an arm when he was shot as he came out of a protestors' meeting. Lynne is frightened to realize that "her whiteness, the mystique of it, the *danger* of it, the historically *verboten* nature of it, encouraged him to attempt to destroy her without any feelings of guilt."[27] She had been in awe of blacks because she viewed them as suffering without hatred. Olds teaches her in the ugliest way that when the defenses of some black men break down under assault, their only comfort is revenge. It is the last straw for him that she pities him for his lost arm.

Complex writers usually strike militant radicals and conservatives as hesitant or equivocal because ideologues reject the binocular vision and the peripheral tendency to see things out of the corners of their eyes that such writers prefer to tunnel vision. It is the spirit of Invisible Man's epilogue:

> I condemn and affirm, say no and say yes, say yes and say no. I denounce because though implicated and partially responsible, I have been hurt to the point of abysmal pain, hurt to the point of invisibility. And I defend because in spite of all I find that I love. In order to get some of it down I *have* to love.[28]

In a similar spirit, Alice Walker's ending for her novel takes account of Martin Luther King's funeral in April 1968 by noticing out of the corner of Meridian's eye that the blacks following the casket on the mule-drawn cart are not only singing a song that the dead man loved, they are also beginning to engage each other in conversation, drink Coca-Colas, and eat popcorn and hotdogs with a sense of relief. Meridian's binocular vision troubles her radical friends. She concedes that revolutionary murder might sometimes be the "correct" thing to do, but she still remembers that "the right thing is never to kill." Unlike most people, "who did what they had to do to survive," Meridian still struggles with the question of how to reconcile the political with the ethical.[29]

Meridian's exemplary character is capable of acting with courage and cogency. When the city officials close the public swimming pool, which was ordered by the federal government to be open to blacks as well as whites, black children have no recourse but to use the reservoir, which overflows during excessive rains and drowns the children. Meridian, carrying one of the corpses in her arms, leads a march to the mayor's office. She makes her supporters promise to use their vote, though the townspeople, who "had done nothing before beyond complaining among themselves and continually weeping," protest that they will be laughed at for not doing something radical, "choosing to believe radicalism would grow over their souls, like a bright armor, overnight."[30]

After King's murder, Meridian begins going irregularly to various churches and discovers that, as a result of the civil rights movement, the black church has changed. Inspired by King, it is now the place where both political and moral questions are taken seriously. Only there can she promise herself that she would kill to prevent the political murder of an activist son, whose death has driven his father insane. But her act would require "spiritual work, and the historical background and present setting must be right. Only in a church surrounded by the righteous guardians of the people's memories could she even approach the concept of retaliatory murder."[31] But her dedication to her promise is not constant, because she is conflicted, a "*flawed* revolutionary," the only kind, as Walker says, who is worth following.[32]

Meridian charges Truman Held with believing that "revolution, like everything else in America, was reduced to a fad." She knows the evidence for his disenchantment, yet asks: "But don't you think that the basic questions raised by King and Malcolm and the rest still exist?"[33] He answers "No," but Meridian, in the penultimate chapter, "Settling Accounts," learns from her old friend Anne-Marion that a tiny branch is growing out of the gigantic stump of the Sojourner Tree. It is Walker's symbolic tribute to the power of tradition, which can survive (as it does in Meridian) even our collective failures to be faithful to it.

At the end of the novel, Truman Held, generously forgiven by Meridian for his irresponsibility, sees her as returning to the world, like Lazarus, cleansed of sickness. He knows her now for the first time and realizes that her ambivalence will be deplored by revolutionists and traditionalists alike. In this sense, he sees her as being alone, but, like the lonely Invisible Man, she is sustained by the idea of a communal future: "All the people who are as alone as I am will one day gather at the river. We will watch the evening sun go down. And in the darkness maybe we will know the truth."[34] Feeling dizzy, Truman shakily climbs into her sleeping bag and puts her hat on his head as he imagines Anne-Marion returning some day to him.

Walker's last lines in her novel make Meridian as representative a figure as Ellison made Invisible Man. Truman wonders if she knew that "the sentence of bearing the conflict in her own soul which she had imposed on herself—and lived through—must now be born in terror by all the rest of them." Ellison had put a similar truth, connected to a similar fear, into the mouth of Invisible Man. In his last line he says that he is frightened to think: "Who knows but that, on the lower frequencies, I speak for you?"[35] Walker's *all the rest* and Ellison's *you* testify to the burden they lay on the reader. "Her struggle," as Walker has said, "is the struggle each of us will have to assume in our own way."[36] Meridian's conflict and Invisible Man's invisibility must be "worked through" by all the readers of their stories.

Meridian has a recurring dream of being a character in a novel with her existence posing an insoluble problem that could be solved only by her death. Reading novels encouraged that solution. That was what usually happened to independent female characters, such as Hawthorne's Zenobia in *The Blithedale Romance* or Kate Chopin's heroine in *The Awakening*. It happens as well to fictional black males: Harriet Beecher Stowe in *Uncle Tom's Cabin* could imagine no solutions for her black protagonists other than to send George and Eliza in exile to Liberia and Uncle Tom to a martyr's death. Richard Wright's Bigger Thomas awaits execution. Invisible Man has a dream in which all his tormentors castrate him, but he awakens to realize that he cannot go back home, to the college, to Mary Rambo, or to the Brotherhood; he can only move ahead or stay underground: "The end was in the beginning." The reader is returned in the epilogue to the prologue's extensive meditations on invisibility. He now knows that he must come out of hibernation; we know no more than that.

Walker's novel deliberately avoids death, martyrdom, or hibernation for her heroine. The new part of her has "grown out of the old" and so she can go home again in the sense of returning to the South. But Walker's ending is also indeterminate: Meridian, who "owned nothing to pack," leaves her house to Truman, and sets out alone with no specific destination, no concrete social identity. These inconclusive and abstract endings to *Invisible Man* asnd *Meridian* give their protagonists a penumbra of vagueness that prevents them from having any continuing concrete attachments, which are essential to having a credible individual and social identity. In this sense, the two novels illustrate W. H. Auden's generalization about American literature's being "a literature of lonely people." But the unsettled fate of Invisible Man and Meridian is part of the difficulty of their being representative figures of a race whose collective presence in American society is still profoundly problematical, given the persistence of a black underclass, untouched by the success of the civil rights movement.

That is why the last lines in both books are associated with a feeling of fright (*Invisible Man*) and terror (*Meridian*). The people called Negroes, blacks, or African-Americans have always been the litmus test for the integrity of the principles of freedom and equality, which were spoken for so eloquently by Jefferson, Madison, Lincoln, and King. The point of the American story, however, can be lost, leaving the American people adrift, whenever they fail to incorporate those principles into their common life. The hope and promise in the grand words and ideas are therefore balanced by the burden and difficulty of realizing them. The fear of failure, which is also the risk of losing the meaning of our collective selves and our history, must haunt all the readers of Ellison's and Walker's stories. It is our burden, our risk, and our fear, because they are the price of our hope.

My chapters have attempted to show that responding to the visions of others engenders a process that is revisionary. Precisely how it is revisionary cannot be summed up in any single generalization; it is an empirical question to be answered only by close inspection of particular examples, which have their own shape and point. Alice Walker's emphasis is on the help the ancestor gives: "The spirit of our helpers incarnates in us, making us more ourselves by extending us far beyond." She says it is "always a hello" from the spiritual ancestor "you may not even have known you had" and "never a good-bye."[37] Nevertheless, there is usually something of a good-bye in the later work, for revision is also finding a new point of departure, though the mood of the departing good-bye may cover a wide range from respectful tribute to rivalrous criticism, and elements of both may modify each other. There is no better evidence than *Meridian*'s relation to *Invisible Man*. The eagles look alike, but they look in different directions.

Notes

Introduction

1. Fred Lewis Pattee, *Penn State Yankee* (State College: Pennsylvania State College Press, 1953), 165.

2. Cushing Strout, "Tocqueville's Duality: Describing America and Thinking of Europe," *American Quarterly* 21 (Spring 1969), 87–99; François Furet, "Naissance d'un paradigme: Tocqueville et le voyage en amérique (1825–1831)," *Annales: Economies, Sociétiés, Civilizations* 39 (March-April 1984), 225–237.

3. Alexis de Tocqueville, *Democracy in America,* ed. J. P. Mayer and Max Lerner, tr. George Lawrence (New York: Harper & Row, 1966), 439.

4. Ibid., 454–455.

5. Ibid., 455.

6. Cushing Strout, "Tocqueville and the Idea of an American Literature (1941–1971)," *New Literary History* 18 (1986–1987), 115–127.

7. Edmund Wilson, "The Critic Who Does Not Exist," *The Shores of Light: A Literary Chronicle of the Twenties and Thirties* (New York: Farrar Straus Giroux, 1952), 371–372.

8. Charles Feidelson, *Symbolism in American Literature* (Chicago: University of Chicago Press, 1966), 4, 75–76.

9. Cynthia Ozick, "Science and Letters: God's Work—and Ours," *New York Times Book Review* (Sept. 27, 1987), 3.

10. Ibid. For an hilarious and knowledgeable spoof of the literary fashionableness of Structuralist and Post-Structuralist concepts and jargon see Malcolm Bradbury, *My Strange Quest for Mensonge* (New York: Penguin Books, 1988).

11. Sacvan Bercovitch, *Reconstructing American Literary History* (Cambridge, Mass.: Harvard University Press, 1986), vii–viii. The work of Bradbury's fictional Mensonge is typically "filled with all those gaps, ruptures, fractures, lacunae and apertures that have become a Deconstructionist mannerism, and then a few more." *My Strange Quest for Mensonge,* 65.

12. Henry Louis Gates, Jr., "Reclaiming Their Tradition," *New York Times Book Review* (Oct. 4, 1987), 34.

13. Quoted in Luther Stearns Mansfield, "Literary Life in Nineteenth Century Berkshire County," *Berkshire History* 2 (Spring 1976), 21.

14. For fertile suggestions for new meanings of "influence," see Douglas N. Archibald, "Yeats's Encounters: Observations on Literary Influence and Literary History," *New Literary History* 1 (Spring 1970), esp. 442–455.

15. Harold Bloom, *Agon: Towards a Theory of Revisionism* (New York: Oxford University Press, 1982), 19.

16. William Dean Howells, "Of Originality and Imitation," in *W. D. Howells as Critic,* ed. Edwin H. Cady (London: Routledge and Kegan Paul, 1973), 446.

17. John W. Miller, Letter to Cushing Strout, Oct. 23, 1951. That is why "influences" cannot be treated as if they were physical causes.

18. Maurice Mandelbaum, *The Anatomy of Historical Knowledge* (Baltimore, Md.: Johns Hopkins University Press, 1977), 20, 36.

19. Umberto Eco, *The Name of the Rose,* tr. William Weaver (New York: Harcourt Brace Jovanovich, 1983), 286.

20. Jacques Barzun, "Shaw versus Stendhal," *Partisan Review,* 50th Anniversary Ed. (New York: Stein and Day, 1985), 131.

21. John William Miller, "History," Box 4, Folder 5 and Box 23, Folder 7, Miller Papers, Stetson Library, Williams College.

22. Quoted from Eric Hobsbawm in Gertrude Himmelfarb, *The New History and the Old: Critical Essays and Reappraisals* (Cambridge, Mass.: Belknap Press, 1987), 10.

23. Ibid., 12.

24. Himmelfarb, "Social History in Retrospect," *The New History and the Old,* 99.

25. Alfred Kazin, *On Native Grounds: An Interpretation of Modern American Prose Literature* (New York: Reynal and Hitchcock, 1942), xi.

26. Quoted from Michael Oakeshott, *On History and Other Essays,* in Himmelfarb, "Is National History Obsolete?" *The New History and the Old,* 122; quoted from Marc Bloch, *Strange Defeat* in ibid., 132.

27. Carol Gelderman, *Mary McCarthy: A Life* (New York: St. Martin's Press, 1988), 142.

28. William C. Spengemann, *A Mirror for Americanists: Reflections on the Idea of American Literature* (Hanover, N.H.: University Press of New England, 1989), 69, 121, 162.

Chapter One

1. *Benjamin Franklin's Autobiography,* ed. J. A. Leo Lemay and P. M. Zall (New York: W. W. Norton, 1986), 59–61.

2. On role playing as a benign form of Franklin's social consciousness, see John Griffith, "Franklin's Sanity and the Man Behind the Masks," in *The Oldest Revolutionary: Essays on Benjamin Franklin,* ed. J. A. Leo Lemay (Philadelphia: University of Pennsylvania Press, 1976), esp. 128–131.

3. Quoted by Julian Smith, "Coming of Age in America: Young Ben Franklin and Robin Molineux," *American Quarterly,* 17 (Fall 1965), 551, n.4. Cf. A. B. England, "Robin Molineux and the Young Ben Franklin: a Reconsideration," *Journal of American Studies,* 6 (August 1972), 181–188, where the differences in point of view are stressed.

4. *Benjamin Franklin's Autobiography,* 64; Herman Melville, *Israel Potter: His Fifty Years of Exile* (New York: Warner Books, 1974), 24.

5. *Israel Potter,* 70.

6. Ibid., 79.

7. Ibid., 115.

8. Ibid., 72.

9. Ibid., 130.

10. Ibid., 159, 172.

11. Ibid., 195.

12. Ibid., 21, 32, 145.

13. See S. Gorley Putt, *Henry James: A Reader's Guide* (Ithaca, N.Y.: Cornell University Press, 1966), 110; Cornelia Pulsifer Kelley, *The Early Development of Henry James* (Urbana: University of Illinois Press, 1965), 239–240.

14. Quoted by Martha Banta, Introduction, *New Essays on "The American"* (New York: Cambridge University Press, 1987), 19.

15. Letter to Madame Lavoisier, October 23, 1788, *Benjamin Franklin's Autobiographical Writings,* ed. Carl Van Doren (New York: Viking, 1945), 761.

16. *The Notebooks of Henry James,* F.O. Matthiessen and Kenneth B. Murdock, eds. (Chicago: University of Chicago Press, 1981), 26.

17. Henry James, *The American,* (1879; New York: New American Library, 1963), 321.

18. Ibid., 35.

19. Ibid., 322.

20. Ibid., 305, 322.

21. Ibid., 24.

22. F. Scott Fitzgerald, *The Great Gatsby,* in Dorothy Parker, ed., *The Portable F. Scott Fitzgerald* (New York: Viking Press, 1945), 126.

23. Harry Salpeter, "The Next Fifteen Years Will Show How Much Resistance There Is in the American Race," an interview, April 3, 1927, reprinted in *F. Scott Fitzgerald In His Own Time: A Miscellany* Matthew J. Bruccoli and Jackson R. Bryer, eds., (Kent, Ohio: Kent State University Press, 1971), 275–277.

24. Joyce A. Rowe, *Equivocal Endings in Classic American Novels* (New York: Cambridge University Press, 1988), 26.

25. *Benjamin Franklin's Autobiography,* 7–8.

26. On the significance of this polarity for Americans, see Ferner Nuhn, *The Wind Blew from the East: A Study in the Orientation of American Culture* (New York: Harper, 1942).

27. Letter to Polly Stevenson, March 23, 1763, *Autobiographical Writings,* 139.

28. Letter to Joseph Galloway, February 25, 1775, quoted in Carl Van Doren, *Benjamin Franklin* (New York: Viking, 1938), 517.

29. Brian M. Barbour, "*The Great Gatsby* and the American Past," *Southern Review,* 9 (January 1973), 288–299.

30. Joel Porte, *Representative Man: Ralph Waldo Emerson in His Time* (New York: Oxford University Press, 1979), 38, 57–63.

31. Fitzgerald, *The Great Gatsby,* 167.

32. Carl Becker, "Benjamin Franklin," *Dictionary of American Biography,* vol. 6 (1943), 597.

33. Rowe, *Equivocal Endings,* 126.

Chapter Two

1. Richard H. Brodhead, *The School of Hawthorne* (New York: Oxford University Press, 1986), 9.

2. Quoted in James R. Mellow, *Nathaniel Hawthorne in His Times* (Boston: Houghton Mifflin, 1980), 490–491.

3. Brodhead, *School of Hawthorne,* 9–10.

4. For Anne Hutchinson, see David Leverenz, *The Language of Puritan Feeling: An Exploration in Literature, Psychology, and Social History* (New Brunswick, N.J.: Rutgers University Press, 1980), 152. For the historical pertinence of Hawthorne's use of sexuality, see Michael J. Colacurcio, " 'The Woman's Own Choice': Sex, Metaphor, and the Puritan 'Sources' of *The Scarlet Letter,*" in *New Essays on "The Scarlet Letter,"* ed. Michael J. Colacurcio (New York: Cambridge University Press, 1985), 101–135. For the traditional novel of adultery in contrast to Hawthorne's, see Carol Bensick, "His Folly, Her Weakness: Demystified Adultery in *The Scarlet Letter,*" *New Essays,* 137–159.

5. Quoted in Clara M. and Rudolf Kirk, *William Dean Howells* (New York: Twayne Publishers, 1962), 87.

6. W. D. Howells, "Henry James, Jr.," in Cady, *W. D. Howells as Critic,* 68.

7. Ibid., 70.

8. R. W. B. Lewis, "Hawthorne and James: The Matter of the Heart," *Trials of the Word: Essays in American Literature and the Humanistic Tradition* (New Haven, Conn.: Yale University Press, 1965), 79–85; Robert Weisbuch, *Atlantic Double-*

Cross: American Literature and British Influence in the Age of Emerson (Chicago: University of Chicago Press, 1986), 279–290; Clara M. and Rudolf Kirk, *William Dean Howells,* 84–88; Richard Brodhead, *The School of Hawthorne,* 94–103.

9. W. D. Howells, *Literary Friends and Acquaintance,* ed. David F. Hiatt and Edwin H. Cady (Bloomington: Indiana University Press, 1968), 53.

10. Quentin Anderson, *The Imperial Self: An Essay in American Literary and Cultural History* (New York: Knopf, 1971), 70.

11. Edwin H. Cady, *The Road to Realism* (Syracuse: Syracuse University Press, 1956), 212. For the view that Atherton speaks for Howells, see Henry Nash Smith, "The Theology of Realism," *Democracy and the Novel: Popular Resistance to Classic American Writers* (New York: Oxford University Press, 1978), 95–102. He ignores the female criticism of Atherton, and Howells also describes Halleck's "desperate retreat" as a failure of nerve. See Howells, *A Modern Instance* (New York: New American Library, 1964), 417–418.

12. See Gertrude Himmelfarb, *On Liberty and Liberalism: The Case of John Stuart Mill* (New York: Knopf, 1974), 273–275.

13. Nina Baym, *Novels, Readers, and Reviewers: Responses to Fiction in Antebellum America* (Ithaca, N.Y.: Cornell University Press, 1984), 241.

14. See "Sex in Literature," in Cady, *W. D. Howells as Critic,* 149–155.

15. Quoted in Samuel Eliot Morison, *Builders of the Bay Colony* (Boston: Houghton Mifflin, 1930), 335.

16. Ernest Samuels, Introduction, Henry Adams, *Democracy and Esther* (New York: Anchor Books, 1961), xviii–xix; on Esther's troubled sexual identity see Strout, "Personality and Cultural History in the Novel: Two American Examples," *New Literary History,* 1 (Spring 1970) 426–432.

17. Nathaniel Hawthorne, "Mrs. Hutchinson," *Biographical Sketches, The Complete Works of Nathaniel Hawthorne,* Riverside Ed. (Boston: Riverside Press, 1888), xii, 218–219, 222.

18. Austen Briggs, Jr., *The Novels of Harold Frederic* (Ithaca, N.Y.: Cornell University Press, 1969), 132.

19. Van Wyck Brooks, Introduction, Harold Frederic, *The Damnation of Theron Ware* (New York: Premier Books, 1962), vi.

20. Briggs, *Novels of Harold Frederic,* 132–133.

21. Nathaniel Hawthorne, *The Scarlet Letter,* 2nd Norton Critical Ed., (New York: Norton, 1978), 168–169.

22. Abbott is quoted in H. Shelton Smith, *Changing Conceptions of Original Sin* (New York: Scribner's, 1955), 180; Beecher is quoted in Lyman Beecher Stowe, *Saints, Sinners, and Beechers* (New York: Blue Ribbon Books, 1934), 259.

23. John Updike, "On One's Own Oeuvre," *Hugging the Shore: Essays and Criticism* (New York: Knopf, 1983), 855.

24. Updike, "Hawthorne's Creed," *Hugging the Shore,* 73–74.

25. See Updike, "To *Soundings in Satanism,*" *Picked-Up Pieces* (New York: Knopf, 1975), 91.

26. Updike, "To the Tram Halt Together," *Hugging the Shore,* 828–829. He also notes that Karl Barth offers some "strikingly undemanding and almost apologetic theology on the subject of sexual disorder," which characterized his own relationship to his female assistant. Loc. cit.

27. For the second-sight puzzle, see David Lodge, "Chasing After God and Sex," *New York Times Book Review* (August 31, 1986), 1,15; for suspicion about Updike in Roger see Frederick Crews, "Mr. Updike's Planet," *New York Review of Books* (December 4, 1986), 7–14. Crews notes the Hawthorne analogy, as Lodge does not.

28. Updike, "One Big Interview," *Picked-Up Pieces,* 505; "An Interesting Emendation," ibid., 443.

29. Updike, "Edmund Wilson's Fiction: A Personal Account," *Hugging the Shore,* 196, 199.

30. Updike, "More Love in the Western World," *Assorted Prose* (New York: Fawcett Crest, 1966), 233.

31. Updike, *Roger's Version* (New York: Fawcett Crest, 1986), 326.

32. Ibid., 310–311.

Chapter Three

1. Lionel Trilling, "Family Album" and "An American View of English Literature," in *Speaking of Literature and Society,* ed. Diana Trilling (New York: Harcourt Brace Jovanovich, 1980), 238, 262, 265; Lionel Trilling, "Manners, Morals, and the Novel," *The Liberal Imagination: Essays on Literature and Society* (New York: Scribner's, 1952, reprinted 1976), 212.

2. Quentin Anderson, *The Imperial Self,* 77, 86. Lionel Trilling, "William Dean Howells and the Roots of Modern Taste," *The Opposing Self* (New York: Harcourt Brace Jovanovich, 1955, reprinted 1979), 67–91; Lionel Trilling in "Hawthorne in Our Time," *Beyond Culture: Essays on Literature and Learning* (New York: Viking, 1965), 179–208.

3. To Henry James, January 19, 1870, *The James Family,* ed. F. O. Matthiessen (New York: Knopf, 1961), 319. For a summation of the commentary on the Hawthorne-James connection see Thaddeo K. Babiiha, *The James-Hawthorne Relation: Bibliographical Essays* (Boston: G.K. Hall, 1980).

4. T. S. Eliot, "Reflections on Contemporary Poetry IV," *Egoist* 6 (July 1919), 39–40.

5. T. S. Eliot, "The Hawthorne Aspect," in *The Question of Henry James,* ed. F. W. Dupee (London: Allan Wingate, 1947), 127, 129, 130, 133.

6. John Carlos Rowe, "What the Thunder Said: James's *Hawthorne* and the American Anxiety of Influence: Centennial Essay," *Henry James Review* 4 (Winter 1983), 103.

7. Peter Buitenhuis, "Henry James on Hawthorne," *New England Quarterly,* 32 (June 1959), 207–225. He identifies five different views. Quoted in Babiiha, *James-Hawthorne Relation,* 57. See, for a recent example, Robert Emmet Long, *The Great Succession: Henry James and the Legacy of Hawthorne* (Pittsburgh: University of Pittsburgh Press, 1979), 155–156, 171.

8. Bloom, *Agon,* viii.

9. Henry James, *Autobiography,* ed. Frederick W. Dupee (New York: Criterion Books, 1956), 477–478, 480.

10. Brodhead, *The School of Hawthorne,* 150. The book deals very perceptively with the full story of Hawthorne's meaning for James.

11. Alfred Kazin, Introduction, *The Blithedale Romance* (New York: New American Library, 1981), xi.

12. See Howard Kerr, *Mediums, and Spirit-Rappers, and Roaring Radicals: Spiritualism in American Literature, 1850–1900* (Urbana: University of Illinois Press, 1972), passim; James, *Autobiography,* 364; Leon Edel, *Henry James: The Untried Years, 1843–1870* (Philadelphia: Lippincott, 1953), 110.

13. W. D. Howells, "My Favorite Novelist and His Best Book," in Cady, *W. D. Howells as Critic,* 275; Howells, *The Undiscovered Country* (Boston: Houghton, Mifflin, 1880, 1900), 110.

14. Kerr, *Mediums and Spirit-Rappers,* 146. For James's story, see Peter Buitenhuis, *The Grasping Imagination: The American Writings of Henry James* (Toronto: University of Toronto Press, 1970), 72–74.

15. Letter from E. E. Hale, Feb. 28, 1880, cited in *Selected Letters of W. D. Howells,* ed. George Arms and Christopher K. Lohmann (Boston: Twayne Publishers, 1979), 2: 1873–1881, 245, n. 2; to James R. Lowell, June 22, 1879, 231. *The Notebooks of Henry James,* ed. F. O. Matthiessen and Kenneth B. Murdock (Chicago: University of Chicago Press, 1981), 47.

16. Quoted in Louise Hall Tharp, *The Peabody Sisters of Salem* (New York: Pyramid Books, 1968), 334. Tharp herself sees Miss Birdseye as "Miss Peabody to the life," 337.

17. See George Dimock, "Caroline Sturgis Tappan: A Study in American 19th-Century Sensibility," in Dimock, *Caroline Sturgis Tappan and the Grand Tour* (Lenox, Mass.: Lenox Library Association, 1982), 41–73.

18. July 20 (1880), *Henry James Letters,* ed. Leon Edel (Cambridge, Mass.: Belknap Press, 1975), vol. 2, 299; April 18 (1880), 286.

19. Kerr, *Mediums, and Spirit-Rappers,* 197–203.

20. Henry James, *Hawthorne* (Ithaca, N.Y.: Cornell University Press, 1963), 108.

21. Dimock, "Caroline Sturgis Tappan," 48.

22. See my review of Jean Strouse, *Alice James: A Biography* (Boston: Houghton Mifflin, 1980): "James's Daughter and Shakespeare's Sister," *The Henry James Review* 3 (Fall 1981), 59–63; Alice James, *The Diary of Alice James,* ed. Leon Edel (New York: Dodd, Mead, 1964), 230; Kay H. Blacker and Joe P. Tupin, "Hysteria and Hysterical Structures: Developmental and Social Theories," in *Hysterical Personality,* ed. Mardi J. Horowitz (New York: Jason Aronson, Inc., 1977).

23. *The Blithedale Romance,* 96, 192.

24. Judith Fryer, *The Faces of Eve: Women in the Nineteenth Century* (New York: Oxford University Press, 1976, 1978), 225. See W. R. Martin, "The Use of Fairy-Tale: A Note on the Structure of *The Bostonians,* a Novel by Henry James," *English Studies in Africa* 2 (1959), 98–109.

25. Henry James, *The Bostonians* (New York: Modern Library, 1956), 273–274, 345, 412.

26. Quoted in Ernest Samuels, *The Young Henry Adams* (Cambridge, Mass.: Harvard University Press, 1948), 264; Erik H. Erikson, *Insight and Responsibility* (New York: Norton, 1964), 172.

27. Ronald Bush, "Nathaniel Hawthorne and T. S. Eliot's American Connection," *Southern Review* 21:4 (October 1985), 924–933; *T. S. Eliot: A Study in Character and Style* (New York: Oxford University Press, 1983), 4, 8; Stanley Sultan, "Eliot and the Concept of Literary Influence," *Southern Review* 21:4 (October 1985), 1071–1093.

Chapter Four

1. Quoted in David F. Hiatt and Edwin H. Cady, eds., Howells, *Literary Friends and Acquaintance,* xiv.

2. Quoted in James R. Mellow, *Nathaniel Hawthorne in His Time,* 472.

3. October 31, 1895, *The Notebooks of Henry James,* 226.

4. To John M. Howells, July 27, 1894, *Life in Letters of William Dean Howells,* ed. Mildred Howells (New York: Russell and Russell, 1968), 52–53.

5. To William Dean Howells, August 10, 1901, *The Ambassadors,* S.P. Rosenbaum, ed. (New York: Norton Critical Ed., 1964), 406.

6. Leon Edel, *The Treacherous Years: 1895–1901* (New York: Avon Books, 1978), 151.

7. October 10, 1901, *The Notebooks,* 313.

8. *The Notesbooks,* 374.

9. Leon Edel, "Jonathan Sturges," *Princeton University Library Chronicle* 15 (Autumn 1953), 3, 9.

10. Edel, *The Treacherous Years,* 150.

11. To Thomas Bailey Aldrich, July 3, 1902, *Life in Letters,* vol 2, 121.

12. Notebook Entries, *The Ammbassadors,* 375.

13. To William James, March 29, 1870, *The James Family,* 261.

14. *The Notebooks,* 371.

15. To William Dean Howells, January 8, 1904, *The Letters of Henry James,* vol. 2, 10; to Charles Eliot Norton, August 9, 1871, quoted in Kirk, *William Dean Howells,* 201.

16. William M. Gibson, Introduction, William Dean Howells, *Indian Summer* (New York: E.P. Dutton, Everyman, 1958), xv.

17. *Indian Summer,* 195.

18. *The Ambassadors,* 323.

19. Ian Watt, "The First Paragraph of *The Ambassadors:* An Explication," *The Ambassadors,* 472.

20. *The Ambassadors,* 331.

21. Henry James, Preface to "The Ambassadors," *The Art of the Novel: Critical Prefaces* (New York: Scribner's, 1934), 310.

22. See Cushing Strout, *The American Image of the Old World* (New York: Harper & Row, 1963), 191–192.

23. William Dean Howells, *The Rise of Silas Lapham* (New York: Modern Library, 1951), 314.

24. Abraham Cahan, *The Rise of David Levinsky* (New York: Harper Torchbooks, 1960), 529–530.

25. Quoted from a letter to his father on August 10, 1884, in Kirk, *William Dean Howells,* 105.

26. Rudolf and Clara M. Kirk, "Abraham Cahan and William Dean Howells: The Story of a Friendship," *American Jewish Historical Quarterly* 52 (September 1962), 30, 42.

27. Kirk, "Abraham Cahan and William Dean Howells," 41; to F. A. Duneka, September 20, 1917, ibid., 42, n.20.

28. *The Rise of Silas Lapham,* 176.

29. Kirk, "Abraham Cahan and William Dean Howells," Appendix III, 57.

30. Edith Wharton, *A Backward Glance* (New York: Appleton Century, 1934), 146–147.

31. Percy Lubbock, *Portrait of Edith Wharton* (New York: Appleton-Century-Crofts, 1947), 8.

32. Millicent Bell, *Edith Wharton and Henry James: The Story of a Friendship* (New York: Braziller, 1965), 295.

33. *A Backward Glance,* 190.

34. Bell, *Edith Wharton and Henry James,* 309.

35. Cynthia Griffin Wolff, *A Feast of Words: The Triumph of Edith Wharton* (New York: Oxford University Press, 1977), 311–313.

36. *The Notebooks,* 15, 18; Preface to "The Portrait of a Lady," *The Art of the Novel,* 51.

37. Edith Wharton, *The Age of Innocence* (New York: D. Appleton, 1920), 293.

38. R.W.B. Lewis, *Edith Wharton: A Biography* (New York: Harper & Row, 1975), 317.

39. Henry James, *The Portrait of a Lady,* ed. Robert D. Bamberg (New York: Norton Critical Ed., 1975), 39.

40. *The Portrait of a Lady,* 41.

41. *The Age of Innocence,* 42–43.

42. Ibid., 172, 350.

43. *The Portrait of a Lady,* 481.

44. Ibid., 54.

45. *The Age of Innocence,* 360.

46. *A Backward Glance,* 366.

47. Cynthia Propper Seton, *A Glorious Third* (New York: W. W. Norton, 1979), 26.

48. Lewis, *Edith Wharton,* 433.

49. To William James, March 8, 1870, *Letters of Henry James,* vol. 1, 26–27. Quentin Anderson notes the connection between James's praise of the women and of his father's article in *The American Henry James* (New Brunswick: Rutgers University Press, 1957), 137.

50. Henry James, Sr., "Is Marriage Holy?" *Atlantic Monthly* 25 (March 1870), 360–368.

51. Henry James, Sr., "Woman and the 'Woman's Movement,'" *Putnam's Monthly* 1 (1853), 283.

52. Henry James, Sr., "The Woman Thou Gavest With Me," *Atlantic Monthly* 25 (January 1870), 68–69.

53. Cushing Strout, "Complementary Portraits: James's Lady and Wharton's Age," *The Hudson Review* 35 (Autumn 1982), 415.

Chapter Five

1. Perry Miller, "From Edwards to Emerson," *Errand into the Wilderness* (New York: Harper Torchbooks, 1964), 197; Harold Bloom, "Emerson: The American Religion," *Agon* 145; Richard Poirier, *A World Elsewhere: The Place of Style in American Literature* (New York: Oxford University Press, 1966), 69; Quentin Anderson, *The Imperial Self,* 3–58. Anderson criticizes and Poirier celebrates Emerson's "imperial self."

2. Quoted in Jerome Loving, *Emerson, Whitman, and the American Muse* (Chapel Hill: University of North Carolina Press, 1982), 93, 96.

3. Quoted in ibid., 10.

4. Ralph Waldo Emerson, "The Poet," *Selected Writings of Ralph Waldo Emerson*, ed. William H. Gilman (New York: New American Library, 1965), 324.

5. Quoted in Loving, *Emerson, Whitman, and the American Muse*, 92, 97.

6. To James Elliot Cabot, September 26, 1855, *The Letters of Ralph Waldo Emerson*, ed. Ralph L. Rusk (New York: Columbia University Press, 1939), 531.

7. Quoted in Loving, *Emerson, Whitman and the American Muse*, 99.

8. Ibid., 178.

9. Bloom, *Agon*, 167.

10. August 27 (?), 1841, Emerson, *Selected Writings*, 105.

11. Howard M. Feinstein, *Becoming William James* (Ithaca, N.Y.: Cornell University Press, 1984), 67–68.

12. Quoted in Ralph Barton Perry, *The Thought and Character of William James* (Boston: Little, Brown, 1936), vol. 1, 43.

13. Feinstein, *Becoming William James*, 73–75.

14. Jonathan Bishop, *Emerson on the Soul* (Cambridge, Mass.: Harvard University Press, 1964), 167–176.

15. Feinstein, *Becoming William James*, 245.

16. To Mrs. Louis Agassiz, December 15, 1902, *Letters of William James*, Henry James, ed. (Boston: Atlantic Monthly Press, 1920), vol. 2, 181.

17. Cushing Strout, "William James and the Twice-born Sick Soul," *The Veracious Imagination: Essays on American History, Literature, 2nd Biography* (Middletown, Conn.: Wesleyan University Press, 1981), 202–207.

18. Perry, *Thought and Character*, vol. 1, 143.

19. Henry James, "Mr. Emerson," *The Literary Remains of the Late Henry James*, ed. William James (Boston: James R. Osgood, 1885), 296, 302.

20. Quoted in *Letters of William James*, vol 2, 174–175.

21. To Mrs. William James, July 9, 1898, ibid., 76–77.

22. "The Poet," 318.

23. William James, *The Varieties of Religious Experience: A Study in Human Nature* (New York: Longmans, Green, 1902), 513.

24. *The Varieties*, 360.

25. Ibid., 110–111.

26. Ibid., 333.

27. Ibid., 234.

28. Ibid., 165, 176.

29. Cushing Strout, "The Pluralistic Identity of William James: A Psychohistorical Reading of *The Varieties of Religious Experience*," *American Quarterly* 23 (May 1971), 151.

30. Strout, "William James and the Twice-born Sick Soul," 209.

31. *Literary Remains*, 11.

32. Ibid., 116.

33. Ibid., 117–118.

34. Quoted in Strout, "William James and the Twice-born Sick Soul," 213.

35. *Literary Remains,* 119.

36. Perry, *Thought and Character,* vol. 2, 324.

37. *The Varieties,* 25, 299, 163–165.

38. Emerson, "Fate," *Selected Writings,* 381.

39. Ibid., 401.

40. *The Varieties,* 33.

41. Ibid., 167.

42. Ibid., 239–240, n. 1.

43. Emerson, "The Divinity School Address," *Selected Writings,* 256.

44. Ibid., 448, n. 1.

45. *The Varieties,* 525.

46. To Theodore Flournoy, April 30, 1903, *The Letters of William James and Theodore Flournoy,* ed. Robert C. Le Clair (Madison: University of Wisconsin, 1966), 141.

47. Perry, *Thought and Character,* vol. 2, 376.

48. To Henry James, May 3, 1903, *Letters of William James,* vol 2., 190–191.

49. William James, Address at the Emerson Centenary in Concord," in *Emerson: A Collection of Critical Essays,* ed. Milton R. Konvitz and Stephen E. Whicher (Englewood Cliffs, N.J.: Prentice-Hall, 1962), 18–23.

50. Perry, *Thought and Character,* vol. 1, 441. He resigned in the spring of 1907.

51. To Henry James, May 4, 1907, *Letters,* vol. 2, 280.

52. To Henry James and William James, Jr., February 14, 1907, *Letters,* vol. 2, 265.

53. February 7, 1839, in Edward Waldo Emerson, *Emerson in Concord: A Memoir* (Boston: Houghton Mifflin, 1889), 166.

54. Emerson, *Miscellanies,* James's edition of Emerson's works, William James Collection, Houghton Library, Harvard University.

55. For detailed, helpful use of James's annotations, see Frederick I. Carpenter in "William James and Emerson," *American Literature* 11 (March 1930), 39–57 and "Points of Comparison Between Emerson and William James," *New England Quarterly* 2 (July 1929), 458–474.

56. Emerson, "Experience," *Selected Writings,* 337.

57. To Frances R. Morse, May 26, 1903, *Letters of William James,* vol. 2, 194; to Henry W. Rankin, June 10, 1903, ibid., 197; to Mrs. Henry Whitman, August 22, 1903, ibid., 199; ibid., 172.

58. To W. C. Brownell, September 2, 1909, in Perry, *Thought and Character,* vol. 1, 144.

59. William James, *Pragmatism: A New Name for Some Old Ways of Thinking* (New York: Longmans, Green, 1907), 260. See my commentary on James's approach to a philosophy of history in "The Unfinished Arch: William James and the Idea of History," in *The Veracious Imagination*, 44–56.

60. *Pragmatism*, 269, 277, 278, 292, 294.

61. Ibid., 295–296, 299.

62. To Dickinson S. Miller, November 10, 1905, *Letters*, vol. 2, 234–235.

63. To Frances R. Morse, May 26, 1903, *Letters*, vol. 2, 194.

Chapter Six

1. Perry, *Thought and Character*, vol. 2, 277–278. For the role of Wilkinson and Robertson, see Feinstein, *Becoming William James*, 258–267.

2. To F. G. Brombert, June 30, 1884, Perry, *Thought and Character*, vol. 2, 297.

3. Robert Penn Warren, *The Legacy of the Civil War* (New York: Random House, 1961; Cambridge, Mass.: Harvard University Press, 1983), 47, 72.

4. Robert Penn Warren, Introduction to the Modern Library Edition of *All of the King's Men*, in *Twentieth Century Interpretations of "All the King's Men,"* ed. Robert H. Chambers (Englewood Cliffs, N.J.: Prentice-Hall, 1977), 97; "In the Time of 'All the King's Men,' " *New York Times Book Review* (May 31, 1981), 39.

5. Frederick A. Olafson, *The Dialectic of Human Action: A Philosophical Interpretation of History and the Humanities* (Chicago: University of Chicago Press, 1979), 79–81.

6. Warren, Introduction, 97. Cf, Ladell Payne, "Willie Stark and Huey Long: Atmosphere, Myth, or Suggestion?" *Twentieth Century Interpretations*, 98–115.

7. Quoted in T. Harry Williams, *Huey Long* (New York: Knopf, 1969; Vintage Books, 1981), 868.

8. Warren, Introduction, 94; "In the Time of 'All the King's Men,' " 42. A dramtic version of *All the King's Men* was performed in New York on October 16, 1959. See *All the King's Men: A Play* (New York: Random House, 1960).

9. Long's message in the speech Warren heard in 1935 was: "You will find out that you cannot do without politicians. They are a necessary evil in this day and time." See Charles East, "The Death of Huey Long: A Photographic Essay," *Southern Review* n.s. 2 (Spring 1985), 255.

10. Warren, "In the Time of 'All the King's Men,' " 42.

11. Albert E. Stone, Jr., "Seward Collins and the *American Review:* Experiment in Pro-Fascism, 1933–37," *American Quarterly* 5 (Spring 1960), 3–19. There were also a few pragmatic liberals, notably Lincoln Steffens, who defended Mussolini.

See John Diggins, "Flirtation with Fascism: American Pragmatic Liberals and Mussolini's Italy," *American Historical Review* 71 (January 1966), 487–506.

12. Quoted in Ken Bode, "Hero or Demagogue," *New Republic* 194 (March 3, 1986), 37.

13. I was present at this showing in April 1986, when Ken Burns made this remark.

14. Robert Penn Warren, *All the King's Men* (New York: Harcourt, Brace, 1946), 168.

15. I draw in this chapter on my "*All the King's Men* and the Shadow of William James," *Southern Review* n.s. 6 (October 1970), 920–934.

16. Perry, *Thought and Character,* vol. 2, 575, 577.

17. Quoted in ibid., 299.

18. *All the King's Men,* 273–274.

19. William James, "The Moral Philosopher and the Moral Life," *Essays on Faith and Morals,* ed. Ralph Barton Perry (New York: Longmans, Green, 1947), 206–207.

20. Ibid., 208; *All the King's Men,* 417.

21. *All the King's Men,* 330.

22. William James, "Great Men and Their Environment," *Selected Papers on Philosophy,* Everyman Ed. (New York: E. P. Dutton, 1917), 166, 176, 179, 189.

23. Sidney Hook, *The Hero in History: A Study in Limitation and Possibility* (New York: John Day, 1943), 16. James West Davidson and Mark Lytle have used both James and Hook on the hero in history to discuss Huey Long as an "event-making man" in *After the Fact: The Art of Historical Detection* (New York: Knopf, 1982), 296–319. They also consider Warren's novel an unrivalled source for "a feeling for Long's Louisiana." Ibid., 319.

24. Robert T. Heilman, "Williams on Long: The Story Itself," *Southern Review* 6 (October 1970), 951, 953.

25. *All the King's Men,* 346.

26. Ibid., 417–418.

27. Ibid., 425, 452.

28. James, "The Moral Philosopher and the Moral Life," 214.

29. *All the King's Men,* 462.

30. Marshall Walker, "Robert Penn Warren: An Interview," *Journal of American Studies* 8 (August 1974), 234.

31. James, *The Varieties of Religious Experience, 138.*

32. Warren, *The Legacy of the Civil War,* 98.

33. William James, "The Dilemma of Determinism," *Essays on Faith and Morals, 158.*

34. *All the King's Men,* 195–196, 442, 464.

35. Walker, "Robert Penn Warren," 230.

Chapter Seven

1. Quoted in Ian Hamilton, *Robert Lowell* (New York: Random House, 1982), 70.

2. Robert Lowell, "Visiting the Tates," *Collected Prose,* ed. and intro. Robert Giroux (New York: Farrar Straus Giroux, 1987), 59; "An Interview with Frederick Seidel," ibid., 256.

3. Lowell, "Visiting the Tates," 60.

4. Quoted from a talk c. 1960 in Hamilton, 86.

5. Quoted from Jean Stafford and Robert Lowell in Hamilton, 87, 96.

6. To President Roosevelt, September 7, 1943, Lowell, *Collected Prose,* 368, 369.

7. Lowell, "Memories of West Street and Lepke," *Selected Poems,* rev. ed. (New York: Farrar Straus Giroux, 1977), 91; "Robert Lowell in a Conversation with A. Alvarez," *London Observer* (July 21, 1963), 19.

8. Richard J. Fein, *Robert Lowell,* 2nd ed. (Boston: Twayne Publishers, 1979), 59.

9. Quoted from "From the Steps of the Harvard Gym," in Hamilton, *Robert Lowell,* 41; ibid., 80.

10. Lowell, "For the Union Dead," *Selected Poems,* 135–137. See Paul C. Doherty, "The Poet as Historian: 'For the Union Dead' by Robert Lowell," *Concerning Poetry,* 1 (Fall 1968), 37–41.

11. Quoted in Hamilton, *Robert Lowell,* 281.

12. Lowell, "New England and Further," *Collected Prose,* 188–189, 197.

13. Michael Colacurcio, *The Province of Piety: Moral History in Hawthorne's Early Tales* (Cambridge, Mass.: Harvard University Press, 1984), 227, 264; Amasa Delano, "Voyage in the Ship *Perseverance,*" in *Five Sea Captains,* ed. Walter Teller (New York: Atheneum, 1960), 73–101.

14. Nathaniel Hawthorne, "The May-pole of Merry Mount," *The Scarlet Letter and Other Tales of the Puritans,* ed. Harry Levin (Boston: Houghton Mifflin, 1961), 303.

15. Nathaniel Hawthorne, "Endicott and the Red Cross," *The Scarlet Letter and Other Tales of the Puritans,* 291.

16. Colacurcio, *The Province of Piety,* 231.

17. Robert Lowell, "Endecott and the Red Cross," *The Old Glory,* rev. ed. (New York: Farrar Straus Giroux, 1968), 45, 48, 50.

18. Ibid., 77.

19. Hamilton, *Robert Lowell,* 312.

20. To the Editors, February 4, 1968, *New York Review of Books* (February 29, 1968), 32.

21. See Peter Shaw, "Fathers, Sons, and the Ambiguities of Revolution in 'My

Kinsman, Major Molineux,' " *New England Quarterly* 49 (December 1976), 569–576; Michael Colacurcio, *The Province of Piety*, 134–153.

22. Michael Kammen, *A Season of Youth* (New York: Knopf, 1978), 186–220.

23. Colacurcio, *The Province of Piety*, 137.

24. Director's note (1965), *The Old Glory*, 221.

25. Lowell, "My Kinsman, Major Molineux," *The Old Glory*, 127.

26. Ibid., 119.

27. Nathaniel Hawthorne, "The Whole History of Grandfather's Chair," *A Wonder-Book, Tanglewood Tales, and Grandfather's Chair*, Riverside Ed. (Boston: Houghton Mifflin, 1883), 619.

28. Nathaniel Hawthorne, "My Kinsman, Major Molineux," *The Snow Image and Other Twice-Told Tales*, 6th ed. (Boston: Houghton Mifflin, 1879), 254.

29. Hamilton, *Robert Lowell*, 343.

30. "A Conversation with Ian Hamilton," in Lowell, *Collected Prose*, 289.

31. Robert Brustein, Introduction (1965), *The Old Glory*, 217; Director's note, ibid., 220.

32. "A Conversation with Ian Hamilton," 289.

33. Herman Melville, *Benito Cereno*, in R.W.B. Lewis, ed., *Herman Melville* (New York: Dell, 1962), 212; cf. *The Old Glory*, 143.

34. Eric J. Sundquist, "*Benito Cereno* and New World Slavery," in Sacvan Bercovitch, ed., *Reconstructing American Literary History*, 106.

35. *Benito Cereno*, 258.

36. Ibid., 213, 273.

37. Sundquist, "*Benito Cereno*," 119.

38. Stephen B. Oates, *Let the Trumpet Sound: The Life of Martin Luther King, Jr.* (New York: New American Library, 1982), 247.

39. Introduction, *The Old Glory*, xii.

40. "A Conversation with Ian Hamilton," 288.

41. *The Old Glory*, 204, 213.

42. *Benito Cereno*, 297.

43. *The Old Glory*, 214.

44. *Benito Cereno*, 252, 294.

45. *The Old Glory*, 214; Director's note, *The Old Glory*, 223.

46. Edmund Wilson, *Patriotic Gore: Studies in the Literature of the American Civil War* (New York: Oxford University Press, 1962), xxxii.

47. To Edmund Wilson, March 31, 1962, quoted in Hamilton, *Robert Lowell*, 302.

48. *London Observer* (July 21, 1963), 19.

49. "A Conversation with Ian Hamilton," 289.

50. Robert Brustein, Introduction (1965), *The Old Glory*, 215, 217.

51. Hamilton, *Robert Lowell*, 311.

52. Hamilton, *Robert Lowell*, 327; "Robert Lowell in a Conversation with A. Alvarez," 19.

Chapter Eight

1. Avrom Fleishman, *Fiction and the Ways of Knowing: Essays on British Novels* (Austin: University of Texas Press, 1978), 10.

2. Tony Tanner, *City of Words: American Fiction 1960–1970* (New York: Harper & Row, 1971), 242, 245. For White's view, see his "The Fictions of Factual Representation," in *The Literature of Fact,* ed. Angus Fletcher (New York: Columbia University Press, 1976), 21–44. On Mailer, see Ronald Weber, "Recording Angel and Amateur Philosopher," *The Literature of Fact: Literary Nonfiction in American Writing* (Athens: Ohio University Press, 1980), 80–88.

3. Walter Clemons, "Houdini, Meet Ferdinand," *Newsweek* (July 14, 1975), 73.

4. See John Ditsky, "The German Source of *Ragtime:* A Note," *E. L. Doctorow: Essays and Conversations,* ed. Richard Trenner (Princeton, N.J.: Ontario Review Press, 1983), 179–181.

5. Walter L. Reed, *An Exemplary History of the Novel: The Quixotic versus the Picaresque* (Chicago: University of Chicago Press, 1981), 222.

6. Marcus Cunliffe, "Mark Twain and his 'English' Novels," *London Times Literary Supplement* (Dec. 25, 1981), 1503–1504.

7. Justin Kaplan, *Mr. Clemens and Mark Twain* (New York: Simon and Schuster, 1966), 276.

8. E. L. Doctorow, *Ragtime* (New York: Random House, 1975), 153.

9. Mark Twain, *A Connecticut Yankee in King Arthur's Court* (New York: Modern Library, 1949), Preface.

10. *Ragtime,* 3–5.

11. Ibid., 238.

12. *Connecticut Yankee,* 63, 66.

13. *Ragtime,* 143.

14. Ibid., 225.

15. *Connecticut Yankee,* 108, 382.

16. *Ragtime,* 71, 111.

17. Cf. *Ragtime,* 113 and *Connecticut Yankee,* 147.

18. Cf. *Connecticut Yankee,* 407, 449 and *Ragtime,* 156.

19. *Connecticut Yankee,* 171.

20. Ibid., 429–430.

21. Ibid., 78–79.

22. To Clemens, Nov. 12, 1889, quoted in *Selected Mark Twain—Howells Letters,* ed., Frederick Anderson, William M. Gibson, Henry Nash Smith (Cambridge, Mass.: Belknap Press, 1967), 285, n. 2; to Howells, Sept. 22, 1889, ibid.; to Clemens, Dec. 29, 1889, ibid., 292.

23. *Connecticut Yankee,* 150, 382, 419.

24. Reed, *An Exemplary History of the Novel,* 229.

25. *Mark Twain's Notebook,* Authorized Ed. (New York: Harper and Brothers, 1935), 348–351.

26. *Ragtime,* 270.

27. Ibid., 97–99.

28. E. L. Doctorow, "False Documents," in Ditsky, *Doctorow,* 24–25.

29. Quoted in Alice Wexler, *Emma Goldman in America* (Boston: Beacon Press, 1984), 199.

30. Doctorow, "False Documents," 24.

31. For an extended discussion of the historical status of *The Book of Daniel,* see Cushing Strout, "Hazards of the Border Country," *The Veracious Imagination,* 173–179.

32. *Ragtime,* 29.

33. Ibid., 233.

34. Richard Trenner, "Politics and the Mode of Fiction," *E. L. Doctorow,* 53–54.

35. *Ragtime,* 259.

36. John Lukacs, "Doctorowurlitzer or History in *Ragtime,*" *Salmagundi* 31–32 (Fall 1975–Winter, 1976), 290.

37. "E. L. Doctorow: 'I Saw a Sign,'" *New York Times Book Review* (Sept. 28, 1980), 45.

38. Gerald Graff, "The Politics of Anti-Realism," in *The Salmagundi Reader,* ed., Robert Boyers and Peggy Boyers (Bloomington: Indiana University Press, 1983), 416.

39. John Clayton, "Radical Jewish Humanism," *Doctorow,* 118.

40. *Connecticut Yankee,* 301.

41. See the review of 1970s historical literature on the Progressives in Daniel T. Rodgers, "In Search of Progressivism," *Reviews in American History* 10:4 December 1982), esp. 123–132.

42. Quoted in Sam B. Girgus, *The New Covenant: Jewish Writers and the American Idea* (Chapel Hill: University of North Carolina Press, 1984), 22. Girgus thinks Doctorow, like Bellow, participates in a "New Covenant" dedication to the American experiment, but this comparison blurs important differences between them regarding their image of America.

Chapter Nine

1. "Bush's Bows to the Right," *New York Times,* Sunday, Sept. 11, 1988, sec. 1.

2. Stephen B. Oates, *Abraham Lincoln: The Man Behind the Myths* (New York: New American Library, 1985), 59, 63, 77, 81.

3. Eulogy on Henry Clay, in *Abraham Lincoln: Selected Speeches, Messages, and Letters,* ed. T. Harry Williams (New York: Rinehart, 1958), 36.

4. To Messrs. Nehemiah Dodge and Others, Jan. 1, 1802, in *Thomas Jefferson,* ed. Merrill D. Peterson (New York: Library of America, 1984), 510. For a critical history of the reading of the Amendment in the light of the statute, see Cushing Strout, "Jeffersonian Religious Liberty and American Pluralism," in *The Virginia Statute for Religious Freedom: Its Evolution and Consequences in American History,* ed. Merrill D. Peterson and Robert C. Vaughan (New York: Cambridge University Press, 1988), 218–229.

5. Martin E. Marty, "The Virginia Statute Two Hundred Years Later," in Peterson and Vaughan, *Virginia Statute,* 4.

6. Ralph Lerner, "Jefferson's Pulse of Republican Reformation," *The Thinking Revolutionary: Principle and Practice in the New Republic* (Ithaca, N.Y.: Cornell University Press, 1987), 61.

7. *Bacon* Case, 7 Va. 604, 609, 611, 612 (1850). See Cushing Strout, "Jeffersonian Religious Liberty and American Pluralism," in Peterson and Vaughan, *Virginia Statute,* 205.

8. Rhys Isaac, " 'The Rage of Malice of the Old Serpent Devil': The Dissenters and the Making and Remaking of the Virginia Statute for Religious Freedom," in Peterson and Vaughan, *Virginia Statute,* 162–163.

9. Willie Lee Rose, "The Impact of the American Revolution on the Black Population," in *Legacies of the American Revolution,* ed. Larry R. Gerlach (Logan and Cedar City: Utah State University, 1978), 188.

10. J. R. Pole, *Paths to the American Past* (New York: Oxford University Press, 1979), 219.

11. Thomas Jefferson, "Notes on the State of Virginia," in Peterson, *Thomas Jefferson,* 288–289.

12. Ibid., 187.

13. Ibid., 264–265.

14. Ibid., cf. 266 and 269–270.

15. Ibid., 270.

16. Ibid., 264.

17. "A Declaration by the Representatives of the United States of America," in Peterson, *Thomas Jefferson,* 19.

18. "Notes on the State of Virginia," in Peterson, *Thomas Jefferson*, 269.

19. See Herbert J. Storing, "Slavery and the Moral Foundations of the Republic," in *The Moral Foundations of the American Republic*, ed. Robert H. Horwitz, 3d ed. (Charlottesville, Va.: University Press of Virginia, 1986), 319.

20. To Benjamin Banneker, Aug. 30, 1791, in Peterson, *Thomas Jefferson*, 982–983.

21. Pole, *Paths to the American Past*, 73.

22. To Edward Coles, Aug. 25, 1814, in Peterson, *Thomas Jefferson*, 1346. See John Chester Miller, *The Wolf by the Ears: Thomas Jefferson and Slavery* (New York: Free Press, 1979), 205–209.

23. To M. de Meusnier, June 22, 1786, in *Jefferson Himself: The Personal Narrative of a Many-Sided American*, ed. Bernard Mayo (Boston: Houghton Mifflin, 1942), 109. Miller's otherwise reliable book mistakenly attributes this remark to Jefferson's autobiography; see Miller, *Wolf by the Ears*, 28.

24. Miller, *Wolf by the Ears*, 259.

25. To John Holmes, April 22, 1820, in Peterson, *Thomas Jefferson*, 1434. On the Tallmadge Amendment issue see Miller, *Wolf by the Ears*, 225–232.

26. To Albert Gallatin, Dec. 26, 1820, in Peterson, *Thomas Jefferson*, 1450.

27. "A Declaration," in Peterson, *Thomas Jefferson*, 22; "Autobiography," ibid., 18.

28. To Jean Nicolas Démeunier, June 26, 1786, in Peterson, *Thomas Jefferson*, 592.

29. Quoted in Thomas E. Buckley, S.J., "The Political Theology of Thomas Jefferson," in Peterson and Vaughan, *Virginia Statute*, 80, 95.

30. "First Inaugural Address," in Peterson, *Thomas Jefferson*, 493–494.

31. Pole makes this point about Lincoln in "Abraham Lincoln and the American Commitment," *Paths to the American Past*, 152.

32. To William Branch Giles, Dec. 26, 1825, in Peterson, *Thomas Jefferson*, 1511.

33. To James Heaton, May 20, 1826, in Peterson, *Thomas Jefferson*, 1516.

34. To Roger C. Weightman, June 24, 1826, in Peterson, *Thomas Jefferson*, 1517.

35. Robert Penn Warren, *Brother to Dragons* (New York: Random House, 1953), 6, 194.

36. See Julian P. Boyd, "The Murder of George Wythe," in Boyd and W. Edwin Hemphill, *The Murder of George Wythe* (Williamsburg, Va.: Institute of Early American History and Culture, 1955), 29–31.

37. Speech at Peoria, Illinois, Oct. 16, 1854, in *The Life and Writings of Abraham Lincoln*, ed. Philip Van Doren Stern (New York: Modern Library, 1940), 340.

38. From a Speech in Springfield, Illinois, June 26, 1857, in Stern, *Life and Writings*, 423.

39. From a Speech in Springfield, June 26, 1857, in Stern, *Life and Writings,* 424–425.

40. From a Speech at Chicago, July 10, 1858, in Stern, *Life and Writings,* 448–449.

41. Speech at Peoria, Oct. 16, 1854, in Stern, *Life and Writings,* 362–363.

42. First Inaugural Address, in Peterson, *Thomas Jefferson,* 493, 495.

43. Letter to H. L. Pierce and Others, April 6, 1859, in Stern, *Life and Writings,* 539–540.

44. Lord Charnwood, *Abraham Lincoln* (New York: Pocket Books, 1948), 165.

45. Pole, *Paths to the American Past,* 162.

46. Charnwood, *Abraham Lincoln,* 146.

47. From a Speech at Chicago, July 10, 1858, in Stern, *Life and Writings,* 447.

48. See Don E. Fehrenbacher, "Only His Stepchildren," *Lincoln in Text and Context: Collected Essays* (Stanford, Cal.: Stanford University Press, 1987), 106.

49. Speech at Peoria, Oct. 16, 1854, in Stern, *Life and Writings,* 361.

50. From Lincoln's Reply in the Last Joint Debate at Alton, Oct. 15, 1858, in Stern, *Life and Writings,* 530.

51. From a Speech in Springfield, June 26, 1857, in Stern, *Life and Writings,* 422.

52. Speech at Independence Hall, Philadelphia, Feb. 22, 1861, in Stern, *Life and Writings,* 644–645.

53. From the Annual Message to Congress, Dec. 1, 1862, in Stern, *Life and Writings,* 745.

54. Letter to Governor Andrew Johnson, March 26, 1863, in Stern, *Life and Writings,* 752.

55. See Glen E. Thurow, *Abraham Lincoln and American Political Religion* (Albany: State University of New York Press, 1976), 75–77.

56. From Lincoln's Reply in the Fifth Joint Debate at Galesburg, Oct. 7, 1858, in Sterns, *Life and Writings,* 504.

57. Cf. Meditation on the Divine Will, Sept. 1862, in Stern, *Life and Writings,* 728, and Letter to A. G. Hodges, April 4, 1864, ibid., 809.

58. Second Inaugural Address, March 4, 1865, in Stern, *Life and Writings,* 841–842.

59. Robert N. Bellah, "To Kill and Survive or to Die and Become: The Active Life and the Contemplative Life as Ways of Being Adult," in *Adulthood,* ed. Erik H. Erikson (New York: Norton, 1978), 77.

60. To Jean Nicolas Démeunier, June 26, 1786, in Peterson, *Thomas Jefferson,* 592.

61. Letter To Anson G. Chester, Sept. 5, 1860, in Stern, *Life and Writings,* 618.

62. Draft of the Kentucky Resolutions, Oct. 1798, in Peterson, *Thomas Jefferson,* 453.

63. First Inaugural Address, in Stern, *Life and Writings,* 650.

64. To William Branch Giles, Dec. 26, 1825, in Peterson, *Thomas Jefferson,* 1510–1511.

Chapter Ten

1. Robert A. Jelliffe, ed., *Faulkner at Nagano* (Tokyo: Kenkyusha, 1956), 88.

2. *Mark Twain's Notebooks and Journals,* ed., Frederick Anderson, Michael B. Frank, Kenneth M. Sanderson (Berkeley: University of California Press, 1975), vol. 1, 39, n. 51; Dixon Wecter, *Sam Clemens of Hannibal,* Sentry Ed. (Boston: Houghton Mifflin, 1961), 235, 313, n.29; Mark Twain, "The Late Benjamin Franklin," in *Sketches Old and New* (Hartford, Conn.: American Publishing Co., 1899), 211, 213.

3. Wecter, *Sam Clemens of Hannibal,* 265.

4. Foreword to *Sherwood Anderson & Other Famous Creoles,* in James B. Meriwether, ed., *Essays, Speeches, and Public Letters by William Faulkner* (New York: Random House, 1965), 174.

5. Frederick L. Gwynn and Joseph L. Blotner, eds., *Faulkner in the University* (Charlottesville: University of Virginia Press, 1959), 15.

6. Mark Twain, "Tom Sawyer's Conspiracy," in Walter Blair, ed., *Mark Twain's Hannibal, Huck, & Tom* (Berkeley: University of California Press, 1969), 163–242.

7. Gwynn and Blotner, *Faulkner in the University,* 142.

8. Quoted by Patrick H. Samway, S.J., *Faulkner's Intruder in the Dust: A Critical Study of the Typescripts* (Troy, N.Y.: Whitston Publishing Company, 1980), 6.

9. Irving Howe and Michael Millgate have both made this suggestion, and for an analysis of the comparison see Philip J. Skerry, "*The Adventures of Huckleberry Finn* and *Intruder in the Dust:* Two Conflicting Myths of the American Experience," *Ball State University Forum* 13:1 (Winter 1972), 4–13. Skerry uses R.W.B. Lewis's idea of an Adamic hero to polarize the two stories with Chick being "Huck Finn fully grown and totally aware of the loss of innocence in twentieth-century America." Ibid., 13.

10. "Huck Finn and Tom Sawyer among the Indians," in Blair, *Mark Twain's Hannibal, Huck & Tom,* 81–140.

11. Ralph Ellison, "Change the Joke and Slip the Yoke," *Shadow and Act* (New York: New American Library, 1966), 65.

12. John Seelye, *The True Adventures of Huckleberry Finn* (Urbana: University of Illinois Press, 1987), xii.

13. Gwynn and Blotner, *Faulkner in the University,* 244–245.

14. Compare Lionel Trilling, "The Greatness of Huckleberry Finn," in *Adven-*

tures of Huckleberry Finn, 2d Norton Critical Ed. (New York: Norton, 1977), 321, with his "An American View of English Literature (1951)," in Diana Trilling, ed., *Speaking of Literature and Society* (New York: Harcourt Brace Jovanovich, 1980), 261–262.

15. William Faulkner, *Intruder in the Dust,* Vintage Books Ed. (New York: Random House, 1972), 138, 151, 209–210.

16. "William Faulkner," in *Writers at Work,* ed. Malcolm Cowley, Compass Books Ed. (New York: Viking, 1965), 141.

17. *Intruder,* 26–27.

18. Ibid., 21.

19. *Huckleberry Finn,* 102.

20. Ibid., 177.

21. *Intruder,* 21, 194, 206.

22. Gwynn and Blotner, *Faulkner in the University,* 139.

23. *Intruder,* 25.

24. Ibid., 89, 112.

25. Gwynne and Blotner, *Faulkner in the University,* 140.

26. *Intruder,* 239–240.

27. Ibid., 156.

28. Ibid., 216–217.

29. Ibid., 194.

30. Ibid., 244. The most relentless criticism of the uncle's ideology is in Walter Taylor, *Faulkner's Search for a South* (Urbana: University of Illinois Press, 1983), 154–164. Taylor overdoes it by finding the whole book "an incredible performance."

31. Gwynn and Blotner, *Faulkner in the University,* 223.

Chapter Eleven

1. Richard Wright, *Native Son* (New York: Harper & Row, Perennial, 1966), xxxiv.

2. See Donald B. Gibson, "Ralph Ellison and James Baldwin," in *The Politics of Twentieth-Century Novelists,* ed. George A. Panichas (New York: Thomas Y. Crowell, 1974), 307.

3. Larry Neal, "Ellison's Zoot Suit," in *Ralph Ellison: A Collection of Essays,* ed. J. R. Hersey (New York: Prentice Hall, 1974), 79.

4. Ralph Ellison, "Richard Wright's Blues," *Shadow and Act* (New York: New American Library, 1966), 104. For Ellison's relation to Wright see Ellison's "Remembering Richard Wright," *Going to the Territory* (New York: Random House, 1986), 198–216. For a biography of Wright see Michael Fabre, *The Unfin-*

ished Quest of Richard Wright, tr. Isabel Barzun (New York: William Morrow, 1973).

5. Quoted by Ellison, "The World and the Jug," *Shadow and Act,* 122.

6. Ibid. 124.

7. Richard Wright, *Black Boy: A Record of Childhood and Youth* (New York: Harper, 1942, 1945), 219.

8. Ellison, "Brave Words for a Startling Occasion," *Shadow and Act,* 111.

9. Richard Wright, *Native Son,* 388.

10. See Dan McCall, *The Example of Richard Wright* (New York: Harcourt, Brace, and World, 1969), 166–170.

11. Quoted in Harold Cruse, *The Crisis of the Negro Intellectual* (New York: William Morrow, 1967), 182, 184.

12. Ralph Ellison, "Remembering Richard Wright," *Going to the Territory,* 210, 214.

13. For critical accounts of the black political opposition to Ellison see John Wright, "Dedicated Dreamer, Consecrated Acts: Shadowing Ellison," *Carleton Miscellany* 18 (Winter 1980), 142–198; Cruse, 235, 506–510.

14. Ellison, "The World and the Jug," *Shadow and Act,* 125.

15. Wright, Introduction, *Native Son,* xiii.

16. Quoted by McCall, *The Example of Richard Wright,* 145.

17. Ellison, " 'A Very Stern Discipline,' " *Going to the Territory,* 303.

18. Ellison, "Remembering Richard Wright," 216.

19. Ellison, " 'A Very Stern Discipline.' " 303.

20. Ellison, "Remembering Richard Wright," 198.

21. Ellison, "Richard Wright's Blues," *Shadow and Act,* 96. On the psychological role of fire in *Black Boy,* see Albert E. Stone, "The Childhood of the Artist," *Autobiographical Occasions and Original Acts: Versions of American Identity from Henry Adams to Nate Shaw* (Philadelphia: University of Pennsylvania Press, 1982), 124–142.

22. Ellison, "The Little Man at Chehaw Station," *Going to the Territory,* 13.

23. Ellison, "Going to the Territory," *Going to the Territory,* 131–137. On his relationship to Twain's best novel, see Alan Nadel, *Invisible Criticism: Ralph Ellison and the American Canon* (Iowa City: University of Iowa Press, 1988), 124–146.

24. The most detailed account of Ellison's use of folklore in *Invisible Man* is Robert G. O'Meally, *The Craft of Ralph Ellison* (Cambridge, Mass.: Harvard University Press, 1980), 78–104.

25. Ellison, "Harlem is Nowhere," *Shadow and Act,* 283–284.

26. *Invisible Man,* 196.

27. Ibid., 221.

28. *Native Son,* 334–335.

29. Ibid., 362, 364, 366.

30. Marcus Klein, *Foreigners: The Making of American Literature 1900–1940* (Chicago: University of Chicago Press, 1981), 287.

31. *Native Son*, 391–392.

32. McCall, *The Example of Richard Wright*, 153.

33. Richard Wright, *American Hunger* (New York: Harper & Row, 1977), 120, 122.

34. *Native Son*, xxiv–xv, 367.

35. *Invisible Man*, 13–14, 433.

36. Ibid., 422.

37. Ibid., 118–120.

38. Ibid., 437. See Gibson, "Ralph Ellison and James Baldwin," 309. Taking the story literally, he reads it as saying: "There is no way for black people to deal with the racial problem, the novel asserts, and the best that can be done is for us to withdraw into the inner recesses of our own psyches."

39. Ellison, "Society, Morality, and the Novel," *Going to the Territory*, 243.

40. *Invisible Man*, 361, 377, 333.

41. Ibid., 11.

42. C.W.E. Bigsby, *The Second Black Renaissance: Essays in Black Literature* (Westport, Conn.: Greenwood Press, 1980), 66.

43. Ibid., 5.

44. Ellison, "An American Dilemma," *Shadow and Act*, 301.

Chapter Twelve

1. Ralph Ellison, "Society, Morality, and the Novel," *Going to the Territory*, 243, 248; Patricia Caldwell, *The Puritan Conversion Narrative: The Beginning of American Expression* (New York: Cambridge University Press, 1983), 134.

2. Caldwell, *Puritan Conversion Narrative*, 107.

3. See the collection of essays in Peterson and Vaughan, *Virginia Statute;* my contribution to it is "Jeffersonian Religious Liberty and American Pluralism," 201–235.

4. Adam Fairclough, *To Redeem the Soul of America: The Southern Christian Leadership Conference and Martin Luther King, Jr.* (Athens: University of Georgia Press, 1987), 153–154.

5. David J. Garrow, *Bearing the Cross: Martin Luther King, Jr., and the Southern Christian Leadership Conference* (New York: Random House, 1986; Vintage Books, 1988), 219.

6. Martin Luther King, Jr., "An Autobiography of Religious Development," King Papers, Mugar Memorial Library, Boston University, Box 106; John Cogley, "An Interview with Reinhold Niebuhr," *McCall's* 93:5 (February 1966), 171.

7. Richard Wightman Fox, *Reinhold Niebuhr: A Biography* (New York: Pantheon Books, 1985), 288–289.

8. Garrow, *Bearing the Cross,* 587–588.

9. Ibid., 587–588; Reinhold Niebuhr, "Epilogue: A View from the Sidelines," in *The Essential Reinhold Niebuhr: Selected Essays and Addresses,* ed. Robert McAfee Brown (New Haven: Yale University Press, 1986), 251; Fox, *Reinhold Niebuhr,* 273.

10. Reinhold Niebuhr, *Moral Man and Immoral Society: A Study in Ethics and Society* (New York: Scribner's, 1932, 1947), 254–255; "The Mounting Racial Crisis," *Christianity and Crisis,* 23 (July 8, 1963), 121.

11. Fox, *Reinhold Niebuhr,* 282.

12. Walter Rauschenbusch, *A Theology for the Social Gospel* (New York: Macmillan, 1917), 273.

13. Reinhold Niebuhr, "Introduction: Changing Perspectives," *Man's Nature and His Communities* (New York: Scribner's, 1965), 18–19.

14. Fox, *Reinhold Niebuhr,* 91–92.

15. Quoted in Fox, *Reinhold Niebuhr,* 119.

16. Reinhold Niebuhr, *Leaves from the Notebooks of a Tamed Cynic* (New York: Willet, Clark, 1929; Hamden, Conn.: Shoe String Press, 1956), 195–196.

17. Niebuhr, *Leaves,* 85–86.

18. Niebuhr, *Man's Nature and His Communities,* 23.

19. Niebuhr, *Moral Man,* 199.

20. Ibid., 244, 248, 249–250.

21. Ibid., 252, 254.

22. Quoted in Fox, *Reinhold Niebuhr,* 168–169.

23. Martin Luther King, Jr., "Reinhold Niebuhr's Ethical Dualism," May 9, 1952, King Papers, Box 113, 3–4, 13–14.

24. Martin Luther King, Jr., "Reinhold Niebuhr," King Papers, Box 113, # 20, 11.

25. Martin Luther King, Jr., "How Modern Christians Should Think of Man," ibid., 1,4,5.

26. Martin Luther King, Jr., "Pilgrimage to Nonviolence," *The Christian Century* (April 13, 1960), 439–441.

27. On Niebuhr, see John E. Smith, *Themes in American Philosophy: Purpose, Experience, and Community* (New York: Harper Torchbooks, 1970), 217–221.

28. Quoted in Taylor Branch, *Parting the Waters: America in the King Years, 1954–63,* (New York: Simon and Schuster, 1988), 141.

29. Quoted in Garrow, *Bearing the Cross,* 75.

30. King, "Pilgrimage to Nonviolence," 440–441.

31. Fairclough, *To Redeem the Soul of America,* 24–26.

32. Martin Luther King, Jr., *Stride Toward Freedom: The Montgomery Story* (New York: Ballantine Books, 1958, 1961), 78–79.

33. Niebuhr, *Moral Man*, 248.

34. Reinhold Niebuhr, "The Power of Love and the Will to Justice," *Advance* 148: 18 (Oct. 5, 1956), 9, 24; "What Resources Can the Christian Church Offer to Meet Crisis in Race Relations?" *The Messenger* (April 3, 1956), reprinted in *Love and Justice: Selections from the Shorter Writings of Reinhold Niebuhr*, ed. D. B. Robertson (Philadelphia: Westminster Press, 1957), 154.

35. Reinhold Niebuhr, "Reply," in *Reinhold Niebuhr: His Religious, Social, and Political Thought*, ed. Charles W. Kegley and Robert W. Bretall (New York: Macmillan, 1956), 450.

36. "The Way of Nonviolent Resistance," *Christianity and Society* 21 (Spring 1956), 3, reprinted in *Reinhold Niebuhr on Politics*, ed. Harry R. Davis and Robert C. Good (New York: Scribner's, 1960), 236–237. The Niebuhr-Baldwin debate is quoted in Branch, *Parting the Waters*, 896. Branch also rightly points out (without elaborating) that the relation between Niebuhr and King is "obscured by complicated twists of time, race, and popular imagery." Ibid., 81.

37. Reinhold Niebuhr, "A Question of Priorities," *Faith and Politics*, ed. Ronald Stone (New York: Braziller, 1968), 268.

38. Reinhold Niebuhr, "The Struggle for Justice," *New Leader*, 47:14 (July 6, 1964), 11.

39. Martin Luther King, Jr., *Where Do We Go From Here?: Chaos or Community* (New York: Harper & Row, 1967), 143, 190.

40. Niebuhr, *Man's Nature and His Communities*, 105.

41. Reinhold Niebuhr, "The Ark and the Temple," *Beyond Tragedy: Essays on the Christian Interpretation of History* (New York: Scribner's, 1937), 67.

42. Reinhold Niebuhr, "The Religion of Abraham Lincoln," *The Christian Century*, 82: 6 (Feb. 10, 1965), 172–175. See also his "The Image of America," *New Leader*, (Feb. 23, 1959), 8–10, where he celebrates Lincoln in contrast to the neutralism of Nehru and the self-righteousness of Dulles.

43. Cogley, "An Interview," *McCall's*, 171.

44. See Julius Lester's moving account, "Black and White—Together," *Salmagundi* 81 (Winter 1989), 174–181.

45. Martin E. Marty, "Reinhold Niebuhr's Public Theology and the American Experience," in *The Legacy of Reinhold Niebuhr*, ed. Nathan A. Scott, Jr. (Chicago: University of Chicago Press, 1975), 16, 22. On the role of the black churches and differences among them over the movement, see C. Eric Lincoln, *Race, Religion, and the Continuing American Dilemma* (New York: Hill and Wang, 1984), 94–122, 241–260.

46. For an extensive analysis of *The Irony of American History*, see Richard

Reinitz, *Irony and Consciousness: American Historiography and Reinhold Niebuhr's Vision* (Cranbury, N.J.: Associated University Presses, 1980), 90–112.

47. Branch, *Parting the Waters,* 702.

48. Quoted in ibid., 216; ibid., 887.

49. Quoted in ibid., 743. On the movement's resonance with the black church, see Fairclough, *To Redeem the Soul of America,* 404.

50. Quoted in Branch, *Parting the Waters,* 824.

51. Quoted in Garrow, *Bearing the Cross,* 420.

52. Ibid., 563–564.

53. Cf. King, quoted by Garrow, *Bearing the Cross,* 453, and Niebuhr, quoted in Fox, *Reinhold Niebuhr,* 285.

54. Quoted in Garrow, *Bearing the Cross,* 524.

55. Quoted in Stephen B. Oates, *Let the Trumpet Sound,* 467.

56. Niebuhr, *Leaves,* 166, 193.

57. "Epilogue," in Brown, *The Essential Reinhold Niebuhr,* 250.

58. Quoted in June Bingham, *Courage to Change* (New York: Scribner's, 1961), 224. Cf. Fox's judgment that "Niebuhr's apologetics came straight out of William James's pragmatism, as it had ever since his B.D. thesis," in *Reinhold Niebuhr,* 163. But this judgment makes too little out of the European theological influences and misses James's personal agnosticism. He credited religious believers without really being one himself, and their beliefs did not have to be Christian.

59. Reinhold Niebuhr, intro., James, *Varieties of Religious Experience* (Collier Books ed., 1961), 7–8.

60. James, *Varieties of Religious Experience,* 355–357; Martin Luther King, "Loving Your Enemies," in *Strength to Love* (New York: Pocket Books, 1964), 47.

61. James, *Varieties of Religious Experience,* 355–357, 360, 364.

Chapter Thirteen

1. Alice Walker, "A Name Is Sometimes an Ancestor Saying Hi, I'm With You," *Living by the Word: Selected Writings 1973–1987* (New York: Harcourt Brace Jovanovich, 1988), 97, 98.

2. Alice Walker, Journal, Jan. 8, 1984, *Living by the Word,* 95.

3. See Larry Neal, "Ellison's Zoot Suit," 58–79. See also Cushing Strout, " 'An American Negro Idiom': *Invisible Man* and the Politics of Culture," in Susan Resneck Parr and Pancho Savery, eds., *Approaches to Teaching Ellison's Invisible Man* (New York: Modern Language Association, 1989), 79–85.

4. Walker, "All the Bearded Irises of Life: Confessions of a Homospiritual," *Living by the Word,* 165. See also in the same volume "Oppressed Hair Puts a

Ceiling on the Brain," "Journey to Nine Miles," and "Not Only Will Your Teachers Appear, They Will Cook New Foods for You."

5. Walker, "Everything Is a Human Being," *Living by the Word,* 145.

6. Walker, "The Universe Responds: Or How I Learned We Can Have Peace on Earth," *Living by the Word,* 192.

7. Walker, Journal, *Living by the Word,* 180–181.

8. Ellison, "Hidden Name and Complex Fate," *Shadow and Act,* 154, 167, 168.

9. Ellison, "The Little Man at Chehaw Station," *Going to the Territory,* 17.

10. Alice Walker, *Meridian* (New York: Harcourt Brace Jovanovich, 1976; Pocket Books, 1977), 121.

11. Walker, "Everyone Is a Human Being," *Living by the Word,* 144–145.

12. Ellison, "The Myth of the Flawed White Southerner," *Going to the Territory,* 77.

13. Walker, "The Dummy in the Window," *Living by the Word,* 32; "On Seeing Red," Ibid., 128.

14. Interview with Alice Walker, *Essence* (July 1976), 33.

15. "Alice Walker," *Black Women Writers at Work,* ed., Claudia Tate (New York: Continuum, 1983), 179; Walker, "My Big Brother Bill," *Living by the Word,* 43.

16. Walker, "In the Closet of the Soul," *Living by the Word,* 82, 84.

17. Ibid., 87–89; "Alice Walker," *Black Women Writers,* 178; Ellison, "The Little Man at Chehaw Station," *Going to the Territory,* 13.

18. Ellison, "The Art of Romare Bearden," *Going to the Territory,* 234, 235, 237.

19. "Alice Walker," *Black Women Writers,* 176, 178.

20. Quoted in Pancho Savery, " 'Not like an arrow, but a boomerang': Ellison's Existential Blues," in *Approaches to Teaching Ellison's Invisible Man,* 71, and in Cushing Strout, " 'An American Negro Idiom': *Invisible Man* and the Politics of Culture," ibid., 84.

21. Barbara Christian, "An Angle of Seeing: Motherhood in Buchi Emecheta's *The Joys of Motherhood* and Alice Walker's *Meridian* (1984)," in Christian, ed., *Black Feminist Criticism: Perspectives on Black Women Writers* (New York: Pergamon Press, 1985), 225. The feminist reading I have found most insightful is Kelly Albert's "Alice Walker's *Meridian:* A Quest for New Patterns," a Cornell University undergraduate honors thesis.

22. Walker, *Meridian,* 27–28.

23. Ibid., 125.

24. Ibid., 51, 59.

25. Ellison, *Invisible Man,* 438. Cf. *Meridian,* 91.

26. *Meridian,* 48.

27. Ibid., 162.
28. *Invisible Man,* 437–438.
29. *Meridian,* 189.
30. Ibid., 191.
31. Ibid., 200.
32. "Alice Walker," *Black Women Writers,* 184.
33. *Meridian,* 189.
34. Ibid., 220.
35. *Meridian,* 220; *Invisible Man,* 439.
36. "Alice Walker," *Black Women Writers,* 180.
37. Walker, "A Name Is Sometimes an Ancestor," *Living by the Word,* 98.

Index

Abbott, Lyman, 22

Adams, Henry: *Democracy*, 89; *Esther*, 29–32; and Hawthorne, 32; and W. James, 32; "The Primitive Rights of Women," 50; on sex, 33

Adams, John, 140

Adams, Marion Clover Hooper, 31, 70

Adventures of Huckleberry Finn, The (Twain), 154–156; compared with *Intruder in the Dust*, 156–160; Ellison on, 155; Faulkner on, 152, 153, 156; and *Invisible Man*, 169

Age of Innocence, The (Wharton), 53; compared to *Portrait of a Lady*, 64–69; and Pulitzer Prize, 69; Wolff on, 64

Agrarians, 91

Albert, Kelly, "Alice Walker's *Meridian:* A Quest for New Patterns," 237n21

Alcott, Bronson, 45

"Alice Walker's *Meridian:* A Quest for New Patterns" (Albert), 273n21

Alien and Sedition Laws, 150

Allen, Ethan, 13–14

All the King's Men (Warren), 88–99; and W. James, 88–89, 92–99; and Long, 88–91, 95

Ambassadors, The (H. James), 53; compared to *Indian Summer*, 56–59; and Howells, 53–56, 59; and Sturges, 53–55

American, The (H. James), 14–17, 19–20, 60; and Franklin, 14, 15, 16

American Dilemma, An (Myrdal), 176

American Hunger (Wright), 172

American Indian Movement, 199

American Indians: and Jefferson, 136–137; and Walker, 199, 202

"American James, The" (Howells), 52

American Place Theater, 103

American Renaissance (Matthiessen), 2, 42

American Review, 91

"Americans Abroad" (H. James), 15

"American Scholar, The" (Emerson), 85

"Ancestral Footstep, The" (Hawthorne), 41

Anderson, Margaret, 129

Anderson, Quentin, 2, 27, 40

Armies of the Night, The (Mailer), 117

As You Like It (Shakespeare), 28

Auden, W. H., 2, 207

Australia, 1

Autobiography (Jefferson), 140

Autobiography of Benjamin Franklin, The, 9–10; and *The American*, 14, 16; and *The Great Gatsby*, 17, 19; and *Israel Potter*, 11–13; and "My Kinsman, Major Molineaux," 11

Awakening, The (Chopin), 206

Bacon, Jarvis C., 135

Baldwin, James, 188

Banneker, Benjamin, 138, 199

Barth, John, *The Sot-weed Factor,* 117

Barth, Karl, 38, 214n26

Barthes, Roland, 128

Barzun, Jacques, 5–6

Beard, Dan, 124, 126

Bearden, Romare, 200–201

Becker, Carl L., 21

Beecher, Henry Ward, 46

Bell, Millicent, 63–64

Bellah, Robert N., 149

Bellow, Saul, 132; *Henderson the Rain King,* 132

Benito Cereno (Lowell), 111, 113–114

Benito Cereno (Melville), 103, 104, 111–114

Bethel Evangelical Church, 181

Bewley, Marius, 2

Beyond Tragedy (Niebuhr), 189

Bible, The, 140, 149, 168

Bigsby, C.W.E., 175–176

Bill of Rights, 172, 177. *See also* First Amendment; Thirteenth Amendment

Biographical Stories for Children (Hawthorne), 11

Black Boy (Wright), 164, 165, 169

Blankenship, Tom, 156

Bliss, W.D.P., 59

Blithedale Romance, The (Hawthorne), 7, 42, 206; and *The Bostonians,* 43, 45–47, 48, 50; Howells on, 44; James on, 47; and *The Scarlet Letter,* 49; and *The Undiscovered Country,* 44–45

Bloch, Marc, 7

Bloom, Harold, 4, 42, 72, 74

Bon Homme Richard, 13

Book of Daniel, The (Doctorow), 129

Boston Arts Festival, 102–103

Bostonians, The (H. James), 42, 70; and *The Blithedale Romance,* 43, 45–47, 48, 50; and Alice James, 48; and *The Undiscovered Country,* 44–45, 46; and Warren, 89

Boston University, 184

Bradstreet, Anne, 30

Branch, Taylor, *Parting the Waters: America in the King Years, 1954–63,* 192, 235n36

Brodhead, Richard H., *The School of Hawthorne,* 43

Brook Farm, 44

Brooks, Cleanth, 101

Brooks, Van Wyck, 33

Brother to Dragons (Warren), 141

Brunner, Emil, 182

Brustein, Robert, 111, 115

Buitenhuis, Peter, 42

Bunker Hill, 12

Burns, Ken, "Huey Long," 91

Butterfield, Herbert, 3

Butzel, Fred, 181

Byron, George Gordon Noel, 2

Cable, George Washington, 119

Cahan, Abraham, 53, 59–60, 61–62; on Howells, 61, 62–63; *The Rise of David Levinsky,* 60–63

Caldwell, Patricia, 177

Calhoun, John C., 134, 144

Calvinism: and Beecher, 35; and Hawthorne, 23; and Howells, 24; and Henry James (theologian), 76; and William James, 82; and Jefferson, 140; and King, 185. *See also* Puritanism

Canada, 1

Catcher in the Rye, The (Salinger), 156

Cather, Willa, *The Professor's House,* 7

Cervantes, Miguel de, *Don Quixote,* 119

Charnwood, Lord, 145

Chase, Richard, 2

Chateaubriand, François René, 2, 58

Chesnutt, Charles Waddell, *The Marrow of Tradition,* 164

Chesterton, G. K., 177

Chiaromonte, Nicola, 7

Chopin, Kate, *The Awakening,* 206

Christianity, 78, 82. *See also* Calvinism; King, Rev. Martin Luther, Jr.; Niebuhr, Reinhold; Puritanism

Christianity and the Social Crisis (Rauschenbusch), 185

Christian Science, 78

Church of the Carpenter, 59

civil disobedience, 180, 183–184, 186–187, 190. *See also* King, Rev. Martin Luther, Jr.; Niebuhr, Reinhold

Civilization and Its Discontents (Freud), 27

Civil Rights Movement, 8, 112, 176; and Alice Walker, 201. *See also* King, Rev. Martin Luther, Jr.; March on Washington; Niebuhr, Reinhold

Civil War, 8, 115, 133; and Lincoln, 148, 151; and Twain, 120; and Warren, 88, 89, 97

Clay, Henry, 134, 147, 150

Clemens, Samuel L. *See* Twain, Mark

Clergy and Laymen Concerned About Vietnam, 193

Cleveland, Grover, 127

Cohen, Morris, 132

Colacurcio, Michael, 105, 109

Cold War, 184, 191

Coles, Edward, 138

Collins, Seward, 91

Columbia University, 84

Columbus, Christopher, 111

Compromise of 1850, 144

Concord Sonata (Ives), 103

Confederacy, 99, 127, 157

Connecticut Yankee in King Arthur's Court, A (Twain): and Bellow, 132; and *A Campaign That Failed,* 120; and "dream self," 127, 131; forerunners of, 118–119; and Progressive movement, 131; and *Ragtime,* 118–125, 128, 130, 132; and revolutions, 122, 126

Constitution of the United States, 142–143, 177, 192, 198. *See also* Bill of Rights

Cooper, James Fenimore, 16

Cotton, John, 22

Couples (Updike), 36–37

Cowley, Malcolm, 22

Crozer Theological Seminary, 179, 184, 185

Cuba, 112

Cunliffe, Marcus, 119

Czolgosz, Leon, 123

Damnation of Theron Ware, The (Frederic), 32–35; and *Esther,* 33; and *Roger's Version,* 39; and *The Scarlet Letter,* 33–35

Darwinism, 35, 60

Daudet, Alphonse, 24, 43

Debatable Land between This World and the Next, The (Owen), 44

Declaration of Independence: and Beard, 126; and Ellison, 174, 175, 198; and Jefferson, 134, 135, 136, 137, 139, 141–142; and King, 178; and Lincoln, 143, 146, 147, 148; and Wright, 173

Decline of the West, The (Spengler), 18

Delano, Capt. Amasa, "Voyage in the Ship *Perseverance*," 104
Democracy (Adams), 89
Democracy in America (Tocqueville), 1–2
Derrida, Jacques, 3
determinism: and W. James, 80, 94, 98; and Warren, 94, 97–98
Devil in Miss Jones, The, 37
Dewey, John, 74, 89
DeWolf, Dr. L. Harold, 184
"Dilemma of Determinism, The" (W. James), 80, 98
Dimock, George, 47
"Divinity School Address" (Emerson), 82, 85
divorce, 23, 28–29, 70
Dr. Jekyll and Mr. Hyde (Stevenson), 127
Doctorow, E. L.: and Barthes, 128; and *The Book of Daniel*, 129; on history, 128–129; and Jewishness, 129–130; Lukacs on, 130; *Ragtime*, 118–126, 128–130, 132; and television technique, 130; and Twain, 130–131
Don Quixote (Cervantes), 119
Dostoevsky, Feodor Mikhailovich, *Notes from Underground*, 166
Douglas, Sen. Stephen A., 142, 145, 146, 147, 148
Dred Scott decision, 144
Dreiser, Theodore, 166
Dudley, Thomas, 29–30
Dumas, Alexandre, 14

Eco, Umberto, 5
Edel, Leon, 54, 55
Edwards, Jonathan, 72, 81, 101
Ehrlichman, John, 179
Eisenhower, Dwight D., 180
Eliot, George, 24

Eliot, T. S., 41, 42, 50–51, 168; *The Family Reunion*, 166
Ellison, Ralph: on American literary ancestors, 177, 198; and black culture, 168–170; compared with Walker, 197–200; compared with Wright, 165–166, 167–169, 175; on Harlem, 170, 200; helped by Wright, 165; and Howe, 165, 167; *Invisible Man*, 166–167, 169–171, 173–175; on Myrdal, 176; as native son, 168–169, 198; "Richard Wright's Blues," 165; and symbolists, 166; on Twain, 155; on Wright, 165–166, 167–169
Emancipation Proclamation, 147, 148
Emerson, Ralph Waldo, 21, 46, 72; "The American Scholar," 85; centenary of, 82–85, 87; "The Divinity School Address," 82, 85; and Ellison, 198; "Experience," 85; "Fate," 81; and Franklin, 21; "History," 86; H. James (theologian), 74–75; and W. James, 74–78, 81–87; and "Lectures on the Times," 85; "Literary Ethics," 85; *Miscellanies*, 85; "Nature," 77; "Prospects," 85; "Spiritual Laws," 81–82; and Warren, 97; and Whitman, 72–74
Endecott and the Red Cross (Lowell), 106–107
Endicott, John, 105, 107
"Endicott and the Red Cross" (Hawthorne), 105–106
Erikson, Erik H., 50
Esther (Adams), 29–32; and Marion Hooper Adams, 31; and Hawthorne, 29–31
"Esther Dudley" (Hawthorne), 29–30
Etrangère, L' (Dumas), 14
Evangéliste. L' (Daudet), 43

Facts, The (Roth), 9

Family Reunion, The (Eliot), 166

fascism, 91, 167, 184

"Fate" (Emerson), 81

Faulkner, William, 22; on *The Catcher in the Rye,* 156; compared with Twain, 157; on humor, 153; *Intruder in the Dust,* 153–154, 156–162; on the Negro, 162–163; on Twain, 152

FBI, 179, 193

Feast of Words, A (Wolff), 64

Federal Writers Project, 165

Feidelson, Charles, 2, 3

Feinstein, Howard M., 75–76

Fellowship of Reconciliation, 184, 187

feminism: and Adams, 31–32, 50; and Hawthorne, 22, 31–32, 48–49; and Howells, 44; and James (novelist), 48–50, 70; and H. James (theologian), 70; and mesmerism, 46; and Walker, 197, 237n21

First Amendment, 134

Fitzgerald, F. Scott: *The Great Gatsby,* 17–18, 20–21; and myth of hero, 18–19, 20, 21

Fleishman, Avrom, 117

Flournoy, Theodore, 82

Ford, Henry, 124

"For the Union Dead" (Lowell), 102–103, 133

Foucault, Michel, 3

Fox, Richard Wightman, *Reinhold Niebuhr: A Biography,* 236n58

Franklin, Benjamin: *Autobiography of,* 9–10; compared with Twain, 152–153; and Gatsby, 17, 19; and H. James, 15; myth of, 10–12, 16, 19–20, 21; and Newman, 14, 16; and parents, 19; and Potter, 12–13; and Revolution, American, 10–11, 20–21; and Robin, 11, 19; *The Works of Benjamin Franklin,* 12; as writer, 10

Frederic, Harold, *The Damnation of Theron Ware,* 32–35; and Hawthorne, 33, and Updike, 35, 39

Freud, Sigmund, 3, 4, 27, 50, 78, 132

Frost, Robert, 72, 74

Fugitives, 91, 100

Fugitive Slave Law, 144

Fuller, Margaret, 45, 46, 47

Fullerton, Morton, 65

Gaines, Ernest, 197

Gandhi, Mohandas, 183, 186–188

Garner, John Nance, 95

Garrow, David J., 178

Garvey, Marcus, 167

George III, King, 139–140

Gettysburg Address (Lincoln), 112, 148, 171

Gibson, William B., 56

Glorious Third, A (Seton), 69

Goldman, Emma, 122–123, 128–129, 131–132

Graff, Gerald, 130

Graham, Rev. Billy, 179

Grant, Gen. Ulysses S., 127

Great Awakening, 178

Great Gatsby, The (Fitzgerald), 17–21; and *The American,* 17; and Emerson, 21; and Franklin, 17, 19, 20

"Great Men and Their Environment" (W. James), 94–95

Haiti, 111–112

Hamilton, Ian, 107, 115

Harlem, 170, 200

Harvard Divinity School, 82

Hatch, Cora, 44, 46

Hawthorne, Nathaniel, 2, 3, 4, 7, 21; "The Ancestral Footstep," 41;

Hawthorne, Nathaniel (*continued*)
Anderson on, 40; *Biographical Sketches,* 31; *The Blithedale Romance,* 7, 42, 44, 45, 47–48; and Eliot, 41, 50–51; "Endicott and the Red Cross," 105–106; "Esther Dudley," 29–30; and Franklin, 11, 19; and Frederic, 33; as hero, 22; and Howells, 24, 29; on Hutchinson, 22–23, 31–32; H. James on, 42; W. James on, 41; R. Lowell on, 103; and Melville, 4, 52; *The Marble Faun,* 41; "The May-pole of Merry Mount," 104–105; "My Kinsman, Major Molineaux," 11, 19, 20, 108, 110; *The Scarlet Letter,* 22–27, 32; and Tocqueville, 2; Trilling on, 42; and Updike, 35; and Warren, 97
Hawthorne (H. James), 42, 47
Hegel, Georg Wilhelm Friedrich, 186, 194, 196
Heilman, Robert T., 95
Hemingway, Ernest, 22, 155; *The Sun Also Rises,* 155
Henderson the Rain King (Bellow), 132
Hero in History, The (Hook), 95
Himmelfarb, Gertrude, 6–7
"History" (Emerson), 86
History (Lowell), 100
Hoffman, Daniel, 2
Hook, Sidney, 89, 95
Hooker, Thomas, 38
Hooper, Clover. *See* Adams, Marion Hooper
Houdini, Harry, 120, 125, 129
Howe, Irving, 165, 167
Howells, William Dean, 4; "The American James," 52; and Cahan, 53, 59–60, 61–63; and Hawthorne, 24, 27, 29, 44; *Indian Summer,* 56–57; and H. James, 24, 52, 54–56;

Literary Friends and Acquaintance, 52; *A Modern Instance,* 23–29; and Owen, 43; *The Rise of Silas Lapham,* 60, 62; *Through the Eye of the Needle,* 63; *The Traveler from Altruria,* 63; and Twain, 126, 152; *The Undiscovered Country,* 43–45
"How Modern Christians Should Think of Man" (King), 185
"Huck Finn and Tom Sawyer among the Indians" (Twain), 155
"Huey Long" (Burns), 91
Hughes, Langston, 165, 197
Hurston, Zora Neale, 197
Hutchinson, Anne, 22–23, 31–32, 49
Hutchinson, Thomas, 10

"I Have a Dream" (King), 192
Independence Hall, 147
Indians. *See* American Indians
Indian Summer (Howells), 53; and *The Ambassadors,* 56–59
"international theme, the," 20, 53, 56, 60, 127
Intruder in the Dust (Faulkner), 153–154, 156–162; compared with *The Adventures of Huckleberry Finn,* 156–160
Invisible Man (Ellison), 166–167, 169–171, 173–175; compared with *Meridian,* 200–207; compared with *Native Son,* 166–167, 170–175; and Tocqueville, 166; and Twain, 169
Irony of American History, The (Niebuhr), 184, 191
Israel Potter (Melville), 11–14, 19
Ivanhoe (Scott), 119
Ives, Charles, 103

James, Alice, 48
James, Henry (father), 70, 74; and Em-

erson, 74–75, 76; *The Literary Remains of the Late Henry James,* 74, 79, 80, 86; on marriage, 70; and Williams, 74–76, 79–80, 82, 87

James, Henry (son), 7; *The American,* 14–17, 19–20; "Americans Abroad," 15; *The Bostonians,* 45–50; Eliot on, 41–50; and father, 70; and Hawthorne, 42–43; *Hawthorne,* 42, 47; and Howells, 24, 46, 54–56; "The Jolly Corner," 7, 51; *The Portrait of a Lady,* 64–70; *Roderick Hudson,* 41; *The Sense of the Past,* 41; and sister, 48; and Sturges, 55; and Sturgis, 46; Trilling on, 40; and Wharton, 63, 68–69; on woman's role, 49–50, 70

James, Wilkinson, 88

James, William, 174; "The Dilemma of Determinism," 80, 98; and Emerson, 74–78, 81–87; at Emerson's centenary, 82–85, 87; and father, 74–76, 79–80, 82, 87; "Great Men and Their Environment," 94–95; and Harvard, 84; on Henry, Hawthorne, and Howells, 41; on hero, 93–95; and liberalism, 92; pluralism of, 79–80, 83, 97; "The Moral Philosopher and the Moral Life," 93, 96; and Niebuhr, 194–195; *Pragmatism,* 79, 84, 86–87, 89; and Shaw memorial, 88, 133; and sister, 48; and Renouvier, 80; *The Varieties of Religious Experience,* 76, 77–82; and Warren, 88–89; 92–99; on Whitman, 83, 86

Jefferson, Thomas, 132, 198; *Autobiography,* 140; on blacks, 137–138; and civil religion, 140; and Coles, 138; colonization policy of, 137; and Declaration of Independence, 134–135,

139–140, 141, 142, 148; and "exceptionalism," 140; on Indians, 137; on judicial review, 144; and Kentucky Resolutions, 149–150; and King, 178, 192; J. C. Miller on, 139; on minority rights, 143–144; on Missouri Compromise, 139; *Notes on the State of Virginia,* 136, 137; and Ordinances of 1784 and 1797, 138, 142; as slaveholder, 134, 136, 137, 138; on slavery, 138, 139–140, 142; and University of Virginia, 134; and Virginia Statute for Religious Freedom, 134; and Warren, 141; as writer, 133; and Wythe, 142. *See also* Lincoln, Abraham

Jefferson Memorial, 178

Jewish Daily Forward, 53

Johnson, Andrew, 147

Johnson, Lyndon B., 114, 190, 198–199

"Jolly Corner, The" (H. James), 7, 51

Jones, John Paul, 11, 13

Joplin, Scott, 118

Journal of John Winthrop, 104

Kammen, Michael, 108

Kansas-Nebraska Act, 134, 144

Kaplan, Justin, 120

Kazin, Alfred, 6, 43

Kennedy, Jackie, 110

Kennedy, John F., 112, 178, 192, 203

Kentucky Resolutions, 149–150

Kerr, Howard, 46

Kierkegaard, Søren, 182, 194

King, Clarence, 31

King, Rev. Martin Luther, Jr., 112, 122; and black power, 191; compared with Niebuhr, 179–180, 187, 189, 191, 193–194, 235n36; funeral of, 204; and Gandhi, 186–187;

King, Rev. Martin Luther (*continued*)
"How Modern Christians Should
Think of Man," 185; "I Have a
Dream," 192; inner conflicts of,
179; and Jefferson, 178, 192; as
leader, 178–179, 191–192; "Letter
from the Birmingham Jail," 192;
and liberal social gospel, 185–186;
and Lincoln, 195; as martyr, 193–
194; and pacifists, 187; "Pilgrimage
to Nonviolence," 186; "Reinhold
Niebuhr's Ethical Dualism," 184; re-
sponse to Niebuhr of, 184–185,
186, 189; as revolutionary, 193;
Stride Toward Freedom, 187; *Where
Do We Go From Here? Chaos or Community*, 188
Kipling, Rudyard, *Kim*, 156
Klein, Marcus, 172
Kleist, Heinrich von, *Michael
Kohlhaas*, 118
Koestler, Arthur, 7

Lafargue Psychiatric Clinic, 170
Lamartine, Alphonse de, 2, 58
Last of the Barons, The (Lytton), 119
"Late Benjamin Franklin, The"
(Twain), 152–153
Leaves of Grass (Whitman), 72, 73
"Lectures on the Times" (Emerson),
85
Legacy of the Civil War, The (Warren),
88–89, 97
Lennon, John, 197
Lerner, Ralph, 134–135
"Letter from the Birmingham Jail"
(King), 192
Levin, Harry, 2
Levison, Stanley D., 192–193
Lewis, John, 201
Lewis, R.W.B., 2, 65

Lewis, Sinclair, 60, 69, 166
liberalism, 8, 28, 33, 92, 132. *See also*
Ellison, Ralph; James, William; Jefferson, Thomas; King, Rev. Martin
Luther, Jr.; Lincoln, Abraham
Library of American Biography, 12
Lincoln, Abraham, 43, 101, 132, 199;
Bellah on, 149; Charnwood on,
145; and Clay, 134; and civil religion, 148, 149, 151; colonization
policy of, 145, 147; on Declaration
of Independence, 143, 146, 148; election of, 147; Emancipation Proclamation, 147; and "exceptionalism,"
140; Gettysburg Address, 148, 171;
and irony of history, 148, 151; and
Jefferson, 142–144, 149–150; and
King, 178, 192, 195; on minority
rights, 143–144; as moderate, 145;
Niebuhr on, 189–190; on political
parties, 144; and race prejudice,
145–146; and slavery, 142–148; on
Union, 150; as writer, 133–134, 149
Lincoln Memorial, 112, 178
"Literary Ethics" (Emerson), 85
Literary Friends and Acquaintance (How-
ells), 52
*Literary Remains of the Late Henry
James, The*, 74, 79, 80, 86
Little Review, 129
Living by the Word (Walker), 198
Long, Huey: and *All the King's Men*,
89–91, 95; biography of, 95; Heil-
man on, 95; Hook on, 95; and
"Huey Long" (film), 91; and Louisi-
ana State University, 91, 100
Loring, Katharine P., 48
Loving, Jerome, 74
Lowell, Col. Charles Russell, 102
Lowell, James Russell, 45
Lowell, Lawrence, 100

Lowell, Robert: ancestry of, 100–101, 102, 103; *Benito Cereno* (*The Old Glory*), 111, 113–114; as Catholic conscientious objector, 101–102; *Endecott and the Red Cross* (*The Old Glory*), 106–107; "For the Union Dead," 102–103, 133; on Hawthorne, 103; and image of violent America, 102, 107–108, 115–116; on Melville, 103; mental illness of, 102, 116; *My Kinsman, Major Molineaux* (*The Old Glory*), 109–110; and Southern mentors, 100; and Stafford, 100; and Vietnam War, 107, 114–115

Lubbock, Percy, 63

Lukacs, John, 130

Lusitania, 121

Luther, Martin, 118, 122

Lynd, Staughton, 201

Lytton, Edward Bulwer, *The Last of the Barons,* 119

McCall, Dan, 172

McCarthy, Mary, *The Oasis,* 7

Machiavelli, Niccolò, 91, 93, 98

McKinley, William, 123

Madison, James, 134, 135, 150

Mailer, Norman, *The Armies of the Night,* 117

Main Street (Lewis), 69

Malcolm X, 112–113, 122, 203

Malory, Sir Thomas, *Morte d'Arthur,* 119

Mandelbaum, Maurice, 5

Man's Nature and His Communities (Niebuhr), 189

"Man Who Lived Underground, The" (Wright), 166

Marble Faun, The (Hawthorne), 41

March on Washington (1963), 112, 178, 192

Marrow of Tradition, The (Chesnutt), 164

Marshall, Thurgood, 189

Marty, Martin E., 191

Marx, Karl, 194

Matthiessen, F. O., 2, 42

"May-pole of Merry Mount, The" (Hawthorne), 104–105

Melville, Herman, 3, 5, 71; *Benito Cereno,* 103, 104, 111–114, 166; on Franklin, 13; and Hawthorne, 4, 52; *Israel Potter,* 11–14, 19, 20

Memoirs of Hecate County (Wilson), 37

Meridian (Walker), 201–207; compared with *Invisible Man,* 200–207

Merry Mount, 102, 104, 107

mesmerism, 43, 46

Michael Kohlhaas (Kleist), 118

Mill, John Stuart, 28, 70, 79

Miller, John Chester, 139

Miller, John William, 6

Miller, Jonathan, 109–111

Miller, Perry, 72

Miscellanies (Emerson), 85

Missouri Compromise, 139, 144, 146

Moby Dick (Melville), 4, 153

Modern Instance, A (Howells), 23–29; Cahan on, 62; and *The Scarlet Letter,* 24–27, 29; and Wharton, 63

modernism, 8, 35, 129–130

monism, 8, 79–80, 81, 85, 87

Montgomery bus boycott, 178, 186, 187, 188

Month of Sundays, A (Updike), 35

Monticello, 136

Moral Man and Immoral Society (Niebuhr), 182–183, 184, 186

"Moral Philosopher and the Moral Life, The" (W. James), 93

Morgan, J. P., 121, 122, 123, 125

Morte d'Arthur (Malory), 119

Morton, Nathaniel, 104; *New England's Memorial,* 104

Morton, Thomas, 104; *New English Canaan,* 104

Mount Marcy, 76

Mue009lder, Dean Walter, 185

Münsterberg, Hugo, 76

Mussolini, Benito, 89, 91, 92, 221n11

Myers, Maj. Mordecai, 102

"My Kinsman, Major Molineux" (Hawthorne): and Franklin, 11, 19; and Lowell, 109–110

Myrdal, Gunnar, *An American Dilemma,* 176

NAACP, 187

Name of the Rose, The (Eco), 5

nation, idea of, 6–7

National Book Award, 166

Native Son (Wright), 166–167, 171–173, 175; compared with *Invisible Man,* 166–167, 170–175

"Nature" (Emerson), 77

Nature and Destiny of Man, The (Niebuhr), 182

Neal, Larry, 197

Nesbit, Evelyn, 124, 129

Nest of Nobelmen, A (Turgenev), 14

New Challenge, 165

New Criticism, 100

New Deal, 95, 180

New England's Memorial (N. Morton), 104

New English Canaan (T. Morton), 104

New Leader, The, 165

New Masses, 165

New York Review of Books, 107

Niagra Falls, 32

Niebuhr, Reinhold: antifascist agenda

of, 184; anxieties of, 179–180; *Beyond Tragedy,* 189; compared to King, 179–180, 187, 189, 191, 193–194, 235n36; and European existentialist theology, 182; on Gandhi, 183, 188; and W. James, 194–195, 236n58; on King, 180, 188, 192; on Lincoln, 189–190; *Man's Nature and His Communities,* 189; Marty on, 190–191; *Moral Man and Immoral Society,* 182–183, 184, 186; *The Nature and Destiny of Man,* 182; on Nixon, 179; on nonviolent resistance, 180, 183–184, 187–188; as pastor of Bethel Evangelical Church, 181; prestige of, 184; as realist, 182–183, 194; "The Religion of Abraham Lincoln," 189–190; as socialist, 182–183; on Vietnam War, 193

Nixon, Richard M., 179

Nixon, Robert, 167

nonviolent resistance. *See* civil disobedience; Gandhi, Mohandas; King, Rev. Martin Luther, Jr.; Niebuhr, Reinhold

Notes on the State of Virginia (Jefferson), 134, 136, 137, 142, 148

Oakeshott, Michael, 6

Oasis, The (McCarthy), 7

Old Glory, The (Lowell): and American violence, 102, 107, 110, 114; Brustein on, 111, 115; Hamilton on, 107; 115; origin of, 103. *See also Benito Cereno; Endecott and the Red Cross; My Kinsman, Major Molineux*

Ordinance of 1784, 138, 142

Ordinance of 1787, 138, 142

Oswald, Lee Harvey, 123

Outsider, The (Wright), 172

Owen, Robert Dale: *The Debatable*

Land between This World and the Next, 44

Ozick, Cynthia, 3

pacifism. *See* King, Rev. Martin Luther, Jr.; Niebuhr, Reinhold

Page, Dr. Inman E., 169

Parting the Waters: America in the King Years, 1954–63 (Branch), 235n36

Patriotic Gore (Wilson), 115

Peabody, Elizabeth, 43, 45, 47

Peirce, Charles S. Sanders, 74

Perry, Ralph Barton, 76, 80, 86

Personalism, 185

"Pilgrimage to Nonviolence" (King), 186

pluralism, 79–80, 83, 97

Poe, Edgar Allan, 3

"Poet, The" (Emerson), 73

Poirier, Richard, 2

Pole, J. R., 136, 145

Poor Richard's Almanac, 12

Portrait of a Lady, The (H. James), 24, 53, 63; and *The Age of Innocence,* 64–69; author on, 64; and marriage, 70; and Wharton, 64

Portrait of Edith Wharton (Lubbock), 63

"post-structuralist deconstruction," 3

pragmatism, 74; and Emerson, 84–85; in Italy, 92; and W. James, 85–87, 88–89, 93–94, 98, 194; and King, 192; and Niebuhr, 183, 191, 194; Warren on, 88–89, 92

Pragmatism (W. James), 79, 84, 86–87, 89, 98

"Primitive Rights of Women, The" (Adams), 50

"Princess with the Golden Hair, The" (Wilson), 37

"Professor Fargo" (H. James), 43, 44, 46

Professor's House, The (Cather), 7

Progressive movement, 131

"Prospects" (Emerson), 85

Proud Flesh (Warren), 90

Puritanism: and conversion, 177; and Great Awakening, 178; and Hawthorne, 22–23, 24, 28, 29, 104–108

Radical Religion, 184

Ragtime (Doctorow): anachronism in, 120, 122; and *A Connecticut Yankee in King Arthur's Court,* 118–125, 128, 130, 132; and Kleist, 118–119; and Jewishness, 129–130, 132; and television technique, 130; and Walker, 197

Ransom, John Crowe, 100

Rauschenbusch, Walter: *Christianity and the Social Crisis,* 185; *A Theology for the Social Gospel,* 181

realism, literary, 40, 59, 62, 63, 166

Reconstructing American Literary History (Bercovitch), 3

Reconstruction, 186, 190

Reed, Walter, 127

Reinhold Niebuhr: A Biography (Fox), 236n58

"Reinhold Niebuhr's Ethical Dualism" (King), 184

Reivers, The (Faulkner), 153

Renouvier, Charles Bernard, 80

Revolution, American, 8, 9, 11, 20; and Franklin, 10–11, 21; and Hawthorne, 108, 110; and R. Lowell, 109–110, 133; and slavery, 136; and Twain, 126, 130. *See also* Declaration of Independence

Revolution, French, 125, 126

"Richard Wright's Blues" (Ellison), 165

Rise of David Levinsky, The (Cahan), 53; compared with *The Rise of Silas Lapham,* 60–63; Howells on, 61–62

Rise of Silas Lapham, The (Howells): Cahan on, 62; compared with *The Rise of David Levinsky,* 60–63; and Wharton, 63

Roderick Hudson (H. James), 41

Roger's Version (Updike): and *The Damnation of Theron Ware,* 39; and *The Scarlet Letter,* 35–39

"romance," 2, 40, 43, 59, 105, 118

Roosevelt, Franklin D., 95, 102, 199

Roosevelt, Theodore, 130, 164

Roth, Philip, 9

Rowe, John Carlos, 42

Rowe, Joyce A., 19

Rustin, Bayard, 187

Salinger, J. D., *The Catcher in the Rye,* 156

Santayana, George, 87

Santo Domingo, 111–112, 140

Sartre, Jean Paul, 172

Scarlet Letter, The (Hawthorne), 22–24; and *The Damnation of Theron Ware,* 33–35; and *Esther,* 29, 31; and feminism, 22, 31–32; and *A Modern Instance,* 24–27, 29; and *Roger's Version,* 35–39; Updike on, 35

School of Hawthorne, The (Brodhead), 43

Scott, Sir Walter, 23; *Ivanhoe, 119*

Seeing Red, 199

Seelye, John, 155

Sense of the Past, The (H. James), 41

Seton, Cynthia Propper, *A Glorious Third,* 69

Shakespeare, William, 4, 149

Shaw, Col. Robert Gould, 88, 101, 103, 133

Smiley, Glen, 187

Smith Act, 193

socialism, 59, 60, 62, 181, 183, 193

"Song of Myself" (Whitman), 73

Sorel, Georges, 92

Sot-weed Factor, The (Barth), 117

Southern Christian Leadership Conference, 187

Southern Review, The, 100

Spencer, Herbert, 60

Spengler, Oswald, *The Decline of the West,* 18

spiritualism, 43–44, 45, 46

"Spiritual Laws" (Emerson), 81–82

Stafford, Jean, 101, 102

Stark, Gen. John, 102

Stevens, Wallace, 72–74

Stevenson, Robert Louis, *Dr. Jekyll and Mr. Hyde,* 127

Stowe, Harriet Beecher, 164; *Uncle Tom's Cabin,* 206

Stride Toward Freedom (King), 187

structuralism, 3

Sturges, Jonathan, 53, 54, 58

Sturgis, Caroline, 43–44, 46, 47

Subjection of Women, The (Mill), 70

Sullivan, Harry Stack, 169

Sun Also Rises, The (Hemingway), 155

Sundquist, Eric J., 111

Supreme Court of the United States, 144, 156, 175, 189, 189, 201

Swift, Jonathan, 153

Symbolism in American Literature (Feidelson), 3

"synchronicity," 200

Tallmadge Amendment, 139

Taney, Chief Justice Roger, 142, 144

Tate, Allen, 100–101

Temple, Minnie, 55, 70

Thaw, Harry K., 128

Theology for the Social Gospel, A (Rauschenbusch), 181

Thirteenth Amendment, 148

Thoreau, Henry David, 72, 74

Through the Eye of the Needle (Howells), 63

Thurmond, Strom, 160, 161

Tillich, Paul, 36, 182

Time, 184

Tocqueville, Alexis de, 166; *Democracy in America,* 1–2

"Tom Sawyer's Conspiracy" (Twain), 153

Toomer, Jean, 197

"To You" (Whitman), 86

tradition, idea of, 4–5, 7–8, 41, 200

Traveler from Altruria, The (Howells), 63

Trilling, Lionel, 2, 40, 156

Truth, Sojourner, 196

Turgenev, Ivan, 14

Turner, Frederick Jackson, 13

Twain, Mark, 152; *The Adventures of Huckleberry Finn,* 154–156; *A Campaign That Failed,* 120; compared with Faulkner, 157; *A Connecticut Yankee in King Arthur's Court,* 118–127, 130–131; and "dream self," 127, 131; and Ellison, 155; and Franklin, 153; on history, 122, 126, 130–131; and Howells, 126; "Huck Finn and Tom Sawyer among the Indians," 155; "The Late Benjamin Franklin," 152–153; and Paige machine, 126; as Republican Mugwump, 127; "Tom Sawyer's Conspiracy," 153

Uncle Tom's Cabin (Stowe), 206;

Undiscovered Country, The (Howells),

43–45; and *The Blithedale Romance,* 44–45; H. James on, 46; and "Professor Fargo," 44–45

Union: and Jefferson, 139, 140; and Lincoln, 150

Union Theological Seminary, 181

University of Virginia, 134

Updike, John: on adultery, 37; and Apostles' Creed, 36; on K. Barth, 214n26; *Couples,* 36–37; *A Month of Sundays,* 35; *Roger's Version,* 35–39; on *The Scarlet Letter,* 35; on sex, 36–37; on Tillich, 36

Vanderbilt University, 100

Varieties of Religious Experience, The (W. James), 76, 77–82, 84, 194–195

Vaughan, Benjamin, 9–10, 19

Vietnam War, 107, 114, 180, 193

Virginia Resolutions, 150

Virginia Statute for Religious Freedom, 134, 178

"Voyage in the Ship *Perserverance*" (Delano), 104

Walker, Alice: on Bearden, 201; compared with Ellison, 197–200; and counterculture, 197–198; as feminist, 196, 204, 206–207; and Indians, 199; *Living by the Word,* 198; *Meridian,* 201–207; on *Meridian,* 201; and multiracialism, 199; on "synchronicities," 196, 208; traditionalism of, 198–199; and Truth, 196

Walker, Margaret, 197

Warren, Robert Penn: *All the King's Men,* 88–99; on Civil War, 88–89; on Emerson and Hawthorne, 97; and grandfather, 99; and W. James, 88–89, 93–96; *The Legacy of the*

Warren, Robert Penn (*continued*)
Civil War, 88–89, 97; and Long,
89–91, 221n9; and Lowell, 100; on
pragmatism, 88–89; *Proud Flesh,* 90
Washington, Booker T., 122, 164
Washington, George, 22, 198
Webster, Daniel, 22
Wells, H. G., 1
Wharton, Edith: *The Age of Innocence,*
53, 64–69; Bell on, 63; and Fuller-
ton affair, 65; on Howells, 63; and
H. James, 63, 68–69; Lubbock on,
63; marriage and divorce, 65, 68;
and Pulitzer Prize, 69
*Where Do We Go From Here? Chaos or
Community* (King), 188
Whiggism, 3, 122
White, Hayden, 117
Whitman, Walt: and Emerson, 72–74;
W. James on, 83, 86; *Leaves of Grass,*
72, 73; "Song of Myself," 73; "To
You," 86
"Whole History of Grandfather's
Chair, The" (Hawthorne), 108, 110
Williams, Bishop Charles, 181

Williams, Roger, 105
Williams, T. Harry, 95
Wilson, Edmund, 3, 37; *Patriotic Gore,*
115
Wilson, Woodrow, 130
Winthrop, John, 104, 105, 108; *Journal,* 104
Wolff, Cynthia, 64; *A Feast of Words,*
64
Woodhull, Victoria, 46
World War I, 128, 130, 183
World War II, 180
Wright, Richard: *American Hunger,*
172; on American Negro, 164; *Black
Boy,* 164, 165, 169; and black culture, 167–168; and communists,
172; compared with Ellison, 165–
166, 167–169, 175; Ellison on, 165–
166, 167–169; helps Ellison, 165; as
invisible man, 168; and literary realism, 166; "The Man Who Lived Underground," 166; as native son, 167,
175; *Native Son,* 166–167, 171–173,
175; *The Outsider,* 172
Wythe, George, 142